Eat Well For Less Every Day

Eat Well For Less Every Day

Jo Scarratt-Jones

Foreword by **Gregg Wallace** and **Chris Bavin**

BBC
BOOKS

Contents

Foreword

Thank you for watching *Eat Well for Less?*... well, we're guessing you watch it if you've bought this book! Or maybe it's a present and somebody thinks you need a few tips and tricks to get eating well...and, er, for less! If you do watch our show, you'll know we're all about keeping things simple and tasty without breaking the bank. This is our fourth book and it covers lots of the recipes in the recent series – with a few bonus ones thrown in too! We hope it inspires you in the same way that we've inspired the families we've met.

The truth is that, even though all our families are very different, we often hear similar issues: busy lives and no time; no cooking confidence; too many fussy eaters; everybody wants something different; expensive tastes; wedded to the same pricey brands; stuck in a food rut...and we bet you'll identify with at least one of these! But don't worry...help is at hand. Literally, with this book!

With this book, we don't only want to show you delicious, easy recipes that you can put together, we also want to help you do all those things you've talked about doing – saving money on food bills, meal planning, healthy food choices and throwing away less food. Look at the early sections in this book to get savvy. There are also sections on how to deal with children's food habits, from toddlers to teens, plus some of the health issues that you might need to be careful with when cooking. And we make all of it simple – we promise!

One of the things we love to see when we're filming with families is how their confidence grows in the kitchen – even those who have never really cooked before suddenly find enjoyment. Often it can be when you stop thinking about cooking as a chore and more about an activity that you can share as a family. And of course getting busy families to sit down together to eat is always a real triumph, and something we encourage you to do at least once a week if you can't manage more. It's a habit worth getting in to if you can.

If you are a fan of the programme, we thought it might be worth explaining a few of the things you see on the show that we often get questions about. For example, when we pop up and surprise the family while they are doing their supermarket shopping, they really don't know that we're there! Of course, they know they are being filmed as part of the show, but not that we're secretly watching them. It's great seeing their reactions! The other thing people often comment on is the number of different supermarket brands that are spotted, and wonder if we expect you to shop at lots of different supermarkets – we don't! We just want to show you that lots of the supermarkets do own-brand versions and that it really is worth checking out what they have. We bet that sometimes you wouldn't be able to tell the difference!

We really hope you enjoy the book, thank you for buying it and for watching the show. Here's to a new way for you to eat well for less!

Gregg Wallace and Chris Bavin

Let's Get Started!

Use-by/best-before dates

What's the difference?
Surely if it looks ok and smells ok, it's fine? No – the two terms advise very different lifespans, so know the difference and you won't be chucking food out needlessly or, worse, making yourself ill eating it.

Use-by – this is all about safety, so pay attention to this one. Like it says on the packaging, use the product by the date given, otherwise the ingredient/food is no longer safe to eat. This means you can't freeze it or cook it after this date either.

Best-before – you've got a little more latitude here – the product will be at its best before the date shown, but its quality, flavour and texture will deteriorate after that. So it is still safe to eat, but whether you want to or not is your call.

It's easy to get stuck in a bad habit of buying time-saving ready meals to feed the family, but it's also easy to get back on track with healthy eating on a budget. The first thing you need to do is to blitz your kitchen and get a grip on what you've got in your cupboards – out of date, in date; the favourites or the unappealing packets lurking at the back. You will save money on your weekly shopping once you know what you have, because you won't be buying things your cupboards are already overflowing with.

So give yourself an hour or so, and get into those cupboards. Take everything out and set it on a work surface so you can see exactly what you have. If you don't have time to do this all in one go, do a cupboard or two at a time – you might find you get the bug pretty quickly, though, and you'll want to keep going!

Once everything is laid out, go through and check the dates of every package or tin; if they are past their use-by date, you've got no option but to bin them (see box). It might sound odd to throw things out when you're trying to save money, but trust us here, do this and you'll have the perfect clean slate to get started from. Don't beat yourself up about it, just know that you won't let that happen again when you are in your new habits.

If items are in date but you know you won't use them – perhaps you bulk-bought something that no one likes or will eat – set it aside so that you can donate it to a food bank or homeless shelter, so someone else can benefit from it. If you bought a bag of quinoa or tin of mixed beans in a moment of enthusiasm to eat healthily, but they are still sitting there, have a look through the recipes in this book before you ditch them. Go on, give them one last try...

By now you should have thinned out what you have, and it's time to put everything back. Don't just shove it all on the shelves, though; you're going to get really organised now to make life easier later.

It's time to get organised!

Whether you are theming your cupboards or not, think like a supermarket and put the items with the soonest use-by or best-before date at the front so you use them first, and the items with a longer shelf life at the back. You will waste far less this way.

You'll feel really satisfied now – you've got rid of all the clutter and you can see exactly what you've got, and what you need to stock up on.

Everyday **Easy**

Organising ingredients into themed zones will make finding them easier and prepping meals much quicker, as you know exactly where everything is when you need it. For instance, put all the items in one cupboard that you use on a regular or everyday basis, then perhaps the sweet treats and foods you want out of sight and out of mind in another cupboard – preferably high up!

Got the decluttering and organising bug?

If that little purge has inspired you, you could perhaps invest in some cupboard organisers that make it easier to see what you have. Try storing bags of rice, pasta, cereals and dried beans and pulses in clear rectangular containers – not only does this stop the ingredients spilling out over the shelves, but these take up less room, and because they are transparent you can easily see when packets are nearly empty. You can label the boxes to show what's inside, if you like, and even add the expiry date.

Back to basics

Having a well-stocked kitchen will take a lot of stress out of cooking. Keeping a good supply of everyday basic ingredients means you'll never get caught short on a busy night, nor be tempted to reach for that takeaway menu. With a little mix and match, you can have dinner on the table in no time at all without needing to nip out to the shops.

Store cupboard staples

- **Rice** (basmati, long grain white, wholegrain and risotto).
- **Dried pasta** (maybe three or four different shapes and sizes, such as spaghetti, fusilli, etc).
- **Dried egg or rice noodles** (for stir-fries, soups and curries).
- **Grains for salads and packing out dishes** – couscous, bulgur wheat, pearl barley and quinoa.
- **Tinned pulses and beans** – chickpeas, cannellini, red kidney and butter beans and green lentils (for pasta sauces, curries, stews, salads).
- **Tinned chopped tomatoes** (for sauces, stews, curries).
- **Tinned coconut milk** (for curries).
- **Pesto, curry paste, jar of roasted peppers.**
- **Tinned fish** such as tuna, salmon, mackerel (for fishcakes, salads, sandwiches).
- **Tinned fruit** – for pudding or breakfast in a flash!
- **Good selection of dried herbs and spices** for livening up the most humble dish – oregano, smoked paprika, chilli (flakes or powder, mild or hot), cinnamon, cumin, coriander, curry powder or paste, five-spice, turmeric, ginger and fennel seeds are all good.
- **Seasoning and condiments** – sea salt flakes or crystals and black peppercorns for grinding, reduced-salt stock cubes/stock pots, soy sauce (gluten free for coeliacs, or tamari, check the label), tomato purée, Worcestershire sauce, tomato ketchup, mayonnaise, brown sauce, mustard.
- **Oils and vinegars** – vegetable, rapeseed or groundnut oil for cooking; olive oil for dressings; red wine, white wine, cider and balsamic vinegars for marinades, dressings and sauces.
- **Baking kit** – plain flour, self-raising flour, bread flour, baking powder, bicarbonate of soda, dried yeast, cocoa powder, vanilla extract, caster, granulated, soft brown and icing sugars, clear honey, porridge oats, dried fruit, nuts and seeds.

Keeping it fresh with your freezer

- **Bags of frozen veg** (such as peas and mixed veg), **prawns** and **fish pie mix** are perfect for speedy stir-fries, pasta dishes, risottos and stews or curries.
- **Frozen berries** make speedy smoothies, can be whizzed up and eaten immediately as a softly whipped low fat ice cream, or can be added to porridge.
- **Fish, chicken and meat** – defrost fully overnight in the fridge or in the microwave oven for a filling meal.
- **Keeping a sliced loaf** in your freezer means you always have bread for toast or making sandwiches (or breadcrumbs) when you've run out of the fresh stuff.

Get to Grips with Your Gadgets

You've done a great stock check on your food, now let's look at the remainder of the kitchen cupboards…

Cooking from scratch might be new to you, in which case you might not have much equipment, or perhaps you were once a really keen cook until life and work took over and left you reaching for the ready meals, so your cupboards are overflowing with kit that never sees the light of day. If that's you, now's the time to have a blitz. Just as you did for the food, get everything out. I bet there are a few surprises – did you really know what was in there all this time?

So, be honest with yourself, do you really need that dust-covered juicer as well as a blender, hand-held stick blender and food-processor, and how many pans and frying pans do you use? Get out all your gadgets and ask yourself, which do I use on a regular basis? You're going to be cooking a lot more from scratch now, but you don't need everything.

Keeping kit simple

Overwhelmed by all the equipment? Not sure what you're going to need? Here's a handy list of useful stuff to help you get kitted out:

- **Saucepans** – 3–5 pans with lids, preferably non-stick, in various sizes. Ovenproof handles are useful if you want to transfer a one-pot to the oven or grill.
- **Frying pan** – again, non-stick and preferably with a lid. If you make a lot of pancakes or omelettes, get a smaller, thin-edged frying pan, too.
- **Wok** – not essential, but they are brilliant for stir-fries. A decent-quality one will last for ages; you can get them from hardware shops, large supermarkets and online.
- **Colander and sieve** – plastic or metal – great for draining foods and sifting dry ingredients.
- **Mixing bowl** – at least one large and one small. Ideally get a heatproof one that you can add hot ingredients to.
- **A couple of sharp kitchen knives** – one for chopping or carving, another for cutting fruit and veg.
- **Chopping boards** – wooden boards are durable and look

Everyday **Easy**

Pass it on
Don't just chuck everything you don't want or need – keep a box to one side and pack it all away, then either donate the stuff to teenagers heading off to college/ uni or moving out, or to charity shops. That way everyone wins – you get nice clear cupboards and someone else benefits from your clearout.

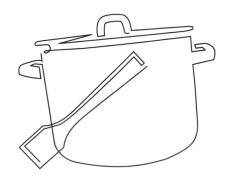

Everyday Easy

Make food prep a breeze at the end of a long day by having all your equipment organised and to hand to save you rummaging around mid-cooking. When you put everything back, know where you put it, and group similar equipment together – i.e. breakfast stuff, such as the kettle and toaster. Put things you use every day out on the worktop, and have cooking spoons and other utensils in a drawer by the oven or in a pot nearby.

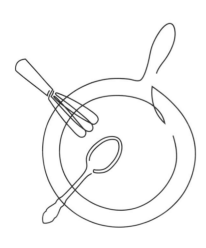

nice but plastic are easy to clean and more hygienic. If you can afford it, get a few in different colours and keep them separate for prepping raw meat, poultry and fish, cooked meats and vegetables.

- Kitchen scissors.
- Speedy/vegetable peeler.
- Tin opener.
- Grater – a simple box grater covers fine and coarse grating.
- Whisk – for whipping cream and whisking egg whites.
- Wooden spoon – good for baking and stirring foods in saucepans.
- Spatula and fish slices – silicone ones are best for non-stick surfaces. Also a slotted spoon for removing food from pans, draining off cooking fat and water.
- Potato masher.
- Hand-held stick blender – a great alternative to an electric worktop blender in smaller kitchens. Good for blending soups, sauces and smoothies.
- Measuring jug – ideally heatproof for measuring out hot water/stock.
- Scales – digital ones are really precise.
- Roasting tin, baking sheets and trays, 12-hole muffin tin, 1kg loaf tin and a couple of cake tins.
- Baking parchment, clingfilm, foil, kitchen paper.
- Ovenproof baking dish for pasta bakes, lasagne, shepherd's pie, etc.
- Pepper and salt mills.
- Oven glove and tea towels.
- Airtight storage/freezerproof and microwaveable containers.
- Resealable food (and freezer) bags.
- Rolling pin.
- Wire rack for cooling cakes, biscuits, etc – or use a clean grill rack.

Kit for the wish list – non-essential (but nice) items

- Food-processor – really useful for blending, making cake batters, pastry or breadcrumbs.
- Slow cooker/pressure cooker – both great time-savers and fantastic for one-pot family cooking. A slow cooker allows you to leave dinner bubbling away all day but uses a fraction of the energy required to cook on the hob, and it is great for getting the best out of cheap cuts of meat.

A pressure cooker does the same thing but in reverse, allowing you to prepare dinner quickly in one pot but still managing to tenderise meat in a fraction of the time.

Start with a plan

Cupboards sorted? You're ready to start planning. Knowing what you are going to cook when and having all the ingredients to hand will make everyday life so much easier. That evening dinner chaos will be a thing of the past – no rushing into the shops on the way home with hungry kids in the car or a famished family waiting at home, just open the fridge or the cupboards and get dinner on.

So, take a look at the recipes in this book, or if you're new to this, check out the menu plans at the back which will get you started for the first few weeks until you're in the swing of it. Then write down the meals you'd like to cook across the week. You can include breakfasts and lunch if you're at home all day or taking packed lunches to work (a real money-saver!) or school.

Top tips

- **Who are you feeding and when?** Is everyone home every evening or is there a steady drift in and out that means meals at different times? Will life be easier if there's a one-pot bubbling away to help themselves to, or something that can be reheated easily?
- **Does anyone have special dietary requirements** or are they fussy eaters? (see page 28)
- If you're all meat-eaters, **how about going meat-free once or twice a week?** Meat tends to be the most expensive item in the shopping trolley, so eating more veggie-based meals not only saves you money but will boost your fibre intake and meet your 5-a-day (see page 24).

- **Mix it up** – vary the menu and ensure you're not eating the same thing every day, or the same ingredients night after night.
- **Think in bulk** – if it's cheaper to buy something in larger packets, ensure you can store what you don't need for another day, or use it in another meal the same week – and don't forget about it!
- **Make a list** of what you need according to the recipes, then check to see if you have any of the ingredients in the cupboards already. While you're at it, check your everyday cupboard and see if you're running low on any of your staples.

Beat the Budget

So you want to save money on food, but do you actually know what you spend each week? Sometimes the reality of this figure can be quite a shock – we might know how much the 'big shop' costs, but those little trips out for milk, snacks or something quick for dinner can really bump up the total.

Ditching these extra spends is a great place to start, but there are many other ways in which you can reduce your shopping bills. So, let's get going.

Where are you going wrong?

Have a look at your last few supermarket receipts or orders and see where you are spending the most. Can you cut back on those items or buy own-brand, cheaper versions? How many items are there that are expensive treats or that you could do without or buy less regularly? Do you actually need everything you bought, or do you already have some of them and popped them into your trolley without checking? How about setting yourself a target to save all food receipts for a week – or even a month! – you might be shocked at just how much those 'little treat spends' add up. If you don't have those receipts, keep track of your spending for one week to give yourself a guide.

Set your budget

Have a look at your spending and decide: do you want to set a weekly budget for food or just an amount by which you'd like to reduce your spending? If it makes it easier to stick to your budget, take cash with you when you go shopping, or order online where you can see the price totting up as you go along. You can even log on to price comparison sites to compare prices of food between supermarkets. Try low-cost supermarkets and own-brand goods, too, which are often just as good as their more expensive rivals. And you never know, you might even prefer them!

Start from scratch

And that means cooking from scratch. Takeaways and ready meals are expensive and will cause a real dent in your finances. Preparing your own food is healthier, cheaper and can even save you time – don't forget that cooking in your microwave is ok if it's something freshly made. You can batch cook for another day, prepare your breakfast the night before, or use leftovers in or for other meals or pack them up for lunch. One meal can stretch to several with a little bit of thought!

What goes where?

Storing fresh food properly can extend its lifespan, so put everything away as soon as it arrives in your kitchen.

In the fridge:
- All packets labelled 'keep refrigerated'!
- Dairy products.
- Meat, poultry and fish – put raw ingredients on the bottom shelf, tightly covered, so they can't contaminate other foods. Once you've cooked these, ensure they are properly covered and stored above raw meats, so there is no chance of raw juices falling onto them.
- Eggs will last for up to 3 weeks if kept in the fridge, but do keep them in the packaging so you can check the use-by date. If in doubt about the freshness of your eggs, pop them in a bowl of cold water; if they sink to the bottom they are very fresh, if they float they are no longer safe to eat.
- Vegetables – pretty much all veg (except winter squash, potatoes, onions and garlic) last longer in the fridge, sometimes you can even double the lifespan quoted on the packet.

- Fruit – although lemons and limes for zesting are best kept at room temperature to keep them juicy.
- Herbs – take these out of their plastic wrapping, trim off the base of the stems and pop them in water, or wrap sturdy herbs, such as thyme and rosemary, with damp kitchen paper.

In the cupboards/at room temperature:
- All tinned/packaged foods.
- Oils, vinegars and unopened condiments – but once opened it is better to store condiments in the fridge.
- Dried herbs and spices.
- Nuts, seeds and dried fruits.
- Fresh foods, such as garlic, onions and shallots, potatoes and winter squash can be kept in a cool, dry place for up to 2 weeks – they will keep their flavour better than when stored in the fridge.

Cooking for Busy Days

For many people, time is what holds them back from cooking at home. There are always going to be nights when you're just too tired to cook or you're home late and need feeding fast. This is where freezing extra food – whether batch-cooked or leftovers – can be a lifesaver. You can just whip it out of the freezer and leave to defrost in the fridge during the day if you know in advance you'll be late, or pop it in the microwave for instant gratification!

So, first up, clear out your freezer. Anything that looks dubious or that might have been there for a while can probably go. Likewise, any meat that has that dry, white colouring on it has got freezer burn and won't taste good when defrosted. Check everything else that's left and organise it properly so you have all fruit and veg together, bread on one shelf, meat, poultry and fish, etc., on another, and so on.

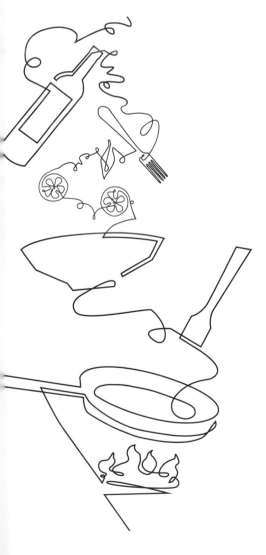

Next, invest in some freezerproof stackable containers or 'store and pour' resealable food bags to decant food into – these are brilliant environmentally friendly options, as you can use them again and again. Get containers in various sizes – little boxes are great for individual portions – and bags take up even less space when frozen flat – which also means food defrosts quicker and there's less waste as you won't be defrosting more than you'll eat. If they are microwaveable, too, even better, then you can transfer the food from freezer to microwave easily. Get yourself some sticky labels so you can mark up what is in each container and add the date, too. Just as in your cupboards, store in the freezer food that needs to be eaten soonest at the front, to reduce wastage.

Cooking in batches isn't as time-consuming as it sounds, and the little extra work will pay dividends when midweek mania hits and everyone is staring at the fridge hopefully. If you've got the time at the weekend, say, spend a couple of hours preparing a few different meals that you can package up and pop in the freezer, or if time is short, just double or treble the quantities of a recipe when you're cooking and store the extra portions – it takes no longer.

Is it worth the effort?

Need convincing that it's worth giving up an afternoon or evening cooking to save you time on another day? Here are a few reasons why:

- You can go to town on those bulk-buy offers without wasting anything. Simply cook them up and pop them in the freezer; ditto for leftovers, if they won't get eaten the next day, pack them up and freeze them.

- Having home-cooked food to hand will keep you on track with your budget and eating healthily. Freezing individual, sensible portion sizes means you won't overeat and you also won't reach for the takeaway menu because you're too tired to cook.

- It's a great way to ensure that anyone who has different nutritional requirements always has something to eat, especially on those nights when you just want to cook one thing for the remainder of the family. Simply freeze in individual portions and label.

Freezing tips

- **Always ensure that food has cooled completely** before you put it in the fridge or freezer – otherwise the heat from the container will raise the temperature of your fridge/freezer, meaning it will have to work hard and use more energy (= more money) to get to its optimum temperature.
- **Freeze fresh food fast!** – food keeps well if it is frozen as soon as possible (and as quickly as possible – use the fast-freeze switch if your freezer has one), so get it in the freezer on the day of purchase and well before the use-by date.
- **Pack it up** – always use appropriate packaging to store foods to protect foods and prevent 'freezer burn'. Don't use glass containers; the extreme temperatures may cause the glass to break. Leave some space at the top of containers before you seal them, as liquids expand during freezing.
- **When defrosting**, ideally defrost, covered, overnight in the fridge, and ensure reheated food is piping hot all the way through before eating.

Everyday Easy

Colour-code or label packages with different marker pens or coloured stickers for meat, fish, or veg dishes to help you identify foods quickly, or even for specific members of your family, so it's quick and easy to whip out what you need.

Foods for freezing

YES!

- **Fruit and vegetables:** Soft fruit, such as raspberries and blueberries, and chopped vegetables should be frozen on baking sheets covered in clingfilm, spaced apart, to prevent them sticking together, then tipped into a freezerproof container once frozen. Blanch super-fresh vegetables before freezing by plunging them first into boiling water, then into cold/iced water to stop the cooking process.
- **Meat and poultry:** Put raw meat and poultry straight into the freezer after purchase – either in its packaging or divide it up into usable portions first.
- **Fish and seafood:** Only freeze super-fresh fish – freeze fillets either wrapped, in freezerproof bags or sealed containers. Freeze seafood in its packaging.
- **Bread and cakes:** Slice loaves or whole cakes before freezing, then double-wrap in foil or pop in a resealable food bag – it can make separating bread/cake slices easier if you pop a little greaseproof paper tab between them, then you can defrost a slice at a time. Buns, bread rolls, pitta breads and home-made pizza bases can be stored wrapped, too.
- **Chicken/meat and vegetable stocks:** Making your own stock after a roast or using odds and ends from the vegetable drawer is a fantastic way to get something from otherwise wasted ingredients. Pour the stock into ice-cube trays or muffin tins to freeze in usable portions, then pop them out into a resealable freezer bag to store easily.
- **Dairy:** Butter, margarine and cheese can all be frozen, as can milk – although if you are freezing milk in its original packaging, pour off a little first as it will expand as it freezes. Cheese can be frozen as whole chunks, or grate it and then you can use it straight from the freezer.
- **Eggs:** Don't freeze eggs in their shells, as they will expand and crack. Separate whites and yolks and freeze in separate containers.

NO!
Some foods don't take well to freezing, as on defrosting they lose their texture or flavour. They're still safe to eat, but might be better off whizzed in a blender to make a smoothie, soup or other dish which doesn't need them to keep their structure.

- **Vegetables with a high water content:** Lettuce, cucumber, radishes, as well as mushrooms.
- **Ingredients with a higher fat content:** Cream, egg-based sauces, yoghurt, full fat and low fat soft cheeses.
- **Soft herbs:** Parsley, basil and chives turn black when frozen, so they are good only for cooking, but not as a garnish.
- **Previously frozen food:** Don't freeze previously frozen food, unless it was raw on previous freezing and you have cooked it into a dish, in which case, it's a yes.

Tips and Tricks for Students

Whether moving out of home for the first time or going to college or uni, cooking on a budget is just one lesson that young adults need to learn – fast! Living within their means is a common issue for students who are on a low income and have a lot of essential expenses.

Setting yourself a budget and sticking to it is vital – do this on paper or set up a spreadsheet. First, you need to include rent and education fees – these are non-negotiable and must be paid before anything else. Then see what you have left and divide it up for food, books, clothes and – going out!

Ensure you set aside money for food, and stick to using it for that purpose – don't be tempted to dip into it for nights out instead. Students often fall into the trap of a weight gain in their first year, that's been dubbed 'fresher's stone', because they have been relying on ready meals, takeaways and sugary snacks to get through the days, not to mention the increased alcohol intake which just piles on the pounds – in more ways than one!

Before you head to college/uni, teach yourself a few recipes that you can make up with minimal ingredients and minimal equipment, which will make it less tempting to pick something up on the way home.

Top tips for staying healthy as a student

- **When you are looking for digs, see if there's a freezer**, and if so, make full use of it – the chances are your housemates won't be using it for much more than ice cubes! Load it up with batch-cooked meals and bags of frozen fruit and veg, so you can get your 5 a day with easy meals or whizz up a smoothie.
- **Take advantage of special offers if they are worth it** – only buy what you know you will eat, or if it's a multi-offer, see if you can share it with fellow students and split the cost.
- **Go veggie a few days a week** – meat is expensive, so find alternative, cheaper protein sources and bulk out meals with other ingredients to make them go further.

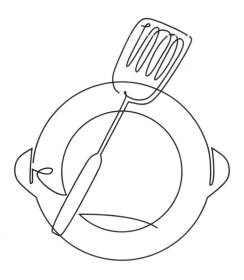

Everyday **Easy**

- **Prepare your own food at home** to avoid spending on takeaways or ready meals – this has the bonus of either cooking extra for the freezer or taking leftovers into college/ uni for lunch the next day.
- **Eat breakfast every morning** – it will keep the hunger pangs at bay and keep you alert through lectures. If you know you might need a boost mid-morning, pack healthy snacks for the day, to save you buying chocolate and unhealthy snacks.
- **Take a refillable water bottle** into lectures so you can top it up throughout the day rather than keep buying water in plastic bottles – it's good for both the environment and your wallet. It's really important to stay hydrated to function properly – aim to drink about 1.2 litres of fluids a day (not alcoholic!).
- **Steer clear of coffee shops** – get yourself a reusable hot drink cup and make your drink in the morning to take into college/ uni if you need that caffeine hit first thing. Don't overdo it on energy drinks or caffeine to burn the candle at both ends – set yourself one or two nights a week when you hit the hay early.
- **Cook with housemates** – maybe create a rota for who cooks when, and all chip in to buy the ingredients. Cooking in bulk will save you money and time, and is a great way to check in with your friends, or even to discuss any 'house' issues.

Eating Healthily Every Day

Eating well for less is not just a solution for those times when you feel the pinch, it's a sensible way of living – permanently. If you aren't used to cooking from scratch every day, or thinking about the cost of your food or what you are eating, adopting this new approach to shopping and eating can seem a bit overwhelming, but as with any lifestyle change, with a little time and commitment it will become part of your life.

Advice for a healthy balanced diet can be summed up with the Eatwell Guide (available online, try www.nhs.uk/live-well/eat-well/the-eatwell-guide), which divides foods into four sections:

1   **Fruit and veg**; at least five separate portions of 80g per day are recommended. This section should take up a third of your daily diet.
2   **Starchy foods**; another third of your diet each day should come from starchy foods, including potatoes (skin on, ideally), bread, rice, pasta or other starchy carbohydrates (preferably wholegrain or high-fibre options).
3   **Dairy or dairy alternatives**; for protein, vitamins and minerals such as calcium. Try sometimes to choose reduced-fat and reduced-sugar options.
4   **Beans, pulses, fish, eggs, meat and other protein**; good sources of vitamins and minerals, too. Pulses make a lower fat alternative to meat, and if you eat fish, try to aim for one portion of oily fish each week.

Not sure how to get this into your daily routine? Here are a few tips:

- **Think positively**; it's not about giving things up or making sacrifices, it's about making a deliberate change for a healthier you and a healthier bank balance.
- **Set yourself a routine to make every day easier**; maybe pick one night on which you will plan your menu and write your shopping list, one night/day on which you will do some batch-cooking, another day on which you will do your weekly shop or have it delivered. Write it on your calendar to make it a fixed part of your week.

Everyday Easy

If you dread clearing up after cooking, these tips will give you back some time after dinner.

- *Clear up as you go – clear away bowls, pans and knives, wipe over work surfaces.*
- *Use less equipment – heat your pasta sauce in the pan you've cooked the pasta in, or use the same frying pan for every stage of a recipe, just give it a wipe clean. Even better, pick a one-pot recipe – these are great for chucking together loads of ingredients and will leave you with just one pan to wash!*

- **Don't beat yourself up over a 'bad' day**; if you slip into old habits, don't dwell on it; get back into the kitchen again.
- **Ease yourself into the change**; if the idea of this being forever is too daunting, tell yourself you'll give this a go for a month, then see where you are at. Taking the pressure off yourself will make it much easier.
- **Start simple**; new to cooking? Not sure where to begin? Turn to the menu planners in this book (see page 213) and use these to get you into the rhythm of your new lifestyle. Choose simple recipes with only a few ingredients until you get kitchen confident.
- **Give yourself a pat on the back**; after two weeks, or a month, check in with yourself and your bank balance and see how well you have done. Do you feel/look healthier? Are you sleeping better or do you have more energy? Do you have more spare cash? Are your cupboards and fridge no longer bulging with uneaten food?
- **Phone a friend**; get someone to do this with you. Having a friend involved will keep you on track and you could even share deals or swap recipes with each other.
- **Remove temptation**; the best way to avoid the old ways? Ditch the junk. If it's not in the cupboard, you won't be tempted by it.

Time saving

You've probably slipped into bad habits because of time – or lack of it. This is often why people opt for convenience foods, because they are just that: convenient. However, in our busy lives full of rush, rush, rush, we are constantly being reminded to take some time out and slow down. Cooking is a fantastic way to do this; it allows you to clear your head and even interact with your family as you cook or eat together.

Still worried about how much time all this is going to take? Here are some time-saving tips:

- **Be organised;** knowing what you are cooking and when saves debate over what's for dinner at the end of a long day, and saves time spent staring into the fridge wondering what you are going to pull together for the hungry hordes (see page 13).
- **Take stock;** keeping your cupboards organised (see page 8)

means you can find food in a flash and also know at a glance what you're running low on.

- **Have a backup plan;** if you're late home and you really don't have time to cook the dish you were planning, try not to resort to ready meals – take something home-made out of the freezer, or whip up a quick and simple dinner from some staples in the cupboard. Remember to cook the meal you skipped on your planner the next night, though, or cook and freeze so you don't waste the ingredients.

- **Fill up your freezer;** batch-cooking will save you time on another busy day (see page 16), and if you store things in portions you will cut back on wastage.

- **Easy everyday kit;** if you can afford to, maybe invest in some time-saving equipment, such as a slow cooker or pressure cooker, and a blender. Time saved in the kitchen will be time you can spend on other things.

- **Get ahead on tomorrow;** while dinner is cooking, prep for the morning. Maybe prepare the ingredients for breakfast in advance, for example, if you like to whip up a smoothie or serve up porridge. If you have packed lunches for school or the office, make a start on these now and pop them in the fridge. It's one less thing to think about in the morning rush.

Hacking meal prep

Cooking from scratch doesn't have to mean loads of preparation; there are a few shortcuts that can make life easier.

- **Buy frozen veg** – carrots, broccoli, cauliflower, green beans and other veg come ready chopped, spinach is already wilted, peas are always a great standby, and all are ready to pop into a recipe straight from frozen.

- **Ditch the peeler** – give root veg and fruit with thin skins a really good wash or scrub and chop up. The skin is where the maximum amount of nutrients are contained, not to mention fibre, so don't chuck it away.

- **Prep two meals in one** – if you're chopping veg and know you'll need more tomorrow, do twice the amount and store the remainder in an airtight container in the fridge ready to go.

- **Don't forget your microwave** – par-cook potatoes before baking to reduce their oven time, and steam veg in microwaveable steamers – it's super speedy and preserves the maximum amount of nutrients.

- **Put lids on pans** – covering pans makes the contents cook quicker – and you'll save money on energy bills, too.

- **Use leftovers** – eat them for your next meal, or as part of it, bulked up with a few freshly prepared ingredients to ring the changes; it will still save on some prep time.

Why 5 a Day?

We all know that fruit and vegetables are a vital component in a healthy diet – and that many of us aren't managing to eat enough of them. The advice from the World Health Organization is that there are significant health benefits to be had by eating at least five separate portions of 80g of different fruit and veg each day (see box).

You can get your 5 a day in many forms – fresh, frozen, canned, dried and juiced (although if you are buying tinned fruits, ensure they are in natural juice, not the sugary syrup). There is a huge variety of fruit and veg to pick from so you can always find something you like, and it won't break your budget. Don't forget that potatoes do not count here, as they mostly contain starch.

And then when you get to five, why stop? There's no harm in eating more…

How much is a portion?

Eating 5 a day sounds daunting, but in fact, it's not that hard when you think about what actually constitutes a portion. There is a lot of confusion about portion sizes, which have got bigger and bigger (see page 27). So let's take the stress out of eating sensibly, and here's a guide to portion sizes:

One portion is roughly equivalent to:
- 1 apple, orange, banana or pear
- 1 large slice of melon or pineapple
- 2 plums, satsumas or kiwi fruit, 3 apricots or 7 strawberries
- 1 glass of pure fruit juice (this includes from concentrate) – note this only counts as one portion no matter how much you drink in a day
- 1 tablespoon dried fruit (be warned that dried fruit can be high in sugar, so don't make this a major source)
- 3 celery sticks, 2 broccoli spears, 1 medium raw carrot, 5cm piece of cucumber, or 7 cherry tomatoes
- 3 tablespoons cooked vegetables – carrots, peas or sweetcorn, 8 cauliflower florets
- A dessert bowl of salad
- 3 heaped tablespoons baked beans or chickpeas

For children, a portion size is even easier – it's as much as they can hold in their hand.

5 a day on a budget

Eating more fruit and veg doesn't have to be expensive.
Try these tips to getting a trolley load within your budget.

- **Choose fruit and veg that are in season** – they are cheaper when they are produced locally, not to mention better for the environment and local farmers.
- **Try local food markets** – you might find they are cheaper
- **When you're in the supermarket**, look for marked-down ingredients and cook them up into stews, soups and casseroles to pop in the freezer.
- **Swap crisps and chocolate bars for fruit** – better for your body and your budget, as a piece of fruit can cost half as much as a sugary snack.
- **Adding vegetables to stews, curries or casseroles** is a really economical way to bulk out meaty dishes, saving money and easily increasing your veg intake.
- **Buy loose fruit and veg** rather than pre-packaged and trimmed – you will buy what you need and not waste any, and not spend on environmentally damaging plastics, too.

Everyday Easy

Sun's out and the barbecue is on, but don't just opt for the usual meat for the grill. If you are making kebabs with red meat, chicken or prawns, alternate these with chunks of vegetables – it reduces the expensive ingredients and bumps up your veg intake. Wrap up sweet potatoes or corn on the cob and bake them on the grill, and for dessert do the same with bananas in their skins.

Stuck for ideas to get that fruit and veg count up?

Here are a few easy ways to do it.

Breakfast

- Add fresh, frozen or tinned berries or sliced apple or banana to pancakes, low fat natural yoghurt or fromage frais, porridge or cereal. Whizz up a smoothie in your blender – you can get up to two portions in one drink if you choose carefully.
- Make your own muesli (or granola) and add your favourite dried fruits; serve with semi-skimmed milk or a dollop of low fat natural yoghurt and some fresh fruit, too.
- Grill some mushrooms or tomatoes.

Snacks

- Snack on dried fruits or fresh fruit (check the portion sizes). Or go for veg snacks – try carrot, celery, pepper or cucumber sticks.
- Give your children fruit for snacks instead of sweets. Bananas, apples, satsumas, small bunches of grapes or small tins of fruit are ideal in lunchboxes, or give them small packets of dried fruit.

Lunch

- Make up a salad, pack a sandwich with lettuce, tomatoes, cucumber, peppers or grated carrot or slice up some raw veg to eat with a low fat dip or houmous. Wash it down with unsweetened fruit juice.
- Whizz up some soup using whatever veg you have in the fridge or follow a recipe. Add some beans and pulses, too (although no matter how many beans, pulses and lentils you eat in a day it still only counts as one portion).

Dinner

- Ensure you have at least two portions of different veg on your plate – potatoes don't count. Serve up a side of peas or green beans or a mixed salad. If you have a spiralizer, why not spiralize some courgettes and serve them with tomato-based sauces as a substitute for pasta.
- Add frozen or chopped fresh vegetables, such as carrots, peas or mushrooms, to soups, stews, bolognaise sauce or home-made burgers.
- Cook up a stir-fry – pack in peppers, onion, broccoli, beansprouts and carrots for a rainbow of veg. It's also a brilliant way to use up any stray vegetables.
- Fruit salad makes a great pudding, and any leftovers can always be eaten for breakfast, or pop squares of fruit onto skewers for children as dessert or a healthy fun snack.

How much is too much?

In the Western world we are guilty of super-sizing portions; reducing the amount of food on our plates is good not only for our waistlines, but also our wallets. To cook less food, you buy less food – simple.

If you're not used to cooking or you're not following a recipe, it's really easy to cook too much. Always weigh out food according to the recipe, and get into the habit of weighing out pasta or rice (one portion is 75g uncooked pasta/rice/noodles – the size of your fist). At first these might seem smaller than you are used to, but you will quickly get used to the new regime, and still feel full! Studies have shown that if you put too much on your plate you will most likely eat it all, so reduce temptation and avoid overeating.

Controlling your portion size is important for everyone to stay healthy, not just those who are trying to lose weight, and it means less wastage, too. The average adult man needs 2,500 kcals a day to maintain a healthy body weight, whereas for women this figure is 2,000 kcals, but obviously this figure might need to be higher if you are particularly tall or very physically active, or lower if you are overweight and trying to lose weight.

Everyday Easy

The British Nutrition Foundation (BNF) has a great free online guide to portion sizes, called Find Your Balance, that you can download and stick on your fridge (www.nutrition. org.uk/healthyliving/ find-your-balance/ portionwise.html). It offers spoon and hand measurements instead of weights, to make it really easy to get the right portion size.

Top tips for getting portions under control

- **Drink a glass of water before eating** – it will fill you up so you want to eat less.
- **Use smaller plates** – try side plates instead of dinner plates, or use your children's plates.
- **Fill half of your plate with vegetables or salad** – this will also help you get to your 5 a day!
- **Eat slowly and mindfully** – focus on eating and don't be distracted by working, reading, watching TV or flicking through your phone, then you'll be aware of how much you're eating and when you feel full.
- **One or two healthy snacks between meals** – such as a piece of fruit, raw veg and dips – will satiate hunger pangs but not fill you up.
- **Serve up onto individual plates as portions** and pack away leftovers immediately to go in the fridge for lunch or the freezer for another day, which will stop you going back for seconds.

Special Diets

The more people there are in your household, the more likely it is that you will have to accommodate a variety of dietary needs. This isn't about fussy eating, this is about tweaking family meals because of medical issues or lifestyle choices, such as allergies or choosing not to eat animal products. If this is your family, you might be feeling a little overwhelmed at trying to plan one meal for everyone, but don't panic – here are a few tips that can make this a whole lot easier!

Putting it all together

Some families might only have to cater for one member with a special dietary requirement, whereas others might have more than one issue, but either way, it doesn't have to mean spending all evening in the kitchen preparing different plates trying to satisfy everyone.

If the issue is an allergy, consider whether it is severe enough that that particular ingredient should be kept out of the house, or if you can still cook it for the remainder of the family.

Put simply, you need to decide whether you change everyone's diet to fit the restriction(s), or whether you just make a few adaptations for it. As with any changes, the way you approach this can make the whole thing easier, so be positive:

- **Flip the picture:** rather than being sad about what you can't eat, think about what you can eat – put it this way and you'll soon see there is still a huge range of foods available to you.
- **Don't always try to replicate favourite dishes** by swapping in an alternative ingredient which sometimes can taste nothing like the original; instead, try some different recipes to find a new favourite. Treat catering for mixed needs as a fantastic opportunity for everyone to broaden their diet and find new flavours.
- **If you don't want to eliminate specific foods** for the remainder of the family, try preparing meals for the majority, with a slight tweak for the person with allergies/dietary choices. Serve gluten free pasta alongside a sauce that everyone shares, or make the main part of the meal vegetarian and serve meat on the side with an alternative for veggies.

Quick meals for the masses

There are a few good options that you can serve to all without having to make too many personalised changes, just offering up a couple of options for allergies or non-meat-eaters.

- **Tacos and wraps** – pile filling ingredients into separate bowls and serve up gluten free wraps alongside wheat or corn ones. Set everything on the table and let everyone help themselves.
- **Pizzas** – serve up gluten free bases for those with allergies, and have a selection of toppings at the ready for everyone to make their own pizzas. It's also a fun way to get the family involved.
- **Red lentils** – a great alternative to mince, they have a slightly chewy texture and rich depth of flavour, and are filling and packed with protein. Make a base sauce and add lentils to some of it rather than mince to make a delicious one-pot veggie bolognaise sauce, curry or shepherd's pie. Or make a big batch and freeze individual portions.
- **Whip up a stir-fry** – so quick to make you can make a couple of versions for dinner, wiping out the pan in between. Add prawns, chicken, red meat or tofu to vegetables and serve with some rice or noodles.

Vegan and Vegetarian

Following a vegan or vegetarian diet isn't as tricky as it sounds, as long as you know what is off-limits.

Vegans and vegetarians have slightly different requirements: a vegetarian usually won't eat meat, poultry and fish but will eat eggs and dairy; a vegan diet is more restrictive and rules out all foods that derive from animals in any form, including dairy products, eggs and often honey, as well as by-products such as rennet (used in cheese-making) and gelatine (used in desserts and sweets).

Cooking for a vegan diet may require a little more planning, because you do need to read the labels on products carefully, but if you are cooking from scratch, both vegetarian and vegan diets are pretty easy to cater for. Essentially, fruit and vegetables form the foundation of any plant-based diet, but these can be varied with a huge selection of easily sourced beans, pulses and grains. There are so many different types of these ingredients to choose from now, so mix it up, rotating your favourite ingredients or trying new ones.

A vegan diet is rich in fibre, vitamin C and folate, but it can be short on other nutrients, including vitamins B12 and D and omega 3 fats, so you need to plan what you eat carefully to ensure you are providing everything your body needs to stay healthy.

Veggie on a budget

If the health and environmental benefits of cutting out meat from your diet aren't enough to convince you to eat veggie, think about the impact it will have on your wallet. Meat, poultry and fish are often the most expensive food items in your supermarket trolley, and according to Office for National Statistics figures for 2016, the average UK family spends a quarter of their weekly food budget on meat and fish, so reducing your meat intake will have a large impact on your expenditure.

If you are a committed meat-eater and cutting it out of your diet is a step too far right now, try reducing the number of days on which you eat it, or use less of it in recipes – bulking out the dish with more vegetables, pulses or beans. You will be getting an equally filling meal, with more fibre, at a much lower cost.

Here are a few tips for eating veggie on a budget:

- **Fresh, frozen, tinned and dried fruit and veg**, and fruit/veg juices, are all healthy and inexpensive options.
- **Buy fruit and veg in season from a local market**, or buy in bulk or when on offer and freeze what you don't need immediately (see page 17).
- **Don't ignore the mark-downs** – for example, overripe fruit can be frozen when you get home or used in smoothies, ice cream, fruit crumbles, etc. Vegetables that have seen better days and are going cheap can be used in soups, casseroles, stews, etc, or blanched and frozen immediately for another day.

Eat your way to 5 a day

One of the huge benefits of a plant-based diet is that it's pretty easy to meet the guideline 5 a day, which is made up of a minimum of 400g of a variety of fruit and veg each day – broken down as at least five separate portions of 80g per day (see also page 24).

Key nutrients for a healthy vegan body

- **Protein** – good sources are whole grains and legumes: lentils, peas, soya, beans, chickpeas and quinoa, as well as nuts and seeds. (Be aware that most Quorn products may contain egg and dairy, so if you are vegan, look for their specialist vegan range.)
- **Vitamins** – in particular it is important to meet your B12 and D requirements; vitamin D is often added to breakfast cereals or fortified vegan spreads, or can be obtained naturally through exposure to sunlight; B12 can be supplemented by including fortified breakfast cereals, soya milks and yeast extract.
- **Iron** – excellent sources are green leafy vegetables, such as cabbage, broccoli, spinach, kale and watercress, or you can get iron from fortified breakfast cereals, muesli, wholemeal bread, beans and pulses, tofu, nuts and pumpkin and sunflower seeds.

- **Calcium** – found in leafy green vegetables (but not spinach), bread and foods containing white or brown flour (although check baked goods for eggs or dairy ingredients), nuts, sesame seeds, raisins, prunes, tofu, pulses and fortified soya drinks.
- **Omega 3** – good sources are seeds, such as flaxseeds/linseeds and chia seeds, nuts and their oils, as well as rapeseed oil.

Everyday **Easy**

Think substitutes; incorporate grains and cereals into your diet, such as quinoa or amaranth (available from health food shops and some supermarkets), polenta, buckwheat, corn, millet and tapioca, which are all naturally gluten free. If you want to use breadcrumbs, swap them for polenta crumbs, and try buckwheat or rice pasta or rice noodles instead of the durum wheat-based versions.

Cooking for Allergies and Illnesses

If members of your family have food intolerances or a more severe reaction with an allergy, you will need to find ways of cooking without the troublesome food that makes them feel unwell.

Unlike allergies, where avoidance of a certain food is best, the symptoms of some illnesses and medical conditions can be alleviated by excluding specific foods from the diet. The key to improving health is understanding what causes the problem in the first place, or what aggravates it.

Coeliac

Gluten is the protein component found in wheat, rye and barley, which can either cause a reaction in the body that is seen as an allergy or intolerance, or result in the body's immune system attacking itself, which is the more serious illness of coeliac disease. If the latter is diagnosed, the best response is removing gluten from the diet in all its forms.

Gluten is found in any wheat-based products, including flour, bread, pasta, breakfast cereals, pastry, pizza bases, couscous, cakes and biscuits. It can also be found in processed foods such as soups, sauces, ready meals and sausages. Be careful, too, of oats, which can become cross-contaminated during production; if you are coeliac, buy gluten free oats to be on the safe side.

Diabetes

There are different types of diabetes, and not everyone with the condition requires the same management of it, but a healthy diet is important for people with both types, and can even prevent Type 2 diabetes.

- **Type 1 diabetes** is less common and usually develops before the age of 40. It must be managed by daily injections of insulin for the rest of the person's life. It occurs when the pancreas stops producing insulin, although it's not known why this happens.
- **Type 2 diabetes** is the non-insulin-dependent condition. It often develops in later life and can be controlled and even avoided with a healthy, balanced diet and regular exercise.

The recommended dietary guidelines for people who diabetic are pretty similar to those suggested for anyone wanting to live a healthy lifestyle: eating a nutritious diet and taking regular exercise. The bonus with adopting this approach is that it also helps you to manage your weight, blood glucose, blood pressure and blood cholesterol levels.

As a quick guide, here are a few top tips on keeping diabetes under control:

- **Cast a critical eye over your carbs** – choose healthier sources which won't make your blood sugar levels soar; whole grains, fruits and vegetables, pulses and dairy, and reduce your intake of white bread, white rice, sugary snacks and processed foods. This is particularly important for those with Type 1 diabetes.
- **Lose the fat** – trim fat from meat and use leaner cuts; spray pans with oil when cooking – you'll use much less – or bake, steam or grill foods instead. Use healthier fats, such as olive, rapeseed or mustard seed oil. Choose reduced-fat yoghurt, cheese, cream or milk.
- **Pump up the pulses** – reduce the amount of red and processed meat in your diet and replace these with poultry, eggs, fish, pulses and nuts. Oily fish is particularly beneficial, because it is rich in omega 3 oils, which help protect against heart disease – try salmon, mackerel, sardines and pilchards.
- **Eat the rainbow** – eat your 5 a day and beyond. Try to eat more fruit and veg with meals or as snacks, to get all the vitamins, minerals and fibre your body needs.
- **Slow down on salt** – too much increases the risk of high blood pressure, which can increase the likelihood of a stroke or heart disease. Aim for a maximum of 6g (roughly 1 teaspoon) a day. Replace salt with other flavourings, such as fresh or dried herbs and spices.
- **Say no to sugar** – try using dried fruit to sweeten cakes naturally or reduce the amount of sugar you use in baking and also in drinks – when added to tea and coffee, and choose unsweetened fruit juices, water and milk.
- **Drink sensibly** – alcohol is high in calories and sugar and people with diabetes should watch their intake carefully; it is not recommended to exceed the maximum weekly limit of 14 units.

Everyday Easy

Cooking from scratch gives you ultimate control over your diet, but if you do buy some ingredients in packets, check the labels. Look for green and orange (amber) flags for the healthier options, and avoid any with lots of red flags.

• **Keep active** – being physically active helps with diabetes management and also protects against heart disease. Aim for 150 minutes of moderate exercise taken in chunks across the week – even if it's just going for a walk.

Arthritis

Arthritis is often thought of as something that your grandparents suffer from, but in fact, it can affect anyone of any age – even children. It is a debilitating condition which causes pain and stiffness in muscles and joints, making movement – such as walking, moving, using your hands, lifting and standing – difficult, not to mention painful.

Although there are no specific diets or dietary supplements that will cure arthritis, a few changes to a diet can sometimes alleviate symptoms and help to manage pain. Being overweight puts an extra burden on the joints – in particular the back, knees, hips, feet and ankles – so losing some weight can also improve the condition. Think of it like this, the pressure on our knee joints is five or six times our body weight when walking, so for an arthritis sufferer this will feel significantly worse, and losing weight will ease that strain a little.

Weight loss for a healthy body and healthy joints

• **Cut down on fats** – fats have twice as many calories as the equivalent amount of protein, and eating just 30g less fat each day can save you as much as 270 calories.

• **Reduce sugar** – this sweetener has no nutrient value and is pure calories. Eating 30g (2 tablespoons) less sugar a day saves you 120 calories; so do without or, if you really need a sweet fix, replace this with artificial or natural sweeteners.

• **Eat the rainbow** – we all know we should eat our 5 a day for the huge number of nutritional benefits we get from fruit and veg, but did you also know that it has been suggested that antioxidants may help to protect joints by 'mopping up' some of the chemicals that cause inflammation? Filling your plate with healthy fruit and veg will also leave reduced room for less nutritious foods that have a higher calorie count.

• **Get out and exercise** – the best way to burn calories is to exercise them off, and this will help you to lose or manage weight, as well as increase your physical strength and suppleness. So find an exercise that you enjoy and that you are comfortable with, then doing it won't feel like such a chore.

There are some key vitamins and minerals that can help to ease the pain of arthritis, as well as a few food supplements:

Calcium

Osteoporosis is a risk for all of us as we age, especially women after the menopause, and many arthritis sufferers could also develop this condition, where bones become fragile and more likely to break. Your best way of preventing this is by ensuring that you have plenty of calcium in your diet – Versus Arthritis recommends a daily intake of calcium of 1,000 milligrams (mg), with added vitamin D if you're over 60.

Good sources are: dairy products, or for vegans calcium-enriched plant-based milks, fish eaten with their bones (sardines and salmon), and green leafy veg.

Iron

Iron is a key mineral for preventing anaemia, and many people with arthritis develop this condition, not least because, although the anti-inflammatory drugs prescribed to arthritic patients ease pain and stiffness of joints, they can also cause bleeding and stomach ulcers, which can lead to anaemia.

Good sources are: lean red meats, darker chicken meat (thighs), oily fish (sardines, salmon, mackerel), pulses (haricot beans and lentils) and dark green veg (spinach, kale and watercress). Your body better absorbs iron if it is taken with vitamin C, so drink fruit juice or eat fruit and veg with your iron-rich meal. Tea, on the other hand, interferes with iron absorption, so wait about an hour before drinking it.

Omega 3

Omega 3 is an essential fatty acid, but it is one you have to get from food as our bodies are not able to make it. It is well known for being useful to protect against diseases like heart disease, but it is also thought to help inflammatory types of arthritis, such as rheumatoid arthritis, as it can reduce joint stiffness.

Good sources are: rapeseed oil, free-range eggs and oily fish, or you can take it in supplement form.

Everyday Easy

You can tick off a lot of the recommended dietary needs by eating a Mediterranean-style diet, which includes fish, pulses, nuts, olive oil and plenty of fruit and vegetables.

Broccoli – the wonder veg

A good source of fibre and protein, and containing iron, selenium, potassium, calcium and magnesium, as well as vitamins A, C, E, K and many B vitamins including folic acid, broccoli has long been known as a bit of a superfood. It has been recommended as part of a healthy diet for its cholesterol-lowering benefits and anti-carcinogenic properties, but now research suggests it contains a compound that can prevent or slow the progress of osteoarthritis. As yet this link hasn't been conclusively proven, but it could be another good reason to eat broccoli!

Toddlers to Teens

Mealtimes can be a warzone when your fussy five-year-old, awkward 8-year-old and suspicious 16-year-old eye your dinner offerings with contempt and disgust. Explaining the nutritional benefits of the lovingly prepared food you've just put in front of them can be met with blank, hungry stares. So what do you do to keep them happy?

Trying to keep calm and carry on cooking a wide variety of home-made nutritious meals can be complicated, stressful and disheartening when your hard work is rejected at every turn. But you can call a truce without complete surrender to their unhealthy food requests. Follow a few simple rules and, armed with some top tips, you can make mealtimes fun and relaxed – and get everyone eating.

Fussy eaters

Most children go through a phase of fussy eating, although this does last longer for some than others. According to Great Ormond Street Hospital, up to a third of children aged two could be termed fussy eaters – and this is quite normal, as their growth rate slows before their first birthday and their appetite decreases, setting a pattern of not wanting to eat as much, not least because they are so busy exploring new things!

The good news is that most children will grow out of this – especially with a little encouragement to broaden their diet – but when they don't it can be easy to fall into a battle of wills. If tension is rising around the dinner table, here are a few tips to restore a bit of calm:

Everyday Easy

Put a reward chart on the fridge and give your child a sticker to put on it every time they try a new food or eat a healthy meal without a fuss. If they can get stickers every day, let them have a treat at the end of the week.

Snack attack!

- Don't offer a wide choice of snacks – offer a limited selection of healthy options.
- Don't let your child snack while doing another activity. Ensure all meals, including snacks, happen at the table.
- Lead by example. Have the same snack as your child.

Avoid distractions

Eating together should be fun, but it is not playtime. So put away the toys and turn off the TV, otherwise children will view eating as an inconvenience that gets in the way of their fun, and it also stops them learning to eat food mindfully and know when they have had enough.

Feeding time!

Routine is a lifesaver for parents and kids. A regular feeding routine of three main meals and two to three healthy snacks is recommended for all children over one. If a child knows when to expect meals and snacks throughout the day, they'll build up hunger in between and be more likely to eat; if there are no set eating times, they will fill up on unhealthy snacks between meals.

Together time

Sitting around the table as a family is not only great nutritionally but also socially, as it's the perfect opportunity to talk without pressure. For younger children, eating with older people means they can watch and mimic feeding actions, as well as seeing a wide range of foods being enjoyed. It's never too early to start!

Team effort

Getting your children involved in every part of mealtimes can make them more invested in what they are eating; from choosing something to cook, writing the shopping list and buying and preparing the food.

It's that or nothing!

How many times did you hear that growing up? That's because it works, and it will keep everyone sane – mostly you. You might have to offer your child a food up to 20 times before they accept it, but keep persevering and don't cave in and give them what they are asking for just because it is easier and saves confrontation. If a food is never offered, they won't learn to like it and will have a very limited diet. So offer a variety of foods and try to combine things they like with things they aren't so keen on in one meal.

Keep (everyone) calm and carry on

Feeding a fussy eater can be deeply frustrating, but it's really important to stay calm and not react to temper tantrums. Remind yourself: you are in charge, not your child. Ignore the behaviours you want to stop and focus on those you want to see more often – offer praise to other family members who eat well or if your fussy eater takes a spoonful of something.

Keep it in perspective

If you worry that taking this approach might mean your child is not getting enough to eat, don't panic. Ultimately, as long as your child is active and is gaining a healthy amount of weight and seems well, they're fine. However, if your child's fussy eating means that they're losing weight, are lethargic and weak or irritable, consult your doctor for advice.

Don't worry if other people's children seem to eat everything; your child will be fine if they are regularly eating one thing from the four major food groups – milk and dairy products, starchy foods, fruit and veg, and protein.

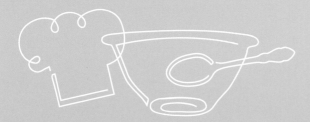

Tired all the time?

If your teenager seems exhausted but is getting early nights and not overdoing it, it could be an iron deficiency. It is thought that almost 50 per cent of girls do not get enough iron, which is vital for making red blood cells which carry oxygen around the body. Check with your GP and encourage your child to eat an iron-rich diet, including fortified breakfast cereals and bread, leafy greens, red meat and beans and lentils.

The Teenage Years

So you get through the fussy eating and the bad news is that it can start all over again! As children get older they start making decisions about all sorts of things – what to wear, what music to listen to and who to be friends with. They also start making decisions about their bodies and what they will eat to achieve the appearance they want. The good news is that sometimes teenagers begin to eat foods that they wouldn't have touched when they were younger.

Your child's body goes through an extraordinary amount of physical change during their teenage years, which needs to be supported by a healthy balanced diet. Sticking to this now is even more important than when they were younger, and if you can get them on side, you will be encouraging them to take on eating and lifestyle habits that will last a lifetime.

Counting the calories

When you have teens in the house, your newly stocked kitchen cupboards and fridge seem to be empty in seconds, as they eat (almost!) everything in sight. Don't be alarmed if your children seem to be constantly eating, but do keep an eye on what it is they are eating. They are growing at a rapid rate right now, and they do need a lot of calories – at the age of 13, boys need around 2,400 kcals a day, while girls need around 2,200 kcals a day, but by the age of 18, the gap has widened, with a daily intake of 3,150 kcals for boys (about 650 kcals more than an average adult man) and 2,400 kcals for girls (about 400 kcals more than an average adult woman).

Food for thought

Growth spurts do not mean teenagers have carte blanche to eat lots of sugar and junk food to bump up their calorie intake. Your child needs a wide range of nutrients to stay healthy and active in body and mind, so encourage them to include as many of these foods into their daily diet as possible:

- **Reduced-fat milk, yoghurt and cheese** – to boost calcium levels and build strong bones and teeth.
- **Fortified orange juice and fatty fish**, such as tuna, mackerel

and salmon, are excellent sources of vitamin D to keep teeth and bones strong.

- **Potassium-rich foods**, such as bananas, dried fruits and broccoli, help lower blood pressure in stressful times.
- **Lean meat, poultry and fish**, along with dairy products, eggs, seeds and nuts, are good sources of protein, necessary for strong growth and development.
- **Iron is crucial**, particularly for menstruating girls, and you'll find it in red meat, spinach, beans and peas, as well as iron-fortified cereals. (Remember, eating vitamin C along with iron helps your body better absorb this mineral.)
- **Wholegrain breakfast cereals, wholewheat pasta, wholemeal bread, oats, barley and rye**, along with a whole host of fruits, beans, nuts and vegetables, including avocados, pears, carrots and sweetcorn, are great sources of fibre.
- **Eat your 5 a day** (see page 24) to ensure you get all those vital vitamins and minerals for healthy growth, hair and skin.
- **Aim to drink 6–8 glasses of fluids (1.2 litres) a day** – water and reduced-fat milk are good choices; tea and coffee also count, but try not to depend on caffeinated drinks or sweetened fruit juices.

Feeling the pressure

Your teenager has a lot to contend with in their high-school years – and a lot of excuses not to eat properly. They're hanging out with their friends, extra-curricular activities take them away from home much more often, there's peer pressure to eat all that junk food marketed at their age group, not to mention issues of body image and the impact that has on diet.

The pressure to conform to size stereotypes has been driven to a new level by social media and can lead to dubious dieting plans and, ultimately, sometimes even eating disorders, with poorly researched information sometimes being offered up to teens by 'influencers'. It's important to approach the issues surrounding food with teens carefully, as their relationship with what they eat is vital for their wellbeing. If you see your child skipping meals or taking on a fad diet, try to talk to them about it, or advise them on a more sensible approach to getting to a healthy body weight which won't exclude important nutrients.

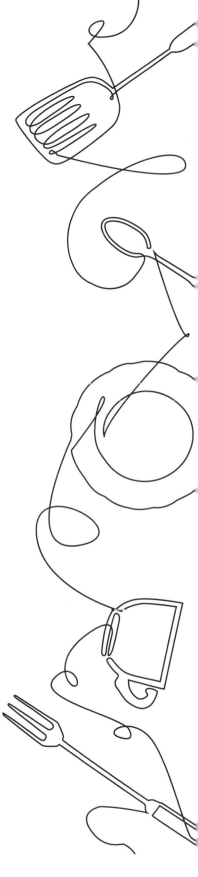

Table talk

Encourage your teenager to eat with the family as often as possible; having them at the kitchen table will give them an opportunity to talk about anything that's worrying them, and to have a healthy meal. Having delicious, nutritious food served up at home might also lure them away from the fast-food restaurants (and takeaways) so often beloved of teens.

Everyday Easy

Ensure that your teenager eats breakfast every day, or at least send them out of the door with a healthy snack they can eat on the go or mid-morning. Pop a small pot of porridge oats and milk in the fridge overnight that they can eat cold, or whizz up a smoothie the night before – teens don't often have time in the mornings to prepare healthy food from scratch!

The teenage years are also when children become young adults and begin to form their own opinions, and this often leads to an interest in issues such as animal welfare. If your child decides to try a vegan or vegetarian diet, ensure they have all the information they need to follow it properly and not deprive themselves of essential nutrients (see page 30 for advice on plant-based diets).

Comfort eating

With exam stress, friendship worries, growth spurts and hormones and the odd heartbreak thrown in, it's a tough time for our children. A bit of comfort is what they need, but this is not the time to suggest that food is a treat, a reward or a solution to a problem.

Don't create a link between treat foods and feeling better emotionally, otherwise you are setting up an unhealthy pattern for life. Equally, don't create a negative connection with treat foods that could lead your child into avoidance, viewing them as fattening – instead remind them that these foods are ok in moderation, and when eaten in combination with exercise and a healthy diet. The earlier you start this message the better – then it won't be such a crutch in later years.

Make your home a food haven

You may not be able to control what your teen eats when they are out and about, but you can ensure that they (and their friends) eat nutritious and delicious food when they are at home. With their metabolism racing they'll want to snack and graze, so ensure your kitchen is well stocked with tasty and healthy snacks, such as fresh and dried fruits, unsalted nuts, raw vegetable sticks or pitta with reduced-fat dips such as houmous, or natural yoghurt with a handful of fresh berries. Even good-quality dark chocolate has health benefits with antioxidants, and in small chunks can make a nice treat to keep sugar cravings at bay.

Also, try to keep a stock of ingredients for speedy meals (no more than 10 minutes start to finish!) that they can prepare themselves. Wholewheat pasta, noodles, wholemeal bread, eggs, tinned fish, beans, lentils and tomatoes, frozen seafood and stir-fry veggies can be whipped up into quick and nutritious meals in minutes. Keep a stash of home-made meals in individual portions in the freezer, too, that they can defrost and reheat for a super-fast supper.

Beating breakouts

The teenage years are often not kind to the skin. A diet of junk food and sugary treats can impact the skin, but you can help keep spot breakouts at bay with plenty of hydration and skin-boosting nutrients, such as zinc, vitamin C and iron. Antioxidants and omega 3 fatty acids are also essential – get these through a combination of vegetables, fruits, nuts, seeds and oily fish.

Breakfast

DIY Breakfast Muesli

Making up a big batch of muesli is so quick and easy to do and will save you time in the morning, too. Simply scoop some into a bowl, top it with fresh or frozen fruit and serve with milk or yoghurt for a healthy start to the day.

Serves 15

For the muesli

1 tbsp ground cinnamon
50g dried cranberries
50g sultanas
50g dried apricots, chopped
50g dried goji berries
50g sunflower seeds
50g pumpkin seeds
50g desiccated coconut
50g flaked almonds
500g porridge oats

To serve (per portion – choose from the following)

100g 0%-fat Greek-style
  yoghurt
80g fresh or frozen berries of
  your choice
80g prepared fresh fruit,
  chopped
300ml semi-skimmed cow's
  milk or dairy-free milk

1 For the muesli, tip all the ingredients, except the oats, into a large, airtight storage container and mix together until evenly distributed. Add the oats and mix well. Cover and store for up to 4 weeks. Use as required.

2 To serve, spoon a portion of the muesli into a bowl and serve with your choice from the list left. If serving with milk, you can have it hot or cold. Simply add the milk to your portion of muesli and eat, or add and then gently heat the mixture in a saucepan until hot and creamy, then serve. Alternatively, the night before, add the milk, stir well, then cover and leave overnight in the fridge before serving the next morning.

Strawberry Fromage Frais

Making your own fruity fromage frais is a very quick job, all done in just 5 minutes. Simply blitz the dates and strawberries together and fold the fruit purée into fat-free natural fromage frais. You can try pineapple or mango flesh, raspberries, blueberries or even cooked apples, instead. Just add a couple of dates to the fruit when you blitz as the fromage frais can be quite tart.

Serves 2

20g stoned dates, roughly chopped

160g ripe strawberries, hulled and roughly chopped

200g 0%-fat high protein natural fromage frais

1   Put the dates and strawberries into a blender or food-processor and blitz to a smooth purée.

2   If you like a really smooth fromage frais, pass the fruit purée through a fine sieve to remove any pips.

3   Spoon the fromage frais into a bowl, then pour the fruit purée over and fold together.

4   Serve immediately in serving bowls or cover and chill in the fridge until needed – it will keep in the fridge for up to 3 days.

Super Speedy Shakshuka

Cooking this in a microwave oven makes it super speedy, so it's perfect for everyday eating. You can prepare the veggie and chickpea base the night before if you like, then it's ready to just pop in the microwave in the morning. High in protein and providing three portions of your 5 a day per serving, this is a great way to start the day.

Serves 5

2 x 400g tins chopped tomatoes

1 tbsp olive oil

2 garlic cloves, finely grated

2½ tsp smoked paprika

3 small red peppers, deseeded and finely chopped

2 x 400g tins chickpeas, drained and rinsed

½ small bunch of coriander

5 eggs

5 wholemeal pitta breads

freshly ground black pepper, to taste

1   Tip the tomatoes into a suitable heatproof mixing bowl. Add the olive oil, garlic, smoked paprika, red peppers and chickpeas and stir well.

2   Keeping the leaves and stalks separate, roughly chop the coriander. Stir the stalks into the tomato mixture (set the chopped leaves aside for later) and season with plenty of black pepper.

3   Cover the bowl with a piece of kitchen paper, place in a microwave oven and cook on high for 6 minutes, then uncover and stir well – the mixture should be hot and the peppers nearly tender.

4   Divide the veg mixture between five suitable small heatproof bowls. Create a little dip in the centre of one portion and crack an egg into it, then carefully pierce the egg yolk with the tip of a sharp knife – just enough to allow the air out (this should stop the yolk from exploding!).

5   Cover with a piece of kitchen paper, place in the microwave and cook on high for 2 minutes. Check to see if the egg is cooked. If not, return to the microwave and cook on high for another 20 seconds, then check and repeat until the egg is cooked to your liking. Repeat with the remaining bowls of veg mixture and the eggs (covering each bowl as before), until all the eggs are cooked.

6   Meanwhile, lightly toast the pitta breads, then cut them into strips.

7   Scatter the bowls of shakshuka with the chopped coriander leaves, and serve with the toasted pitta bread strips.

Eggs Popty Ping

This is a speedy way of poaching eggs for several people at once – up to four mugs can be put in a microwave oven together and cooked, but the mugs do need to be the same size as it affects how the eggs cook. Stick with 30 seconds on high per egg, then check and cook for another 10 seconds on high if necessary – four mugs x 30 seconds, so set the microwave for 2 minutes on high to start with, then check.

Serves 4

4 eggs

4 wholemeal or plain
   English muffins

40g butter, softened

4 tomatoes, roughly chopped

1   Crack each of the eggs into a separate suitable ovenproof mug.

2   Carefully, with the very tip of a sharp knife, pierce the top of each yolk, taking care to only just pierce it – you want the air to be able to escape as it cooks (so it doesn't explode!).

3   Place the mugs, one at a time, into a microwave oven (or see intro above). Cover with a piece of kitchen paper, then cook on high for 30 seconds until the white is set and the yolk is still just runny. If the egg isn't set, cook it on high for another 10 seconds at a time, or until cooked to your liking. Repeat with the remaining eggs (covering each mug as before).

4   Meanwhile, preheat the grill to high. Split the muffins in half, then toast them lightly on each side. Butter the toasted muffins.

5   Divide the muffins between serving plates, then tip the chopped tomatoes on top, followed by the poached eggs, and serve immediately.

Griddle Pan Waffles
with Blueberries and Maple Syrup

Waffles are a lovely treat, and here they're made free-form on a ridged griddle pan – you can make five large ones or numerous smaller ones. Simply ladle the batter into the centre of the pan and let the batter go where it wants – it should naturally form a circle, but don't worry if it doesn't!

Serves 5

(makes 5 large waffles or 10 small ones)

2 tsp vegetable oil

350g spelt flour

1 tbsp baking powder

3 eggs

450ml semi-skimmed milk

2 tsp vanilla extract

50ml rapeseed oil

200g 0%-fat Greek-style yoghurt

400g fresh or frozen (defrosted) blueberries

50g maple syrup

Tip

If you have any leftover waffles, leave them to cool, then transfer to a resealable food bag and keep in the fridge for up to 3 days. To serve, reheat in a toaster until crispy and hot (you may need to cut each one in half to fit in the toaster).

1   Pour a tiny bit of vegetable oil onto a ridged griddle pan, then using kitchen paper, rub the oil all over the cooking surface of the pan. Wipe off any excess with the kitchen paper, then set the griddle pan over a medium-high heat until hot.

2   While the pan heats up, prepare the batter. Tip the flour and baking powder into a large bowl and whisk together.

3   Make a well in the centre and add the eggs, milk and vanilla extract. Whisking from the centre of the bowl outwards, whisk the ingredients together until the mixture forms a thick batter. Add the rapeseed oil and whisk once more.

4   Add a little bit more vegetable oil to the pan and carefully rub it all over as before (remember the pan will be hot!), then wipe off any excess with the kitchen paper, and turn the heat down to medium.

5   Pour one large ladleful (about 175g) of the batter into the centre of the pan (let it spread out on its own) and cook for 2 minutes until you can see bubbles around the outside edge of the waffle and the underside is crispy, then flip it over with a palette knife and cook for a further 1 minute until crispy and cooked through. Remove to a serving plate (and keep warm in a low oven, if you like) while you make the remaining waffles.

6   Repeat with the remaining batter, adding a little more vegetable oil and wiping the griddle pan with the kitchen paper very carefully between each batch. The griddle needs to be lightly oiled but not oily!

7   Serve the warm waffles topped with the yoghurt and blueberries and the maple syrup drizzled over.

Snacks & Light Bites

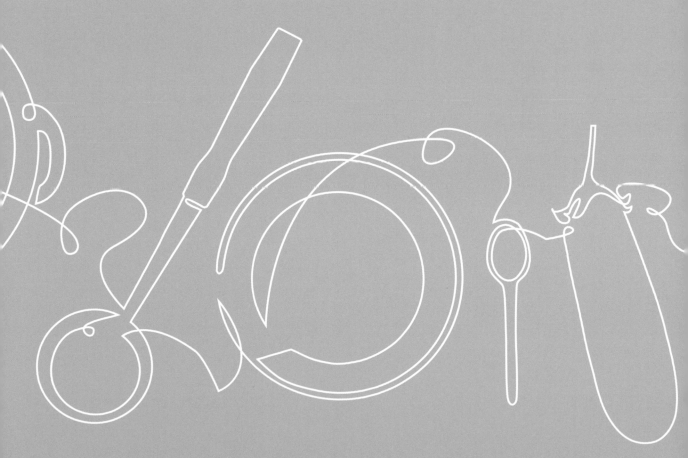

Healthy Flapjacks

These chewy, orange-infused fruit and nut flapjacks are lower in fat and higher in fibre and protein than many traditional ones, plus they're really tasty!

Makes 16

1 tsp rapeseed oil
100g smooth peanut butter
75g clear honey
100g low fat natural yoghurt
150ml orange juice
150g porridge oats
75g dried cranberries
75g roasted unsalted peanuts
75g roasted unsalted cashew
    nuts
75g dried apricots

1   Preheat the oven to 190°C/170°C fan/Gas 5. Grease a deep-sided 20cm square baking tin with the rapeseed oil and line the base and sides with baking parchment.

2   Put the peanut butter and honey into a small saucepan (see Tip) and heat gently until just melted. Whisk together to combine, then whisk in the yoghurt and orange juice.

3   Pour into a large bowl, add the oats and dried cranberries and stir together really well to combine. Set aside to soak while you roughly chop all the nuts and the dried apricots, then add these to the oat mixture and mix well. Tip the mixture into the prepared tin and press down into the corners until level.

4   Bake in the oven for 20–25 minutes until golden brown. Leave to cool in the tin for 10 minutes, before cutting into 16 squares, then leave to cool completely in the tin. Once cold, remove and serve. These will keep in an airtight container for up to 5 days.

Tip
Alternatively, put the peanut butter and honey into a suitable heatproof bowl, cover with a piece of kitchen paper and heat in a microwave oven on high for about 1 minute, until just melted, then continue as above.

Energy Bites

These protein balls are great for all the family – really tasty, yet filling and nutritious, with no added sugar and some good slow-release carbohydrate to keep hunger pangs at bay until the next mealtime. You can mix and match the flavours and coatings – maybe vanilla and pecans, or apple and cinnamon; there's no end to the combos you can enjoy.

Makes 36

For the base mixture
300g stoned dates
75g ground almonds
1½ tsp ground cinnamon
200g jumbo porridge oats

For the carrot and ginger bites
1 medium carrot, peeled and finely grated
½ tsp ground ginger
10g desiccated coconut

For the banana-vanilla bites
40g dried banana chips, roughly chopped
1 tsp vanilla extract
10g freeze-dried raspberries, crushed

For the cranberry and orange bites
finely grated zest and juice of ½ orange
50g dried cranberries, chopped
20g (shelled) pistachio nuts, very finely chopped

1   Make the base mixture. Tip the dates, ground almonds and cinnamon into a food-processor, add 2 tablespoons of cold water, then blitz for 2–3 minutes until it starts to form a ball around the outside of the processor bowl, scraping down the sides a couple of times, if necessary.

2   Add the oats and blitz very briefly until they just break up and you have a rough crumble texture. Add another 4 tablespoons of cold water and blitz again until it just starts to stick to the sides of the processor bowl. Divide the mixture evenly into three separate bowls.

3   For the carrot and ginger bites, add the carrot and ginger to one bowl of the base mixture and mix together really well. Divide the mixture into 12 equal portions, then roll each one into a ball. Tip the coconut into a small bowl, then toss each ball into the bowl, pressing the coconut into each ball to coat all over.

4   For the banana-vanilla bites, add the banana chips and vanilla extract to the second bowl of base mixture and mix together really well. Divide the mixture into 12 equal portions, then roll into balls. Tip the crushed freeze-dried raspberries into a small bowl, then toss each ball into the bowl, pressing the raspberries into each ball to coat all over.

5   For the cranberry and orange bites, add the orange zest and juice to the last bowl of base mixture, then add the cranberries and mix together really well. Divide the mixture into 12 equal portions, then roll into balls. Tip the chopped pistachios into a small bowl, then toss each ball into the bowl, pressing the pistachios into each ball to coat all over.

6   Transfer the coated balls to an airtight container and store in the fridge for up to 1 week. Or they can be frozen for up to 1 month. For a crunchy eat, serve from frozen, or defrost and eat at room temperature.

Packed Lunch Scotch Eggs

Using chicken sausages to coat these eggs turns a traditional Scotch egg into a much healthier one. Combine that with oven-baking instead of deep-frying, and you end up with a Scotch egg that's great served in a packed lunch, as a snack mid-afternoon, or even for breakfast on the go!

Makes 4

5 eggs

450g chicken sausages, skins removed

2 tbsp finely snipped chives

2 tbsp plain flour

50g dried natural breadcrumbs

½ tsp dried thyme

freshly ground black pepper, to taste

1 Preheat the oven to 220°C/200°C fan/Gas 7. Line a baking tray with baking parchment.

2 Bring a saucepan of water to the boil. Add four of the eggs and simmer for 5–6 minutes until soft-boiled. Drain them, return to the pan and run cold water into the pan for a few minutes until the eggs are cool enough to handle. When cool enough, drain and peel them.

3 Put the chicken sausagemeat and chives into a bowl and mix together. Divide and shape into four equal balls, then flatten each one.

4 Wrap one portion of the sausagemeat carefully around each soft-boiled egg, covering the egg completely. You need to ensure that it's a thin, even layer all over the egg, as you want it to cook as quickly as possible so that the egg doesn't overcook.

5 Sprinkle the flour onto a plate and season with black pepper, then crack the remaining egg into a bowl and beat. Combine the breadcrumbs and thyme in another bowl.

6 Carefully roll each sausage-coated egg in the flour, then in the beaten egg and finally in the breadcrumbs, ensuring each one is fully coated each time.

7 Place on the lined baking tray and bake in the oven for 15 minutes until the sausagemeat is cooked through and the outer coating is crispy, but the eggs are not overcooked.

8 Leave to cool, then chill in the fridge and serve cold in a packed lunch, or eat hot or cold as a snack. These will keep in an airtight container in the fridge for up to 3 days.

MINI FRITTATAS TWO WAYS
Mini Quinoa, Cheese and Ham Frittatas

———

Quinoa gives these mini frittatas an added hit of protein as well
as making them nicely substantial, so they are ideal for a healthy
hot snack, or served cold for a tasty lunch on the go.

Makes 12

1 tsp rapeseed oil

180g quinoa

6 eggs

6 spring onions, trimmed and
roughly chopped

6 tomatoes, roughly chopped

120g light mature Cheddar
cheese, grated

120g lean wafer thin ham,
shredded

1 tsp mustard powder

sea salt and freshly ground
black pepper, to taste

1   Preheat the oven to 200°C/180°C fan/Gas 6. Lightly
grease a 12-hole muffin tray with the rapeseed oil, brushing
it up the sides of the holes.

2   Put the quinoa into a large saucepan, add 540ml of cold
water, then bring to the boil. Stir well, then reduce the heat
to a simmer and cook for 20 minutes until all the water has
been absorbed and the quinoa is tender (or cook the quinoa
according to the packet instructions). Run cold water through the
cooked quinoa until it is cool, then drain once more, squeezing
out any excess water, and set aside.

3   Meanwhile, crack the eggs into a large bowl and whisk
well. Add the spring onions, tomatoes, Cheddar and ham and
mix together really well. Add the cooked quinoa, then season
with the mustard powder, a little salt and plenty of black pepper
and stir well. Divide the mixture evenly between the prepared
muffin tray, piling the mixture high in each hole.

4   Bake in the oven for 18–20 minutes until golden brown
and risen.

5   Cool in the muffin tray for a few minutes, then remove the
frittatas to serving plates and serve hot. Any that are not eaten
immediately can be left to cool on a plate, then transferred to
an airtight container and stored in the fridge for up to 3 days
(see Tip).

Mini Roast Veg, Ham and Feta Frittatas

Super tasty and packed with veg, these mini frittatas are great for lunch served with a green salad, but they're equally good served for breakfast or brunch.

Makes 12

3 tsp vegetable oil

1 small courgette, roughly chopped

1 small red onion, diced

1 small pepper (any colour), deseeded and roughly chopped

5 eggs

175ml semi-skimmed milk

180g lean wafer thin ham, shredded

100g salad cheese or feta cheese, roughly chopped

freshly ground black pepper, to taste

1   Preheat the oven to 200°C/180°C fan/Gas 6. Lightly grease a 12-hole muffin tray with 1 teaspoon of the vegetable oil, brushing it up the sides of the holes, then place a small disc of baking parchment in the bottom of each hole.

2   Tip the courgette, red onion and pepper onto a baking tray and drizzle with the remaining oil. Toss together, spread out in a single layer, then roast in the oven for 15 minutes until just coloured and tender.

3   Meanwhile, crack the eggs into a large jug, pour in the milk, add plenty of black pepper, then whisk together until well combined. Set aside.

4   Remove the roasted veg from the oven, add the ham and salad or feta cheese and mix together until combined.

5   Divide the veg mixture evenly between the prepared muffin tray – there will be plenty, so pile it in. Pour the egg mixture over the top so that each hole is just full to the rim.

6   Bake in the oven for 20 minutes until just set and light golden brown.

7   Cool in the muffin tray for a good 5 minutes or so before removing – if you try and take them out immediately, they will probably stick and fall apart! Once cool enough, remove the frittatas to serving plates and serve hot. Any that are not eaten immediately can be left to cool on a plate, then transferred to an airtight container and stored in the fridge for up to 3 days (see Tip).

Tip
Any leftover frittatas can be eaten cold or reheated in a microwave oven. To reheat, place two frittatas at a time on a suitable heatproof plate, cover with a piece of kitchen paper and heat on high for 1 minute. Check if hot; if not, heat on high for another 10 seconds at a time, or until it's hot through, then serve.

Savoury 'Shaky' Crepes

This is a great way of making crepes without having to weigh everything out each time – using a permanent marker, simply mark up the outside of a large, clean jam jar with the levels first time round, then next time, fill, shake and go! These are equally good topped with fruit and a little grated dark chocolate for breakfast or dessert.

Makes 10

150g plain wholemeal flour
1 large egg
375ml semi-skimmed milk
1 tbsp rapeseed oil

For the toppings (quantities given below are enough to top all 10 crepes – just pick and mix your favourites)

150g light mature Cheddar cheese, grated
400g tinned (drained weight) or frozen (defrosted) sweetcorn
400g finely grated carrots
400g finely grated courgettes
150g lean wafer thin ham, shredded

1   Measure the wholemeal flour into a large, clean jam jar. Add the egg and milk, then seal the jar and shake really well until you can see that the batter is completely smooth.

2   To be really organised, you can then divide and mark up the mixture into 10 (see intro) so you know how much to pour out for each crepe!

3   Heat a medium, non-stick frying pan over a medium heat. Add a little of the rapeseed oil and swirl it around the pan, then tip out any excess into a heatproof bowl. You only want enough oil to just coat the pan – you can wipe it out with kitchen paper if you like (but remember the pan is hot, so be careful!).

4   Pour a tenth of the batter into the pan and swirl it around so that it covers the base of the pan in a thin, even layer. Cook over a medium heat for 45–60 seconds until firm and just golden underneath, then flip it over and cook on the other side for another 15 seconds.

5   Tip out onto a plate, then repeat with the remaining oil and batter (stacking the cooked crepes on top of each other), wiping the pan out with kitchen paper between each one.

6   Scatter whichever of the topping ingredients you fancy over the top of each crepe, then fold each one into quarters or roll up into a pinwheel and eat immediately.

> **Tip**
> If you have any leftover crepes, stack them on a plate and allow to cool, then cover with clingfilm or transfer them to a resealable food bag, and chill in the fridge until needed. They will keep in the fridge for up to 3 days. You could even try serving them with a sweet topping, such as chopped banana and peanut butter.

Smoked Salmon, Egg and Potato Traybake

This flavoursome traybake is prepped and cooked in a short space of time and with minimum effort, providing eight generous portions, ideal for brunch, lunch or even a packed lunch! Microwaving the potatoes while you prepare everything else, then grating them into the mixture, means that the whole dish can be made in about 40 minutes. If you're not a fan of smoked salmon, simply leave it out or top with lean ham instead.

Serves 8

vegetable oil, for greasing
2 baking potatoes (about 250g each), scrubbed
16 eggs
½ tsp fine sea salt
100g light mature Cheddar cheese, grated
160g baby spinach leaves
160g cherry tomatoes, halved
120g smoked salmon trimmings
freshly ground black pepper, to taste

1 Preheat the oven to 200°C/180°C fan/Gas 6. Lightly grease and line a medium, deep-sided baking tray (about 24 x 30 x 3.5cm) with greaseproof paper or baking parchment.

2 Pierce each potato with a fork several times, then place them both on a suitable heatproof plate. Cover with a piece of kitchen paper, place in a microwave oven and cook on high for 10 minutes until just tender.

3 Meanwhile, crack the eggs into a large mixing bowl, season with the salt and some black pepper and whisk well until combined. Add the cheese, spinach leaves and cherry tomatoes and stir together until evenly combined.

4 Holding with a piece of kitchen paper (be careful as they will be hot!), coarsely grate each potato and roughly chop any you can't grate, including the skin.

5 Add the grated (and chopped) potatoes to the bowl of eggs and veg and stir really well until everything is mixed together. Pour this mixture into the prepared baking tray, then scatter the smoked salmon trimmings evenly over the top.

6 Bake in the oven for 15–20 minutes until just set and lightly golden around the edges.

7 Remove from the oven and leave to rest for 2 minutes, then slide out onto a chopping board, cut into pieces and serve immediately (see Tip).

Tip
If not eating immediately, leave the traybake portions to cool, then transfer to an airtight container and store in the fridge for up to 3 days. To reheat, transfer one portion to a suitable heatproof plate and cover with kitchen paper. Heat in a microwave oven on high for 1½ minutes until hot through. If not piping hot, heat on high for a further 20 seconds at a time until hot through, then serve.

Veggie Croquettes with Three Easy Dips

This is a great recipe for getting the kids involved – they can help to grate the veggies and then shape the croquettes into sausages. The croquettes are slightly soft when they come out of the oven, so leave them to firm up and cool down a little before serving. And, making dips with frozen veg is the simplest of things – if you like a slight bite to your dips, serve them immediately, or for a softer eat, leave them to defrost and stir well before serving.

Serves 4

(makes 16 croquettes)

For the croquettes

200g cauliflower florets, coarsely grated

200g sweet potato, peeled and coarsely grated

2 carrots (200g total weight), peeled and coarsely grated

1 courgette (200g total weight), coarsely grated

1 red onion, finely chopped

small bunch of parsley, leaves picked and roughly chopped

1 tsp dried onion granules

100g fresh breadcrumbs

2 eggs

sea salt and freshly ground black pepper, to taste

1   Preheat the oven to 200°C/180°C fan/Gas 6. Line a large, shallow baking tray with baking parchment.

2   For the croquettes, place all the grated vegetables into a large bowl and mix together. Add all the remaining ingredients and mix well, squishing it all together until evenly mixed. Set aside to soften for 15 minutes.

3   Mix once more, then divide into eight portions in the bowl. Take one portion, divide it in half and then form into two little sausages. Place on the lined baking tray, then repeat with the remaining mixture to make 16 croquettes.

4   Bake in the oven for 25 minutes until the vegetables are tender and the croquettes are golden brown on the outside.

5   While the croquettes are baking, start preparing the dips to accompany.

6   Place all the ingredients for the pea guacamole into a food-processor and pulse until just broken down, then scrape down the sides of the bowl. Add salt and black pepper to taste, then blitz again until just beginning to get smooth – you want a little texture left. Tip into a serving bowl and taste – you can add more lime/chilli if you fancy.

7   Place all the ingredients for the sweetcorn salsa into a separate bowl and mix together well, seasoning with salt and black pepper, then tip into another serving bowl.

8   For the yoghurt and sweet chilli dip, tip the yoghurt into another bowl, add the sweet chilli sauce, lime zest and some black pepper to taste and mix well. Tip into a third serving bowl.

9   Serve the croquettes warm with the three dips alongside.

For the pea guacamole

240g frozen peas

1 tsp ground cumin

2 garlic cloves, roughly
  chopped

1 red chilli, deseeded and
  roughly chopped

finely grated zest and juice of
  1 lime

½ small bunch of coriander,
  roughly chopped

For the sweetcorn salsa

240g frozen sweetcorn

4 tomatoes, chopped

4 spring onions, trimmed and
  chopped

½ small bunch of coriander,
  chopped

juice of ½ lime

1 tbsp olive oil

*For the yoghurt and sweet
chilli dip*

200g 0%-fat Greek-style
  yoghurt

2 tbsp sweet chilli sauce

finely grated zest of 1 lime

Tips

- Store any unused dips in separate airtight containers
  in the fridge for up to 3 days. Cool any leftover
  croquettes, then transfer them to an airtight container –
  they will keep in the fridge for up to 3 days.
- The croquettes can be eaten hot or cold. To reheat,
  place four croquettes on a suitable heatproof plate and
  cover with kitchen paper. Heat in a microwave oven on
  high for 1 minute until hot through. If not hot enough,
  heat on high for a further 20 seconds at a time until
  hot through.

Gluten Free Bread

This bread is made with some of the liquid from a tin of chickpeas. It's a relatively recent find that the brine from tinned chickpeas can be used as a very effective egg or egg white substitute – perfect if you're following a plant-based diet. Here, it's used to create a tasty, everyday gluten free loaf.

Makes 16 slices

450g gluten free white bread flour

½ tsp fine sea salt

10g fast-action dried yeast

400g tin chickpeas

300ml semi-skimmed milk

1 tbsp clear honey

3 tbsp vegetable oil, plus extra for greasing

2 tsp cider vinegar

1   Grease a 1kg loaf tin with oil and line the base with greaseproof paper or baking parchment. Set aside.

2   Tip the flour, salt and yeast into a large mixing bowl and mix together, then make a well in the middle.

3   Tip the chickpeas into a sieve set over a separate bowl and leave to drain (see Tip). Measure 100ml of the chickpea liquid into a small bowl (discard the remainder), then add the milk, honey, vegetable oil and vinegar and stir together well.

4   Pour this liquid into the flour mixture, stirring all the time, until the mixture forms a sticky batter. Don't worry, it's meant to be quite wet!

5   Spoon the batter into the lined loaf tin, then cover with a clean tea towel and leave to rise at room temperature for about 1 hour, or until doubled in size.

6   Preheat the oven to 220°C/200°C fan/Gas 7.

7   Once the dough has risen, transfer the loaf tin to the oven and bake for 40–45 minutes until golden brown and crusty.

8   To check that the bread is cooked, carefully tip the loaf out of the tin and tap the bottom – it should sound hollow and be golden brown. Transfer the loaf to a wire rack and leave to cool for at least 30 minutes before slicing.

9   Once cold, store the loaf in an airtight container, or resealable food bag (but do not store it in the fridge). The loaf can be sliced and placed in a resealable freezer bag, then frozen for up to 1 month. Simply toast slices straight from the freezer, as required.

Tip
Transfer the chickpeas to an airtight container, store in the fridge for up to 3 days and use for the Aubergine Chilli Traybake recipe (see page 111).

Picnic Sandwiches

Making sandwiches every day can become a bit tiresome, but with this recipe, you can make enough for two days in one go. Mix and match whatever fillings you fancy – ham and cheese are a classic combination, but do try sliced cold beef with tomato and horseradish, tuna and sweetcorn, or pastrami, mustard and gherkins – all pairings that work well with the ciabatta.

Serves 4

2 half ciabattas

1 tbsp reduced-fat salad cream

2 tsp reduced-fat tomato pesto

1 Little Gem lettuce, finely shredded

100g light mature Cheddar cheese, thinly sliced

½ cucumber, thinly sliced

100g lean wafer thin ham slices

1   Split both ciabattas in half horizontally, then lay them, cut-sides up, on the work surface.

2   Spread the cut sides of the bottom ciabatta halves with the salad cream, and then spread the cut sides of the top halves with the tomato pesto.

3   Layer up the lettuce, cheese, cucumber and ham on top of the salad cream halves, dividing evenly. Sandwich them together with the top ciabatta halves and press down lightly.

4   Cut each one in half (to make four sandwiches) and either serve immediately, or tightly wrap each sandwich in clingfilm (or wrap in baking parchment tied with kitchen string) and chill in the fridge overnight, or until needed – they will keep for up to 3 days in the fridge. Remove from the fridge about 30 minutes before serving to allow them to come to room temperature.

Tip
Use mustard (to taste) in place of the salad cream or pesto, and swap in 80g tinned (drained weight) sweetcorn for the cucumber or ham.

Minestrone and Rice Soup

Making minestrone can be a bit of a labour of love, but this one uses tinned tomatoes and vegetable stock as a base. Mixed frozen vegetables, pesto and cooked rice are simmered in the broth to give a tasty, super-quick version, providing two portions of your 5 a day per serving. Rice is used instead of pasta to make it gluten free.

Serves 6

2 tsp vegetable oil

2 onions, roughly chopped

2 gluten free vegetable stock cubes

1.25 litres boiling water

2 x 400g tins chopped tomatoes

640g frozen mixed vegetables with red peppers

120g roasted red pepper pesto

750g cold cooked basmati rice

30g Parmesan cheese or vegetarian Italian hard cheese, finely grated

freshly ground black pepper, to taste

1   Heat the vegetable oil in a large saucepan until hot, then add the onions and cook over a medium heat for 2–3 minutes until just softening.

2   Meanwhile, crumble the stock cubes into a large, heatproof jug, add the boiling water and stir well until dissolved.

3   Add the tinned tomatoes and stock to the onions, then bring to a simmer and cook for 5 minutes. Tip in the frozen mixed vegetables, stir well and return to a simmer, then cook for another 3–4 minutes until the vegetables are hot through.

4   Stir in the roasted red pepper pesto and season to taste with black pepper.

5   If you are serving this now, stir in the cold cooked rice and cook over a high heat for a further 2–3 minutes until piping hot throughout. Serve immediately, topped with the grated cheese and an extra grinding of black pepper.

6   If you are not eating this immediately, don't add the rice, remove the veg soup from the heat and leave to cool. Once cool, transfer to an airtight container and store in the fridge for up to 3 days (alongside the cooked rice, which is stored separately and will keep for up to 24 hours in the fridge). Alternatively, ladle the veg soup into six individual airtight containers and chill (as above) until needed.

7   To reheat, transfer one portion of the veg soup to a saucepan and stir in 125g of the cold cooked rice. Cook over a medium heat for 3–4 minutes, stirring occasionally, until piping hot through, then serve sprinkled with a little of the grated cheese and some black pepper.

Home-made Pork and Apple Rolls

Sausage rolls are a family favourite, but they can be so high in fat. These are a healthier alternative that make a tasty addition to your packed lunch, or serve them hot straight from the oven with a side salad for a light lunch. The grainy mustard packs a punch, but you can change it for some Dijon mustard, or even drop it altogether and use reduced-fat flavoured sausages instead, if you prefer.

Makes 6

6 reduced-fat pork sausages (400g total weight)

1 eating apple, grated (discard the core)

1 tbsp grainy mustard

4 large sheets of filo pastry (about 150g in total), at room temperature (see Tip)

1 egg, beaten

1   Preheat the oven to 200°C/180°C fan/Gas 6. Line a baking tray with baking parchment.

2   Using the tip of a sharp knife, slice through the sausage skins and then tip the sausagemeat out into a large bowl, discarding the skins.

3   Add the grated apple and grainy mustard and mix really well – get your hands in and squish it all together until evenly combined. Set aside and wash your hands thoroughly!

4   Lay one sheet of filo pastry onto the work surface, with the longest side horizontally in front of you. Place another one next to it, in the same position.

5   Brush some beaten egg over both sheets of filo, then lay the other two sheets of filo over the top and brush again with some egg – you'll have two stacks of two sheets of filo. Cut each stack from top to bottom into three rectangles, giving you six rectangles in total.

6   Divide the pork mixture into six equal portions, then form each piece into a fat sausage shape and place one sausage at the bottom short side of each rectangle of filo, positioning it 2cm in from the edge.

7   For each pork roll, roll the filo over the sausage, then fold the filo sides in and continue to roll up until the sausage is totally enclosed in the pastry.

8   Brush the rolls with the remaining beaten egg, then transfer to the lined baking tray, placing them seam-side down. Bake in the oven for 20–25 minutes until golden brown and cooked all the way through.

9   Serve hot or cold. If serving cold, cool completely, then transfer to an airtight container and store in the fridge for up to 3 days.

Tip
You can use chilled fresh or frozen (defrosted) filo pastry for this recipe – just remember to remove it from the fridge about 20 minutes before using, this will make it easier to handle.

Vegetarian

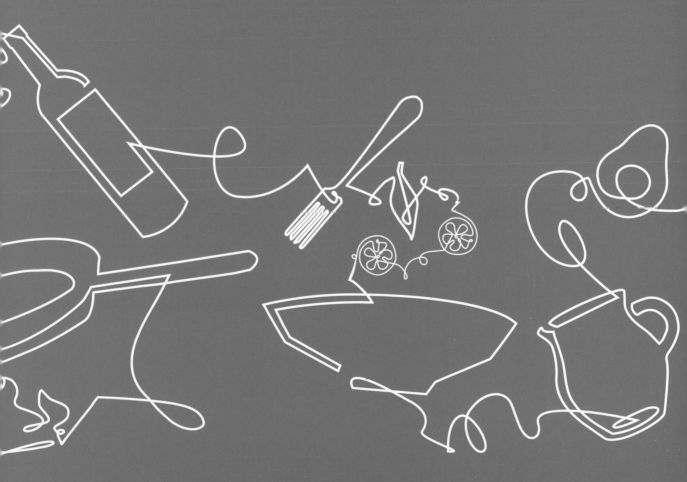

Spiced Roasted Cauliflower
with Romesco Sauce

Tossing cauliflower florets in beaten egg and paprika-spiced flour, then oven-baking them gives them a delicious crispy battered coating. Served with a classic romesco sauce, this is a great everyday vegetarian meal that can be made in the time it takes to boil the rice!

Serves 4

300g brown basmati rice

1 egg

1 medium cauliflower, cut into florets (about 400g prepped weight)

2 tsp smoked paprika

2 heaped tbsp plain flour

3 tsp olive oil

20g fresh breadcrumbs

40g ground almonds

3 roasted red peppers (from a jar), drained and roughly chopped

3 tomatoes, roughly chopped

4 tsp red wine vinegar

½ small bunch of flat-leaf parsley, leaves picked and roughly chopped

sea salt and freshly ground black pepper, to taste

1   Preheat the oven to 200°C/180°C fan/Gas 6. Line a baking tray with baking parchment.

2   Bring a large saucepan of salted water to the boil, add the basmati rice, stir well and return to the boil. Reduce the heat to a simmer and cook for 25 minutes until tender. Drain well, return to the saucepan and keep hot.

3   Meanwhile, crack the egg into a mixing bowl and beat well. Add the cauliflower florets and toss until coated on all sides.

4   Tip 1 teaspoon of the smoked paprika into a separate mixing bowl, then add the flour, a little salt and plenty of black pepper and stir well.

5   Scoop the cauliflower florets out of the egg into the flour bowl, leaving any excess egg behind, and toss the cauliflower in the seasoned flour until completely coated.

6   Transfer to the lined baking tray, spreading out the florets in a single layer, then roast in the oven for 15 minutes until golden brown and tender.

7   In the meantime, make the romesco sauce. Heat a frying pan over a medium heat, add 1 teaspoon of the olive oil and the breadcrumbs and fry for a couple of minutes until toasted and golden brown, stirring occasionally. Tip the breadcrumbs into the bowl attachment of a hand-held stick blender (or into a small food-processor).

8   Add the ground almonds to the frying pan and toast for a couple of minutes, stirring occasionally until golden brown, then add them to the bowl attachment (or processor), along with the red peppers, tomatoes, red wine vinegar, a little salt and the remaining smoked paprika and olive oil. Blitz together until smooth, scraping down the sides if necessary.

9   Serve the spiced roasted cauliflower with the romesco sauce spooned over and the cooked rice alongside, then scatter the parsley over the top to finish.

Falafel Wraps
with Tzatziki and Tahini

These veg-packed wraps count for three portions of your 5 a day per serving, and they are ideal for lunch or dinner. Using 0%-fat Greek-style yoghurt and tinned chickpeas means that they're high in protein, too, keeping you feeling fuller for longer.

Serves 5

2 x 400g tins chickpeas, drained and rinsed

1 bunch of spring onions, trimmed and roughly chopped

3 garlic cloves, roughly chopped, plus 1 garlic clove, peeled

finely grated zest and juice of 1 lemon

1 tbsp ground coriander

1 tbsp ground cumin

1 tsp fine sea salt

2 tbsp roughly chopped flat-leaf parsley

2 tbsp self-raising flour

½ tsp baking powder

3 tbsp tahini

1 cucumber

350g 0%-fat Greek-style yoghurt

3 tbsp finely chopped mint leaves

5 wholemeal or plain tortilla wraps

½ head iceberg lettuce, shredded

3 tomatoes, roughly chopped

freshly ground black pepper, to taste

1   Preheat the oven to 200°C/180°C fan/Gas 6 and line a large baking tray with baking parchment.

2   Tip the chickpeas, spring onions, chopped garlic cloves, the lemon zest, coriander, cumin, ½ teaspoon of the salt and plenty of black pepper into a food-processor. Blitz until just roughly broken down, then add the parsley, flour, baking powder and half of the lemon juice. Blitz again until the mixture just comes together. You want it to be smooth enough to form into balls, but not a purée.

3   Tip out onto the work surface and divide into 20 portions. Roll each portion into a ball and place on the lined baking tray. Bake in the oven for 20 minutes until just golden and crispy.

4   Meanwhile, prepare the tahini sauce and tzatziki. Tip the tahini into a bowl, add the remaining lemon juice and 3 tablespoons of cold water, then whisk together until smooth – you may need more water if you have a juicy lemon, as the acidity thickens the tahini and the water slackens it, so add an extra 1 tablespoon at a time until you have a runny consistency. Set aside.

Tip

The cooked falafel can be served hot or cold. If serving cold, they will keep in an airtight container in the fridge for up to 3 days, as will the tahini sauce and tzatziki (in separate containers). To reheat the falafel, place four falafel at a time on a suitable heatproof plate, cover with a piece of kitchen paper and heat in a microwave oven on high for 1 minute until hot through. If not hot enough, heat on high for a further 20 seconds at a time until hot through.

5   Coarsely grate the cucumber onto a clean tea towel, then gather the tea towel up and hold it over the sink. Twist it until all the liquid comes out of the cucumber. Tip the squeezed cucumber into a separate bowl, then add the yoghurt. Finely grate the remaining peeled garlic clove over the top, add the chopped mint and season with the remaining salt. Stir well to combine.

6   If you like, warm the wraps according to the packet instructions, or serve them as they are. Layer some lettuce and tomatoes down the middle of each wrap. Top with a few dollops of the tzatziki, then divide the hot falafel between the wraps. Finish with a drizzle of the tahini sauce and freshly ground pepper. Fold up and serve immediately.

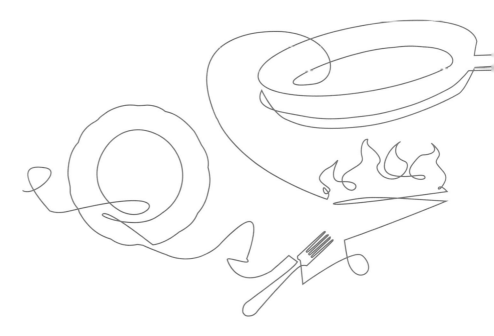

Chana Dahl and Quick Naan

Using tinned green lentils, this dahl is a perfect pick-me-up, full of spices for an authentic-tasting dish. The naan bread recipe is one that can be made so quickly, there's no need for any proving at all, just mix, roll and fry in a pan.

Serves 6

For the dahl

1 tbsp rapeseed oil
1 tsp cumin seeds
1 tsp dried chilli flakes
1 onion, roughly chopped
2 garlic cloves, roughly chopped
5cm piece of fresh root ginger, peeled and roughly chopped
2 tsp ground cumin
1 tsp ground coriander
½ tsp ground turmeric
2 x 400g tins chopped tomatoes
2 x 400g tins green lentils, drained and rinsed
1 vegetable stock cube
small bunch of coriander, roughly chopped
sea salt and freshly ground black pepper, to taste
75g 0%-fat Greek-style yoghurt, to serve

For the quick naan

300g self-raising flour
¾ tsp fine sea salt
2 tbsp sesame seeds
180g 0%-fat Greek-style yoghurt
3 tsp rapeseed oil

1 For the dahl, heat a sauté pan over a medium heat, add the rapeseed oil, cumin seeds and chilli flakes and fry for 20 seconds until the seeds start to pop. Add the onion and cook for 2–3 minutes until just softening, then add the garlic, ginger, ground cumin, ground coriander, turmeric and some salt and black pepper and cook for another 1 minute.

2 Add the tomatoes, lentils, crumbled stock cube and 400ml of cold water and bring to the boil. Reduce the heat and simmer, stirring occasionally, for 10–15 minutes, while you make the naan bread.

3 Tip the flour into a large bowl, add the salt and sesame seeds and mix well. Make a well in the centre and dollop the yoghurt into it, then add 5 tablespoons of cold water and stir everything together to form a soft dough. Tip out onto a lightly floured work surface and knead for 1–2 minutes until you have a smooth dough.

4 Divide into six portions, then roll each piece into a ball. Flatten each ball gently with the palm of your hand, then roll out on a lightly floured surface to about 5mm thick.

5 Heat a large frying pan over a medium heat, add 1 teaspoon of the rapeseed oil and two of the naan breads. Fry on each side for about 1–2 minutes until golden brown and risen. Remove to a clean tea towel, wrap loosely and keep warm.

6 Repeat with the remaining oil and naan breads, cooking them in batches of two each time, as above.

7 Add the chopped coriander to the dahl and stir through, then serve. Add a small dollop of yoghurt to each portion and serve with the naan bread.

Vegetarian Spaghetti Bolognaise

You can use vegetarian mince for this tasty bolognaise – it's high in protein and easily ticks one portion of your 5 a day per serving, plus it's ideal for a midweek meal.

Serves 4

1 tbsp olive oil

1 large onion, chopped

4 carrots, peeled and coarsely grated

4 celery sticks, chopped

1 tsp dried oregano

2 garlic cloves, finely chopped

240g mushrooms, roughly chopped

1 tbsp tomato purée

400g vegetarian mince

250g passata

600ml hot vegetable stock

1 tbsp balsamic vinegar

300g dried spaghetti

sea salt and freshly ground black pepper, to taste

To serve

20g vegetarian Italian hard cheese, finely grated

2 sprigs of basil, leaves picked

1   Heat a large, deep-sided sauté pan or flameproof casserole dish over a medium heat. Add the olive oil, onion, carrots and celery and cook for 5 minutes. You want them to soften but not colour, so it's a good idea to put a lid on the pan to help retain the moisture and steam the vegetables at the same time.

2   Add the oregano and garlic and cook for another minute, then turn the heat up, add the mushrooms and cook them for 2–3 minutes until turning golden. Add the tomato purée, stirring it through all the vegetables, then stir in the vegetarian mince.

3   Pour in the passata and vegetable stock and stir well, then bring to the boil. Reduce the heat to a gentle simmer and cook for 15 minutes until the mince is tender and the sauce has reduced slightly. Add the balsamic vinegar and season to taste with salt and black pepper.

4   Meanwhile, bring a large saucepan of salted water to the boil, then add the spaghetti and cook according to the packet instructions until al dente. Drain the pasta, reserving a little of the cooking water (about 4 tablespoons) in case you need to loosen the sauce.

5   Tip the drained pasta into the sauté pan and mix well with the sauce, adding the reserved pasta water if necessary to coat all the pasta in sauce. Serve immediately, sprinkled with the grated cheese and basil.

Tomato and Veg Sauce

This recipe makes a big quantity of tomato and vegetable sauce, which can then be divided down into four smaller batches, one of which is served with cooked pasta below. The remaining batches can then be frozen for use later, or turned into a flavoursome Chicken and Lentil Curry (see page 143), simmered with meatballs to make Meatballs and Mash (see page 154), or used as the base for a Cheat's Bouillabaisse (see page 186). A truly versatile veg-packed sauce!

Makes 4 batches

(each batch serves 3)

1 tbsp olive oil

2 onions, roughly chopped

2 tbsp smoked paprika

6 garlic cloves, finely grated or crushed

4 large carrots, peeled and coarsely grated

4 celery sticks, finely chopped

3 tbsp tomato purée

4 x 400g tins chopped tomatoes

1 tbsp caster sugar

3 courgettes, coarsely grated

small bunch of basil, roughly chopped

sea salt and freshly ground black pepper, to taste

1   Heat a large, deep-sided sauté pan or flameproof casserole dish over a medium heat, add the olive oil and onions and cook for 5 minutes until softening. Stir in the smoked paprika and cook for another minute. Add the garlic, carrots, celery and tomato purée and cook for 1 minute, stirring, then tip in the tomatoes and sugar and mix well.

2   Bring to a simmer, then cover and cook gently for 5 minutes until the carrots have just softened. Stir in the courgettes, basil and 400ml of cold water. Bring the pan to a simmer again, then cover and cook for a further 10 minutes until all the veg are tender, stirring occasionally. Season to taste with salt and black pepper.

3   Remove from the heat, then using a hand-held stick blender, carefully blitz the mixture in the pan until smooth (or leave it chunky, if you prefer). If not using immediately in other recipes (see intro), leave to cool, then divide evenly between four separate airtight containers. The sauce will keep in the fridge for up to 3 days, or it can be frozen for up to 2 months. If frozen, defrost fully in the fridge overnight, then reheat gently in a pan until piping hot throughout.

Tomato and Veg Sauce with Pasta

This quick and easy pasta dish is ideal for a speedy vegetarian midweek meal.
Serve on its own or with a mixed green salad to accompany, if you like.

Serves 3

225g dried pasta (whatever shape you fancy)

¼ quantity of cold Tomato and Veg Sauce (see opposite)

sea salt and freshly ground black pepper, to taste

1 tbsp finely grated vegetarian Italian hard cheese (see Tip), to serve

1   Bring a large saucepan of salted water to the boil, then add the pasta and cook according to the packet instructions until al dente. Drain the pasta, reserving about 5 tablespoons of the cooking water (to loosen the sauce), then return both to the pan.

2   Add the tomato and veg sauce, toss through until the pasta is coated and then cook over a medium heat for 2–3 minutes, or until hot through, stirring.

3   Serve immediately with the grated cheese sprinkled over and a grinding of black pepper.

Tip
If you are not vegetarian you can use Parmesan cheese, if you prefer.

Speedy Veg Biryani

Frozen vegetables are so versatile – here, they're stirred into brown basmati rice that's been cooked with vegetable stock and tikka masala spice paste to make a speedy veg biryani. Ring the changes and use whatever frozen veg takes your fancy.

Serves 5

375g brown basmati rice

1 vegetable stock cube

3 tbsp tikka masala spice paste

200g frozen sliced roasted mixed peppers

200g frozen peas

200g frozen sweetcorn

200g frozen chopped spinach

150g roasted unsalted peanuts, roughly chopped

1 Tip the rice into a large saucepan, add 750ml of cold water and stir. Crumble in the stock cube and stir in the tikka masala spice paste, then bring to the boil. Turn the heat down to a simmer, stir once more, then cover with a lid and cook for 20 minutes until the rice is just tender and has absorbed all the water (leave it undisturbed during cooking). Without stirring, turn the heat off and leave the rice to steam for 5 minutes until the veg are ready.

2 Meanwhile, tip all the frozen vegetables into a large heatproof bowl, add 2 tablespoons of cold water, stir well, then cover with kitchen paper. When the rice is nearly cooked, place the bowl of frozen veg in a microwave oven and cook on high for 5 minutes.

3 Stir really well, then cover with the paper again and cook on high for another 3 minutes until hot through. If not hot, stir again, cook on high for another 2 minutes, then check again, and repeat if necessary until hot through.

4 Stir the hot vegetables through the cooked rice ensuring they're evenly distributed, then divide between serving bowls. Top with the roasted peanuts to finish.

Baked Sweet Potatoes with Pesto

Pine nuts and walnuts combined with basil and rocket give this pesto a really good flavour, which is a little stronger than a standard pesto. Delicious served with these baked sweet potatoes, the pesto goes equally well stirred through hot pasta or dolloped on tomato soup for a luxurious lunch.

Serves 5

(makes enough pesto for 15)

5 medium sweet potatoes, scrubbed

50g pine nuts

50g walnuts

3 garlic cloves, peeled

100g vegetarian Italian hard cheese (see Tips), roughly chopped

40g basil, roughly chopped

80g rocket

200ml olive oil

1   Preheat the oven to 200°C/180°C fan/Gas 6.

2   Pierce each sweet potato with a fork several times, then place them all on a suitable heatproof plate. Cover with a piece of kitchen paper, place in a microwave oven and cook on high for 5 minutes.

3   Transfer the potatoes to a baking tray, then bake in the oven for 20 minutes while you prepare the pesto.

4   Tip the pine nuts, walnuts, garlic cloves and cheese into a food-processor and blitz until it forms a crumble-like texture.

5   Add the basil, rocket and half of the olive oil and blitz to make a coarse purée, then scrape down the sides of the processor bowl so that all the pesto is at the bottom.

6   With the processor running, pour in the remaining oil in a steady stream until the pesto is nearly smooth.

7   Spoon two-thirds of the pesto into the holes of an ice cube tray and freeze for up to 2 months (see Tips). Or transfer it to an airtight container and store in the fridge for up to 1 week.

8   Once cooked, place the baked sweet potatoes on serving plates. Cut a cross in the top of each one and serve with a dollop of the remaining pesto on top.

Tips

- If you are not vegetarian you can use Parmesan cheese, if you prefer.
- Once frozen, pop the pesto cubes out of the ice cube tray and into a resealable freezer bag, then store like this in the freezer and use as required.
- If serving the leftover pesto from frozen, simply toss a frozen cube or two with hot pasta or pop into the split-open top of a piping hot jacket potato and allow it to melt before serving. The chilled pesto can be served straight from the fridge and used as required.

Lentil and Cumberland Pie

Dried green lentils are a very versatile ingredient – they're cheap, easy to cook and take on the flavours of the other ingredients they're cooked with. Why not try this tempting lentil Cumberland pie for a change, and have a meat-free midweek meal? You'll be surprised how little you miss the meat in this classic pie.

Serves 4

2 tsp vegetable oil

1 onion, roughly chopped

4 carrots, peeled and grated

4 celery sticks, roughly chopped

¼ tsp dried thyme

¼ tsp dried oregano

2 tbsp tomato purée

1 tbsp gluten free yeast extract

160g dried green lentils, rinsed and drained

1 vegetable stock cube

800ml boiling water

800g floury potatoes, scrubbed and roughly chopped

40g butter

100g light mature Cheddar cheese, grated

320g frozen peas

freshly ground black pepper, to taste

1   Heat a large sauté pan or saucepan over a medium heat. Add the vegetable oil, onion, carrots and celery and stir well, then cook for 5 minutes until just beginning to soften.

2   Stir in the dried thyme and oregano, the tomato purée and yeast extract and cook for 1 minute. Add the dried lentils and mix really well, then add the crumbled stock cube and the boiling water and stir well. Bring to the boil, then reduce the heat, cover and simmer for 25 minutes until the lentils are tender and the liquid is reduced, stirring occasionally.

3   Meanwhile, place the potatoes in a separate saucepan and cover with water. Cover with a lid, bring to the boil, then reduce the heat and cook for 15–20 minutes until tender. Drain the potatoes really well, then return to the pan and heat for 1 minute, shaking the pan to drive off any excess moisture.

4   Remove from the heat, add the butter, half of the grated cheese and plenty of black pepper and mash with a potato masher until smooth. Set aside.

5   Preheat the oven to 200°C/180°C fan/Gas 6.

6   By now the lentils should be tender. Stir the frozen peas into the lentil mixture (the peas will heat through in the oven), then tip it into a medium-sized ovenproof dish and spread level across the dish.

7   Spoon the cheesey mash over the lentils, then using a fork, level it out (this creates little ridges that will become nice and crispy) to cover the lentil mixture completely.

8   Sprinkle the remaining cheese evenly over the top, then bake in the oven for 15 minutes until golden and bubbling. Serve immediately.

Mexican Tortilla Baskets

This makes a big batch of tasty bean and lentil stew that can be served in so many ways – here, it's spooned into crunchy tortilla baskets and topped with cheese, avocado and salad. You can also serve it simply with jacket potatoes or rice, or rolled up in wraps, topped with tomatoes and cheese and baked in the oven for healthy vegetarian enchiladas.

Serves 4
(plus 4 portions of leftover stew for the freezer)

For the stew

320g dried split red lentils

1 tsp rapeseed oil

2 onions, roughly chopped

4 garlic cloves, finely chopped

2 red chillies, deseeded and finely chopped

1 tbsp ground cumin

1 tbsp ground coriander

2 tsp smoked paprika

2 tsp freshly ground black pepper

2 tbsp tomato purée

1kg passata

2 vegetable stock cubes

3 large courgettes, grated (about 700g prepped weight)

400g tin black beans or three bean salad, drained and rinsed

4 medium soft wholemeal tortilla wraps (each about 20cm diameter)

sunflower oil spray

1   Preheat the oven to 200°C/180°C fan/Gas 6.

2   For the stew, put the red lentils into a large bowl and cover with cold water. Swish the water around, then leave the lentils to soak for 5 minutes while you start cooking the veg.

3   Heat a large, deep-sided sauté pan or flameproof casserole dish over a medium heat, add the rapeseed oil and onions and fry for 3–4 minutes until just softened. Add the garlic, chillies, cumin, ground coriander, smoked paprika and black pepper and fry for 2 minutes until fragrant.

4   Drain the lentils using a sieve, then rinse and drain again. Add the tomato purée to the sauté pan and fry for 1 minute, then add the lentils, passata, crumbled stock cubes and 600ml of cold water. Stir everything together well, then bring to the boil. Reduce the heat, half-cover the pan with a lid and simmer for 15 minutes until the lentils are nearly tender, stirring occasionally.

5   Stir in the grated courgettes and beans, return to a simmer, then cook for another 10 minutes until everything is tender and thickened slightly.

6   Meanwhile, make the tortilla baskets. For each basket, spray one side of a tortilla wrap with a little sunflower oil, then mould it into a bowl/basket shape by gently pressing it, oil-side down, into one hole of a 12-hole muffin tray (the edges will overhang the top of the hole). Repeat with the other wraps, moulding each one into a hole in a different row of the muffin tray to space them apart.

7   Bake in the oven for 8–10 minutes until just hardened and golden brown. Cool for a couple of minutes in the tray to firm up slightly, then carefully remove to serving plates.

8   While the baskets are baking, get the avocado topping ready. Tip the chopped avocado into a bowl, add the lime juice and two-thirds of the chopped coriander and mix well. Set aside.

For the toppings

2 ripe avocados, peeled,
    stoned and roughly
    chopped
juice of 1 lime
small bunch of coriander,
    roughly chopped
cos lettuce, shredded
salad tomatoes, chopped
60g Cheddar cheese, grated

9   When you are ready to serve, remove half of the stew from the pan and transfer it to an airtight container (see Tip), then set aside to cool.

10 Spoon some of the remaining stew into each of the warm tortilla baskets, dividing it evenly. Serve topped with some lettuce, tomatoes, a spoonful of the avocado mixture and some grated cheese. Finish with a sprinkling of the remaining chopped coriander. Serve immediately.

Tip
Once cool, transfer the leftover stew to the fridge or freezer. It will keep in the fridge for up to 3 days or in the freezer for up to 1 month. If frozen, defrost fully in the fridge overnight. To serve, tip the stew into a saucepan and reheat gently, stirring occasionally, until piping hot throughout.

Gluten Free Squash and Cheese Mac

Can you turn mac 'n' cheese into a healthy dish? You can, by making a purée of butternut squash and sweet potato, then stirring through light extra mature Cheddar cheese to make a silky smooth, vegetable-packed sauce. We've used gluten free pasta – choose whatever shape you like, you don't need to stick to macaroni – then add whatever veg additions you fancy, to suit all tastes. Simply pick and mix between peas, sweetcorn, mushrooms, broccoli, tomatoes and spring onions, stir through each individual serving and heat until hot through.

Serves 12

For the cheese mac

1 tsp vegetable oil

2 onions, roughly chopped

2 gluten free reduced-salt vegetable stock cubes

1 litre boiling water

600g butternut squash, peeled, deseeded and roughly chopped (about 500g prepped flesh)

600g sweet potatoes, peeled and roughly chopped (about 500g prepped flesh)

200ml semi-skimmed milk

1kg dried gluten free pasta

360g light extra mature Cheddar cheese, grated

1 tsp fine sea salt

freshly ground black pepper, to taste

For the optional additions

200g frozen peas, defrosted

200g fried sliced mushrooms

200g cooked broccoli florets

200g cherry tomatoes, halved

1 bunch of spring onions, trimmed and roughly chopped

1   For the cheese mac, heat a large sauté pan over a medium heat. Add the vegetable oil and onions and cook for 5 minutes until just softening.

2   Meanwhile, crumble the stock cubes into a large, heatproof jug, add the boiling water and stir well until dissolved.

3   Stir the chopped butternut squash and sweet potatoes into the onions, then add the stock and milk and stir well. Bring to the boil, then reduce the heat and simmer for 10 minutes until the squash and potatoes are tender.

4   Meanwhile, bring a large saucepan of water to the boil (use your largest pan, or you may need to use two saucepans), then add the pasta and cook for 8–9 minutes until just tender (you don't want to overcook the pasta as you will be cooking it further in the sauce), then drain and set aside.

5   Using a hand-held stick blender, carefully blitz the squash and sweet potato mixture until completely smooth. Stir in the cheese, salt and plenty of black pepper and cook over a medium heat for 2–3 minutes until the cheese has melted, stirring occasionally. Toss in the cooked pasta and cook for another 2 minutes until the pasta is tender and coated in the sauce, stirring occasionally.

6   Serve immediately as it is, or transfer each single portion (separately) to a heatproof bowl and add whichever additions you fancy. Stir well, then cover with kitchen paper and heat on high for 1½ minutes until piping hot.

Aubergine Chilli Traybake

Aubergines are really good at taking on flavours, and here they're mixed with traditional chilli con carne flavours, chickpeas and red kidney beans, then topped with more aubergines to make a delicious one-pot chilli traybake. Finished with bubbling melted cheese, this is a hearty vegetarian dish.

Serves 4

3 aubergines

1 onion, finely chopped

3 garlic cloves, finely grated

½ tsp dried thyme

1 tsp ground cumin

2 tsp mild chilli powder

½ tsp fine sea salt

3 tbsp tomato purée

400g tin chickpeas, drained and rinsed (from Gluten Free Bread recipe – see page 78)

400g tin red kidney beans, drained and rinsed

400g tin chopped tomatoes

2 tsp olive oil

80g light mature Cheddar cheese, grated

freshly ground black pepper, to taste

1 Preheat the oven to 220°C/200°C fan/Gas 7.

2 Roughly chop one aubergine and place in a large, ovenproof dish or baking tin. Add the onion, garlic, thyme, cumin, chilli powder, salt and tomato purée and mix together well, getting your hands in to ensure everything is coated in the spices.

3 Add the chickpeas, kidney beans and tinned tomatoes. Pour 150ml of cold water into the empty tomato tin, swirl it around and add to the dish/tin, then mix once more.

4 Cut the remaining two aubergines in half lengthways and place, skin-side down, on a chopping board. Score the flesh in a criss-cross pattern using the tip of a sharp knife, then place them, skin-side down, in a single layer on top of the bean mixture. Drizzle the scored flesh with the olive oil and season with black pepper.

5 Cover the whole dish/tin with foil and bake in the oven for 45 minutes until the aubergines are tender. Preheat the grill to high.

6 Remove the foil from the aubergine dish/tin and scatter the cheese evenly over the top. Place under the hot grill for 3–4 minutes until golden brown and bubbling. Serve immediately.

7 Cool any leftovers, then transfer to an airtight container and store in the fridge for up to 3 days (see Tip).

Tip
Any leftovers can be eaten cold or reheated in a microwave oven. To reheat, place one portion on a suitable heatproof plate, cover with a piece of kitchen paper and heat on high for 3 minutes until hot through. If not piping hot, heat on high for a further 20 seconds at a time until hot through, then serve.

Stuffed Mushrooms

Stuffed mushrooms are an old-school classic dish, but these ones have a modern low fat twist – all the basic ingredients are there, but with the addition of smoked paprika, jarred roasted peppers and baby spinach, these mushrooms pack a lovely flavour punch and are filling, too. Topped with light mature Cheddar cheese, they are delicious on their own as a starter or light lunch, or they make a great evening meal served with some leftover couscous and Roasted Basil Veg (see pages 169 and 150).

Serves 2

4 large Portobello or flat mushrooms, cleaned

1 tsp olive oil

1 onion, roughly chopped

2 garlic cloves, finely grated

1 tsp smoked paprika

1 tomato, roughly chopped

2 red chillies, deseeded and roughly chopped

80g (drained weight) roasted mixed peppers (from a jar), roughly chopped

80g baby spinach leaves

½ slice of toasted brown bread, roughly chopped

40g light mature Cheddar cheese, grated

sea salt and freshly ground black pepper, to taste

1 Preheat the oven to 220°C/fan 200°C/Gas 7.

2 Remove the stalks from the mushrooms, roughly chop and set aside. Place the whole mushrooms, skin-side down, onto a roasting tray and season with black pepper, then set aside.

3 Heat a frying pan over a medium heat. Add the olive oil and onion and fry for 2 minutes until just softening. Add the garlic and smoked paprika and cook for another minute.

4 Stir in the chopped mushroom stalks, the tomato, chillies and roasted peppers and stir-fry for 2 minutes until hot through and tender. Add the spinach leaves and 2 tablespoons of cold water and stir-fry for 2 minutes until wilted down.

5 Stir in the toasted bread and half of the grated cheese, then season with a little salt and plenty of black pepper. Spoon the mixture into the upturned mushrooms on the roasting tray, dividing it evenly between them.

6 Scatter the remaining cheese over the top, then roast in the oven for 15 minutes until the mushrooms are tender and the cheese is bubbling. Serve immediately.

Store Cupboard Fried Rice

Mastering how to cook rice is an important lesson to learn, but once you've done it, you'll never buy cooked rice again. Cook a 500g batch of basmati rice, divide into single portions and then freeze it until needed. It's perfect to use in this store cupboard fried rice, which is easy to whip up in under 15 minutes, and it provides two portions of your 5 a day per serving.

Serves 1

1 egg

1 tsp gluten free hot chilli sauce

1 tsp gluten free light soy sauce

½ tsp vegetable oil

2 spring onions, trimmed and roughly chopped

80g frozen peas

125g frozen cooked rice (see Tips)

80g tinned (drained weight) sweetcorn

1   Crack the egg into a bowl, add the chilli and soy sauces and whisk together until smooth, then set aside.

2   Heat a large frying pan or wok until hot. Add the vegetable oil and spring onions and stir-fry over a high heat for 30 seconds. Add the frozen peas and 3 tablespoons of cold water and stir-fry for 2 minutes until the peas are just defrosted and the water evaporated.

3   Stir in the frozen cooked rice and sweetcorn and stir-fry for 2 minutes until hot through, then add the egg mixture and stir-fry for 2 minutes until the egg is cooked through and the rice is piping hot. Serve immediately (and do not reheat this dish).

Tips

- To cook basmati rice for the freezer (to make 10 x 125g portions), put 500g basmati rice into a saucepan, add 1 litre of cold water and stir. Cover with a lid and bring to the boil, then reduce the heat to low and simmer for 15 minutes until the rice is just tender and has absorbed all the water (leave it undisturbed during cooking). Without stirring, turn the heat off and leave the rice to steam for a few minutes.
- Carefully fork through the cooked rice, then tip it onto a large baking tray and spread out – it should all be nice and fluffy and separate grains. Set aside to cool for no more than 1 hour, then cover and chill in the fridge. Once chilled, divide into 125g servings using resealable food bags or individual airtight containers, and keep in the fridge for up to 1 day, or freeze for up to 1 month.

Pesto, Pea, Spinach and Pepper Pasta

Sometimes all you fancy is a bowl of pasta and this tasty dish ticks the boxes for both adults and kids alike, in a clever two-from-one meal. Whether you want your pesto simple or pimped with ready-roasted peppers, peas and spinach, this is ready in about 20 minutes.

Serves 4
(2 adults and 2 children)

320g dried tricolore fusilli
    pasta
½ tsp olive oil
160g (drained weight)
    roasted mixed peppers
    (from a jar), thickly sliced
160g frozen peas
160g baby spinach leaves
dried chilli flakes and freshly
    grated or ground nutmeg,
    to taste (optional)
180g basil pesto
40g light mild Cheddar
    cheese, grated
sea salt and freshly ground
    black pepper, to taste

1   Bring a large saucepan of salted water to the boil, then add the pasta and cook according to the packet instructions until al dente. Drain the pasta, reserving about 4 tablespoons of the cooking water, then return both to the pan.

2   Meanwhile, heat a frying pan until hot. Add the olive oil and roasted peppers and stir-fry over a high heat for 2 minutes, then add the peas and cook for 2 minutes until hot through. Stir in the spinach and cook for a further 2 minutes until wilted, then add some chilli flakes and nutmeg to taste, if you like.

3   Add the pesto to the drained pasta and toss through until the pasta is coated. Remove half of the pasta and divide between two serving bowls. Serve these two portions immediately with half of the grated cheese sprinkled over and a grinding of black pepper.

4   Add the pepper and pea mixture to the remaining pasta and stir through until combined, then season well with black pepper.

5   Divide this between another two serving bowls, then serve immediately with the remaining grated cheese sprinkled over.

Gluten free Chilli Bean Quesadillas

Quesadillas are a fun sharing dish to make. Prepare the filling and salsa in advance, then all you have to do is assemble and cook to order when you're ready to eat. You can swap in your favourite tinned beans, just remember to mash them down well so that they stick together.

Makes 4

4 tsp vegetable oil

2 red onions, 1½ sliced and
  ½ diced

2 mixed peppers (any colour),
  deseeded and thinly sliced

2 tsp ground coriander

2 tsp ground cumin

1 tbsp chipotle chilli paste

400g tin cannellini beans,
  drained and rinsed

small bunch of coriander,
  stalks and leaves
  separated, both roughly
  chopped

juice of 1 lime

200g tin chopped tomatoes

8 gluten free tortilla wraps

100g light mature Cheddar
  cheese, grated

80ml sour cream

sea salt and freshly ground
  black pepper, to taste

1   Heat a frying pan over a medium heat. Add 2 teaspoons of the vegetable oil, the sliced red onions and the mixed peppers and stir together, then cover and cook for 5 minutes until just softening.

2   Stir in the ground coriander, cumin and chipotle chilli paste and fry for 1 minute, then stir in the cannellini beans and chopped coriander stalks, along with 100ml of cold water. Cover and cook for about 5 minutes until the peppers are tender.

3   Remove from the heat, stir in half of the lime juice, then mash to as smooth a paste as you can (if it's not smooth, the filling will simply fall out!). Set aside.

4   For the salsa, place two-thirds of the chopped coriander leaves in a bowl, reserving the remainder for garnish. Stir in the tomatoes, the diced red onion and the remaining lime juice and season with a little salt and some black pepper.

5   To assemble, lay four tortilla wraps onto a board and divide the pepper paste mixture between them. Spoon over three-quarters of the salsa, then scatter the cheese on top, going right to the edges – you want to create an even layer to help the quesadillas stick together. Top with the remaining tortilla wraps and press down gently all over so that they stick together.

6   Heat a frying pan over a medium heat. Add ½ teaspoon of the remaining vegetable oil and one of the quesadillas to the pan and fry for 2 minutes until golden brown. Slide out onto a flat plate, then place the frying pan upside-down over the top and flip the whole thing over and back into the pan. Fry for another 1–2 minutes until hot through – the cheese will melt and stick the quesadilla together. Remove to a warm plate and keep hot. Repeat with the remaining oil and quesadillas.

7   To serve, cut each quesadilla into wedges. Top each with a little sour cream, the last of the salsa and the remaining chopped coriander leaves. Serve immediately.

Japanese Vegetable Noodle Soup

Japanese udon noodles and miso paste are becoming more readily available in supermarkets. Miso adds a deep, rich umami flavour to the vegetable stock and the noodles make a filling addition to this quickly prepared veg-packed soup. If you like it spicy, add some red chilli, fresh coriander and pickled ginger to the top to stir through as you eat it.

Serves 4

400g dried udon noodles

1 litre boiling water

2 reduced-salt vegetable stock cubes

2 tbsp brown miso paste

160g sugar snap peas, thinly sliced

160g beansprouts

4 carrots, peeled lengthways into long, thin ribbons (using a speedy/veg peeler)

4 spring onions, trimmed and finely sliced

2 tbsp rice vinegar

2 tbsp hot chilli sauce, or to taste

Optional toppings

1 red chilli, deseeded and finely sliced

1 tbsp roughly chopped coriander

1 tbsp pickled ginger, roughly chopped

1   Bring a large saucepan of water to the boil, then add the noodles, stir well and cook for 8–10 minutes until tender.

2   Meanwhile, prepare the soup. Pour the boiling water into a separate large saucepan, crumble in the stock cubes and bring to a gentle simmer, stirring until the stock cubes have dissolved.

3   Scoop a ladleful of the broth into a heatproof bowl, then add the miso paste and stir well until dissolved. Set aside.

4   Add the sugar snap peas to the simmering broth and simmer for 2 minutes, then add the beansprouts, carrot ribbons and spring onions and simmer for a further 2 minutes until all the veg are tender.

5   Stir the miso stock into the broth and mix well, then stir in the rice vinegar and chilli sauce.

6   Drain the noodles and divide between serving bowls. Ladle the vegetables and broth over the top and serve immediately. Top with the chillies, coriander and pickled ginger, if you like.

Meat & Fish

Coconut Chicken
with Roasted Broccoli

Roasting the broccoli to go with this crispy coconut chicken gives it a more chewy texture, but also a great flavour, with the sesame oil and seeds combining perfectly with the peanut dipping sauce.

Serves 4

2 eggs

8 boneless skinless chicken thighs, each cut into 4 strips

40g desiccated coconut

60g dried natural breadcrumbs

4 spring onions, trimmed and thinly sliced

sea salt and freshly ground black pepper, to taste

For the roasted broccoli

1 head of broccoli, cut into florets

2 tsp toasted sesame oil

1 tbsp sesame seeds

For the dipping sauce

80g smooth peanut butter

4 tsp sweet chilli sauce

80ml light coconut milk

1   Preheat the oven to 200°C/180°C fan/Gas 6.

2   Crack the eggs into a bowl and season with salt and black pepper. Add the chicken thigh strips and mix until completely coated. Set aside.

3   Tip the coconut and breadcrumbs into a resealable food bag, hold it tightly and shake really well until combined.

4   Lift the chicken strips out of the bowl, leaving behind any excess egg, then place into the breadcrumb bag. Shake around, pressing the crumbs onto the chicken strips until they are completely coated.

5   Tip them out onto a non-stick baking tray, spread out in a single layer, then bake in the oven for 15–20 minutes until the chicken is fully cooked through and light golden brown.

6   Meanwhile, for the roasted broccoli, tip the broccoli florets onto a separate non-stick baking tray, drizzle with the sesame oil, scatter over the sesame seeds, then toss together until the broccoli is coated. Spread out in an even layer on the baking tray, then roast in the oven alongside the chicken for 10 minutes until just tender and crispy around the edges.

7   In the meantime, put all the ingredients for the dipping sauce into a small saucepan, then cook over a medium heat for 2 minutes until hot and smooth, stirring. Pour into a serving bowl.

8   Place the chicken on a serving platter and scatter the spring onions over the top. Serve the dipping sauce and roasted broccoli alongside.

Prosciutto and Pesto Chicken
with Rocket Salad

Boneless skinless chicken thighs are a comparatively cheap cut of meat and have bags of flavour. Wrapped in prosciutto with a dollop of pesto, these are served with a light rocket salad combined with ribbons of cucumber – a great recipe to get the kids involved in making.

Serves 4

8 boneless skinless chicken
    thighs, each cut in half
    (to form 2 squares)
8 tsp pesto
8 slices of prosciutto, each cut
    in half widthways

For the salad
1 tbsp balsamic vinegar
1 tbsp olive oil
½ cucumber
160g rocket salad
1 red onion, finely sliced
1 tbsp toasted pine nuts
freshly ground black pepper,
    to taste

1   Preheat the oven to 200°C/180°C fan/Gas 6.

2   Lay the chicken thigh halves on a chopping board, the side up that the skin would have been on. Place ½ teaspoon of the pesto on top of each half, then wrap each one in half a slice of prosciutto, folding it around so the seam is on the bottom.

3   Place on a non-stick baking tray and roast in the oven for 15–20 minutes until golden brown and fully cooked through.

4   Meanwhile, prepare the salad. Pour the balsamic vinegar and olive oil into a large bowl, season with black pepper and whisk together.

5   Peel the cucumber into long, thin ribbons using a speedy/veg peeler, then finely chop the remaining part of the cucumber. Add to the bowl, along with the rocket salad and red onion and toss together, making sure that everything is coated in the salad dressing.

6   Pile the salad onto serving plates, sprinkle over the toasted pine nuts, then serve the chicken alongside.

Asian-style Sticky Chicken
with Chinese Leaf Salad

Soy sauce and honey are a classic pairing in the marinade for these sticky chicken thighs, served with a lightly pickled Chinese leaf salad. It can be served hot, but it's also a great one to serve cold in a packed lunchbox.

Serves 4

½ tsp dried garlic granules

2 tsp toasted sesame oil

2 tsp mirin

2 tbsp soy sauce

2 tbsp clear honey

½ tsp dried chilli flakes

8 boneless skinless chicken thighs, each cut in half (to form 2 squares)

6 spring onions, trimmed and thinly sliced

2 tsp sesame seeds

2 limes, cut into wedges

For the salad

1 small Chinese leaf cabbage, shredded (if unavailable use Spring cabbage)

2 red peppers, deseeded and finely sliced

2 tbsp rice vinegar

1 tbsp caster sugar

small bunch of coriander, roughly chopped

1 Preheat the oven to 200°C/180°C fan/Gas 6.

2 Put the garlic granules, sesame oil, mirin, soy sauce, honey and chilli flakes into a resealable food bag and squish together.

3 Add the chicken thigh halves and mix/squish around in the bag until completely coated with the marinade.

4 Tip the chicken pieces onto a small, non-stick baking tray (about 15 x 25cm in size – any bigger and the marinade will evaporate and burn onto the tray), spreading them out in a single layer and pouring the marinade over. Bake in the oven for 15–20 minutes until the chicken is fully cooked through and light golden brown.

5 Meanwhile, prepare the salad. Tip the Chinese leaves into a bowl, add the red peppers and toss together to mix.

6 Pour the rice vinegar and sugar into a small saucepan and heat over a medium heat for 1 minute, stirring occasionally, until the sugar has just dissolved. Pour straight over the salad and toss together to combine. The salad will wilt slightly. Leave it to macerate while the chicken finishes cooking. Just before serving, stir the coriander through the salad.

7 Turn the chicken over in any remaining marinade on the baking tray, then serve with the spring onions and sesame seeds sprinkled over. Finish with the lime wedges to squeeze over the top, and serve the salad alongside.

Spiced Chicken Tacos with Chilli Sauce

Home-made chilli sauce is a revelation – you can make it as hot and fiery or as mild and fruity as you desire (leave the chilli seeds in for more of a kick).

Serves 4

For the tacos
1 tsp ground cumin
1 tsp ground coriander
1 tsp medium chilli powder
½ tsp smoked paprika
2 garlic cloves, finely grated
juice of ½ lemon
2 tsp rapeseed oil
8 boneless skinless chicken
   thighs
100g 0%-fat natural yoghurt
grated zest and juice of 1 lime
2 Little Gem lettuces, shredded
4 tomatoes, chopped
60g light mild Cheddar cheese,
   grated
4 medium wholemeal tortilla
   wraps
freshly ground black pepper,
   to taste

For the chilli sauce
1 small bunch of spring onions,
   trimmed and roughly chopped
½ large ripe mango, peeled,
   stoned and chopped
4 tbsp cider vinegar
2 garlic cloves, chopped
2 tsp ground coriander
1 tsp ground cumin
½ small bunch of coriander,
   chopped
80g mixed chillies, chopped

1 For the tacos, tip the cumin, coriander, chilli powder and smoked paprika into a medium bowl. Add the garlic, lemon juice, 2 tablespoons of cold water and the rapeseed oil and mix together really well.

2 Add the chicken thighs and toss in the spice mixture until coated. If you have time, cover and leave to marinate in the fridge for 1 hour.

3 Meanwhile, make the chilli sauce. Tip all the ingredients, except the chillies, into a blender, add 2 tablespoons of cold water and blitz until as smooth as possible. Add the chillies, just a few at a time, and blitz until well combined, then check the flavour and heat level – if you like it hotter, add more chillies, if not, stick with just a few milder chillies. Spoon the chilli sauce into a sterilised jar or bottle and seal, then store in the fridge and use as required.

4 Preheat the grill to medium and line the grill tray with foil. Transfer the marinated chicken thighs to the foil-lined tray, then grill for 5–6 minutes on each side until just charred and cooked through (cut a chicken thigh in half – if it's white and hot all the way through, it's cooked).

5 Meanwhile, pour the yoghurt into a serving bowl, add the lime zest and juice and season to taste with black pepper. Put the lettuce, tomatoes and cheese into separate serving bowls, so that people can help themselves.

6 When the chicken has 5 minutes left to cook, heat a frying pan over a medium heat until hot. Add the tortilla wraps, one at a time, and cook for 30 seconds on each side until just golden.

7 When the chicken is ready, cut it into thick slices. For each serving, lay a warm wrap on a serving plate, top with some lettuce, tomatoes, chicken and cheese, then drizzle over some lime yoghurt and chilli sauce. Serve immediately.

Zero Waste Roasted Chicken

Chicken is so versatile – here, one large chicken is used to make several different dishes. The backbone is removed and the chicken is then pressed flat before roasting (also known as spatchcocking) to speed up the cooking time. Once it has cooled enough to handle, the meat is then stripped from the carcass and cooled for use later. The carcass, bones and skin are cut into pieces and used to make the stock for Speedy Chicken Pho (see page 132).

Serves 8

(yields about 800g cooked chicken meat)

2kg (extra large) whole chicken, giblets removed

1   Preheat the oven to 200°C/180°C fan/Gas 6.

2   Place the chicken, breast-side down, on a chopping board. Using a pair of sturdy scissors, cut through the flesh and bone along both sides of the backbone about 5cm wide. Cut from the bottom end up to the head end, cutting through the rib bones as you go, and completely remove the backbone (but reserve it). Open the chicken out and turn it over (so it's skin-side up), then press down on the breastbone to flatten it out.

3   Transfer the flattened chicken (still skin-side up) to a large roasting tray or baking tray, add the backbone alongside and roast in the oven for 45 minutes, or until the chicken is fully cooked through.

4   To check that the chicken is cooked, insert a sharp knife or skewer into the fattest part of a thigh. If the juices run clear, the chicken is cooked through. If any blood comes out, return it to the oven to roast for another 5–10 minutes, then check again.

5   Once cooked, set the chicken (and backbone) aside to cool. When the chicken is cool enough to handle (but still warm), cut down through the leg joints and remove the legs. Strip the meat from the legs and place in a bowl. Place the bones and skin in a separate bowl, along with the backbone (broken into pieces), and set aside to cool (see intro).

6   Cut the breasts from the carcass and tear the meat into strips, then add it to the leg meat. Strip any remaining meat from the carcass and add it to the bowl. Add the carcass (broken into pieces) to the bones and skin in the other bowl (see intro).

7   If not using immediately, leave the chicken meat to cool completely, then transfer to an airtight container and store in the fridge for up to 3 days. Use as required.

One-pot Chicken and Broccoli Pasta Bake

All the rules say that pasta should be boiled in a pan of water – here, against all those rules, pasta is simply tipped into an ovenproof dish and tossed with flour, chicken and cheese, then topped with broccoli and peas. The liquid comes in the form of chicken stock and milk which bind together with the flour to form a delicious creamy sauce – don't worry if it looks slightly grainy, that's just how it goes.

Serves 2

150g dried fusilli pasta

200g skinless, cold, cooked chicken meat, cut into small chunks/strips (from the Zero Waste Roasted Chicken recipe – see page 129)

1 tbsp plain flour

¼ tsp fine sea salt

50g light mature Cheddar cheese, grated

160g broccoli, cut into small florets

160g frozen peas

1 reduced-salt chicken stock cube

250ml boiling water

250ml semi-skimmed milk

2 slices of brown bread

freshly ground black pepper, to taste

1 Preheat the oven to 200°C/180°C fan/Gas 6.

2 Take a medium-sized ovenproof dish and scatter the pasta over the base of it. Add the chicken, flour, salt, cheese and some black pepper, then toss the whole lot together until evenly coated in the flour/cheese. Scatter the broccoli and peas over the top.

3 Crumble the stock cube into a jug, add the boiling water and stir really well. Add the milk and stir once more, then pour the whole lot over the pasta mixture. Cover with foil and bake in the oven for 20 minutes.

4 Remove from the oven, uncover and give it a good stir, then re-cover with the foil and return to the oven for another 20 minutes until hot through and the pasta is tender.

5 Meanwhile, toast the bread in a toaster, then set aside to cool. Blitz the toasted bread in a blender or food-processor to form crumbs.

6 Remove the foil from the pasta dish, sprinkle the breadcrumbs evenly over the top, then return to the oven for another 5 minutes. Serve immediately (see Tip).

Tip
This is best served hot on the day it's made, but if you have any leftovers, leave to cool, then transfer to an airtight container and store in the fridge for up to 3 days. Serve cold and do not reheat.

Speedy Chicken Pho

The last part of the Zero Waste Roasted Chicken recipe (see page 129) is the carcass – here, it's simmered with classic flavourings for just 20 minutes to create a quick version of a Vietnamese pho. Finished with cooked chicken, beansprouts and spring onions, it's served with fine rice noodles for a healthy but substantial soup.

Serves 5

1 large roasted chicken carcass, including skin (leftover from the Zero Waste Roasted Chicken recipe – see page 129), broken into pieces

8cm piece of fresh root ginger, peeled and grated

4 garlic cloves, finely grated

1½ tbsp fish sauce

2 tsp teriyaki sauce

1 tbsp Thai 7 spice seasoning

small bunch of coriander, stalks and leaves separated and roughly chopped

400g skinless, cold, cooked chicken meat, cut into chunks/strips (also from the Zero Waste Roasted Chicken recipe – see page 129)

1 bunch of spring onions, trimmed and finely sliced

200g beansprouts

225g dried rice noodles

juice of 2 limes

1 Place the chicken carcass pieces into a large saucepan and add 1.2 litres of cold water, then add the ginger, garlic, fish and teriyaki sauces, Thai 7 spice seasoning and half of the chopped coriander stalks.

2 Place over a high heat and bring to the boil, then reduce the heat, cover and simmer for 20 minutes.

3 Strain the stock through a fine sieve into a clean saucepan and discard the contents of the sieve. Add the remaining chopped coriander stalks, the cooked chicken, spring onions and beansprouts to the broth and heat gently for 5 minutes until hot through.

4 Meanwhile, put the kettle on to boil. Tip the noodles into a large, heatproof bowl, then pour enough boiling water over until the noodles are submerged. Swirl around, then leave to soak for 3 minutes until tender.

5 To serve, add the lime juice to the chicken broth, then drain the noodles and divide between serving bowls. Ladle the chicken broth over the top and garnish with the reserved chopped coriander leaves.

Chicken and Borlotti Bean Salad

This is a great salad for a packed lunch – simply put the balsamic vinegar and lemon zest and juice in a separate small pot to dress the salad when you want to serve it. With a good portion of protein, this salad also provides two portions of your 5 a day per serving.

Serves 2

½ red onion, thinly sliced

80g cherry tomatoes, halved

80g tinned (drained weight) sweetcorn

400g tin borlotti beans, drained and rinsed

1 tbsp balsamic vinegar

finely grated zest and juice of ½ lemon

80g mixed salad leaves

200g skinless, cold, cooked chicken meat, cut into small chunks/strips (from the Zero Waste Roasted Chicken recipe – see page 129)

freshly ground black pepper, to taste

1   Tip the red onion and cherry tomatoes into a large bowl. Add the sweetcorn and borlotti beans, then stir in the balsamic vinegar and lemon zest and juice and toss together.

2   Stir in the salad leaves and cooked chicken and season to taste with black pepper.

3   Serve immediately or transfer to an airtight container and store in the fridge. This salad will keep in the fridge for up to 1 day.

Spiced Puffed Rice Chicken Goujons
with Sweet Potato Wedges and Green Beans

Puffed rice isn't just for breakfast! Here, it's mixed with fresh thyme to make a tasty crunchy coating for chicken goujons. Served with green beans and roast sweet potato wedges, you get two portions of your 5 a day per serving in this healthier version of a classic breaded chicken and chips supper.

Serves 5

5 medium sweet potatoes, scrubbed and each cut into 2cm-thick wedges

1 tsp olive oil

60g plain flour

1 tsp dried garlic granules

½ tsp fine sea salt

1 lemon

2 eggs

1 tsp smoked paprika

100g puffed rice cereal

2 tsp finely chopped thyme leaves

500g boneless skinless chicken breasts, cut into 1cm-thick strips

400g fine green beans

freshly ground black pepper, to taste

1 Preheat the oven to 200°C/180°C fan/Gas 6 and line two large baking trays with baking parchment.

2 Tip the sweet potato wedges onto one of the lined baking trays and drizzle with the olive oil. Season well with black pepper and toss together, then spread out in a single layer. Roast in the oven for 10 minutes while you prepare the chicken.

3 Tip the flour, garlic granules and salt into a bowl and finely grate the lemon zest over the top, then mix together really well. Crack the eggs into a second bowl, add the smoked paprika and plenty of black pepper and beat together. Tip the puffed rice cereal into a third bowl, add the thyme and stir well, then scrunch the puffed rice in your hands to break it down slightly.

4 Place the strips of chicken into the flour first, ensuring that they are completely coated, then into the beaten egg mixture. Do a few at a time, so you don't end up with sticky fingers.

5 Transfer them, a few at a time, to the puffed rice and toss until completely coated, then transfer to the second lined baking tray in a single layer.

6 Stir the sweet potato wedges around, then return to the oven with the tray of chicken strips and bake both for 15 minutes, or until the chicken is golden brown and cooked through, and the potato wedges are tender.

7 A few minutes before the chicken and wedges are ready, cook the green beans in a saucepan of boiling water for 3 minutes until just tender, then drain. Cut the lemon into five wedges.

8 Serve the chicken goujons and potato wedges with the green beans and lemon wedges alongside.

One-pan Roasted Chicken Dinner

Sometimes all you want is a roast chicken with all the trimmings, but you don't have the time or inclination to make it. Here's a speedy one-tray version that will give you everything you want, in under 45 minutes.

Serves 2

300g potatoes, peeled and cut into small chunks, about 3–4cm

2 parsnips, peeled and cut into small batons, about 5 x 2cm

2 tsp vegetable oil

2 boneless chicken breasts (skin on)

½ reduced-salt chicken stock cube

80g broccoli, cut into florets

80g cauliflower, cut into florets

20g chicken gravy granules

sea salt and freshly ground black pepper, to taste

1   Preheat the oven to 200°C/180°C fan/Gas 6.

2   Put the potatoes and parsnips into a large roasting tray, drizzle with 1 teaspoon of the vegetable oil and season with salt and black pepper.

3   Take a piece of foil about 40cm square and place the chicken breasts, skin-side up, into the centre of it, then pull the foil up around the chicken to create a mini tray.

4   Crumble the stock cube over the chicken, pressing it into the flesh, then pour 200ml of cold water into the bottom of the foil, taking care not to pour it over the chicken and wash off all the stock cube. Scrunch the foil up over the chicken to create a sealed parcel and place on the roasting tray (pushing the veg aside a little to make room for the parcel).

5   Roast in the oven for 15 minutes, then remove from the oven, add the broccoli and cauliflower florets to the tray (on top of the other veg), drizzle with the remaining oil and toss all the veg together. Carefully open up the top of the foil parcel to allow the chicken to colour.

6   Return to the oven and roast for another 15 minutes until the chicken is cooked through and the vegetables are tender.

7   Remove from the oven, put the gravy granules into a heatproof jug, then carefully pour in the hot juices from the chicken parcel and whisk well until smooth and dissolved.

8   Transfer the roasted chicken breasts to serving plates and serve with the roasted veg alongside and the gravy poured over.

Chicken and Lentil Curry

If you have time to marinate the chicken, it will add a greater depth of flavour to this curry, but if not, don't worry, this quick and tasty curry using tinned lentils and a pre-made tomato and veg sauce is ready in the time it takes to boil the rice.

Serves 3

300g boneless skinless chicken breasts, cut into 2cm pieces

1 tbsp medium curry powder

225g long grain white rice

¼ quantity of cold Tomato and Veg Sauce (see page 96)

400g tin green lentils, drained and rinsed

2 tbsp roughly chopped coriander

finely grated zest of 1 lime

1 Place the chicken pieces into a bowl, add the curry powder and toss to coat. If you have time, cover and leave to marinate in the fridge for 4 hours until you are ready to cook.

2 Tip the rice into a medium saucepan, add 450ml of cold water and stir. Cover with a lid and bring to the boil, then reduce the heat to low and simmer for about 15 minutes until the rice is just tender and has absorbed all the water (leave it undisturbed during cooking). Without stirring, turn the heat off and leave the rice to steam until the chicken is ready.

3 Meanwhile, tip the tomato and veg sauce into a separate saucepan and bring to the boil. Add the marinated chicken and lentils and return to a simmer. Cover and cook gently for 15 minutes, or until the chicken is cooked through, stirring occasionally (cut a piece of chicken in half – if it's white and hot all the way through, it's cooked).

4 Divide the rice between serving bowls, then spoon over the chicken curry. Finish with a scattering of the coriander and lime zest.

Turkey Lasagne

Minced turkey can be made from either breast or thigh meat – if you want to keep the fat down, go for minced turkey breast. Here, instead of making a white sauce, Parmesan cheese is mixed with fat-free quark, making this a simple lasagne to prepare. To top this off, toasted bread is blitzed to make some crispy breadcrumbs, but stale bread works equally well.

Serves 8

1 tsp olive oil

750g minced turkey

2 onions, quartered

4 carrots, peeled and cut into chunks

3 garlic cloves, halved

1 tsp dried oregano

1 tsp dried thyme

100g tomato purée

2 reduced-salt chicken stock cubes or 2 x 28g reduced-salt chicken stock pots

2 x 400g tins chopped tomatoes

small bunch of basil, roughly chopped

240g frozen chopped spinach

4 slices of wholemeal bread

750g fat-free quark

50g Parmesan cheese, finely grated

375g no-precook dried lasagne sheets

640g frozen peas

freshly ground black pepper, to taste

1 Heat a large, deep-sided sauté pan or flameproof casserole dish over a medium heat. Add the olive oil and minced turkey and fry for 3–4 minutes until browned all over, stirring regularly.

2 Meanwhile, tip the onions, carrots and garlic into a food-processor and pulse until roughly chopped (or roughly chop them by hand). Add them to the pan and cook over a medium heat for 5 minutes. You want them to soften but not colour, so it's a good idea to put a lid on the pan to help retain the moisture and steam the vegetables at the same time.

3 Add the oregano and thyme and cook for another minute, then add the tomato purée and turn the heat up, stirring it through all the vegetables.

4 Crumble in the stock cubes or add the stock pots, then tip in the tomatoes. Fill both the empty tomato tins with water, swirl around and add to the pan, then stir well and bring to the boil. Turn the heat down to a simmer and cook for 10 minutes until the turkey is tender and the sauce is reduced slightly.

5 Stir in the chopped basil and frozen spinach and heat through for another 5 minutes, stirring occasionally. Meanwhile, toast the bread in a toaster, then set aside to cool.

6 Preheat the oven to 220°C/200°C fan/Gas 7.

7 Tip the quark into a bowl, add the grated Parmesan and plenty of black pepper and mix together really well.

8 Set a large, oblong baking dish (about 32 x 23cm) on a baking tray. Spoon a third of the turkey ragù into the dish and level out so that it covers the bottom of the dish evenly. Lay a third of the lasagne sheets over the top, covering the turkey ragù completely. Spoon a third of the quark mixture over the top of the pasta in an even layer. Repeat the layers until you've used up all the turkey ragù, pasta and quark mixture, ending with a layer of the quark mixture.

9 Blitz the toasted bread in a blender or food-processor to form crumbs, then scatter over the top of the assembled lasagne. Cover with foil and bake in the oven for 30 minutes then uncover and cook for a further 15 minutes until golden brown and bubbling.

10 Remove the lasagne from the oven and leave to stand for 5 minutes while you cook the peas. Bring a saucepan of water to the boil, add the frozen peas and cook for 2–3 minutes until hot through, then drain. Cut the lasagne into portions and serve with the peas alongside.

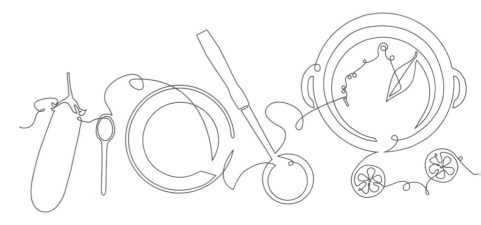

Beef and Lentil Burgers with Onions

Burgers are seen as unhealthy, but here, with the addition of tinned green lentils and some grainy mustard, you can have a burger that provides two portions of your 5 a day per serving and is low in fat, too.

Serves 6

500g lean minced beef

2 x 400g tins green lentils, drained and rinsed

2 eggs

2 tbsp grainy mustard

½ tsp fine sea salt

vegetable oil spray

480g frozen chopped onions

6 large wholemeal buns, split in half

6 tbsp tomato ketchup

2 Little Gem lettuces, leaves separated

freshly ground black pepper, to taste

1 Tip the minced beef into a large bowl, add the green lentils, eggs, mustard, salt and plenty of black pepper and squish together well to ensure that it all binds together – either using your hands or a wooden spoon.

2 Divide the mixture into six even portions in the bowl, scoop out each portion and form into a ball, then press gently to flatten into a round patty about 2cm thick.

3 Spray a little vegetable oil over the burgers and rub all over so they're completely coated in a very fine layer of oil (you don't want the burgers to stick).

4 Preheat the grill to medium and line the grill tray with foil.

5 Place the burgers on the foil-lined tray, then grill for 3–4 minutes on each side until golden brown and cooked through. To check if a burger is cooked, insert the tip of a knife into the centre of the burger, then remove and rest it gently on the inside of your wrist. If it feels piping hot, the burger is ready; if not, cook for another minute on each side and check again. Repeat if necessary until the burgers are fully cooked.

6 Meanwhile, cook the onions. Heat a non-stick frying pan over a medium heat, add the frozen onions and stir-fry for a minute to disperse the ice, then cover and cook over a low heat for 5 minutes until softened and just starting to colour. Remove the lid and turn the heat up, then continue to cook for another couple of minutes until golden, stirring occasionally.

7 Remove the cooked burgers to a plate and leave to rest. Place the burger buns, split-side down on the grill rack and toast under the grill for 20–30 seconds, ensuring they don't burn.

8 Place the bottom half of each bun on a serving plate and spread with the tomato ketchup. Top each with some Little Gem leaves, cooked onions and a burger and finish with the top bun halves. Eat immediately.

Beef and Broccoli Stir-fry

A healthy home-made version of a favourite takeaway dish, this is packed full of flavour and feels really substantial with a generous portion of steak. It's ready in less time than it takes to go to your local takeaway!

Serves 6

450g brown basmati rice

450g frying steak, cut into 1cm-thick slices

1 heaped tsp cornflour

1 tbsp groundnut oil

60g unsalted cashew nuts

1 red onion, thinly sliced

3 garlic cloves, thinly sliced

5cm piece of fresh root ginger, peeled and grated

1 head of broccoli (about 250–275g), cut into small florets, and the central stalk sliced

2 tbsp soy sauce

2 tbsp oyster sauce

½ vegetable stock cube

400ml boiling water

small bunch of coriander, roughly chopped

sea salt and freshly ground black pepper, to taste

1 Bring a large saucepan of salted water to the boil, add the basmati rice, stir well, then return to the boil. Reduce the heat to a simmer and cook for 25 minutes until tender. Drain and return to the pan.

2 Meanwhile, prepare the stir-fry. Season the beef generously with black pepper, then sprinkle over the cornflour and toss well to coat.

3 Heat a wok until hot, then add half of the groundnut oil and when it's just smoking, add the beef and stir-fry over a high heat until browned all over – you don't want it cooked through, just browned on the outside and slightly pink in the middle (you might need to do this in two batches, depending on how big your wok is). Remove and set aside in a heatproof bowl.

4 Add the cashews to the wok and stir-fry over a medium heat for 1–2 minutes until just golden brown, then remove and add to the bowl of beef.

5 Carefully wipe out the wok (remember, it will be hot!), then add the remaining oil and the red onion. Stir-fry over a high heat for 1–2 minutes until just softening, then add the garlic and ginger and stir-fry for another minute.

6 Add the broccoli, soy sauce and oyster sauce and mix well. Stir in the crumbled stock cube and boiling water, then bring to the boil, cover and cook for 2 minutes until the broccoli is just tender (you don't want it to lose its bright green colour).

7 Remove the lid, return the beef and cashews to the wok and stir through. Heat for 1 minute – you just want to heat the beef through and not cook it any further. Stir through the coriander and serve with the basmati rice.

Slow-cooked Beef
with Root Veg Mash

A perfect piece of meat for the slow cooker, the beef brisket breaks down into soft strands during the slow cooking. It's then mixed with the rich cooking juices and served with a carrot, parsnip and swede mash, providing three portions of your 5 a day per serving.

Serves 5

For the beef

1kg beef brisket joint, cut into 4 pieces

1 tsp vegetable oil

½ tsp fine sea salt

28g reduced-salt beef stock pot or 1 reduced-salt beef stock cube

500ml boiling water

2 tbsp Worcestershire sauce

3 tbsp reduced-salt and sugar brown sauce

freshly ground black pepper, to taste

1 Preheat the slow cooker on the high setting, according to the manufacturer's instructions, or preheat the oven (see Tip).

2 Rub the beef brisket with the vegetable oil, then season with the salt and some black pepper. Tip the stock pot into a jug or crumble in the stock cube, add the boiling water and stir to combine.

3 Heat a large frying pan over a medium heat, then add the beef brisket and fry on each side for 2 minutes until browned. Place into the cooking pot of the slow cooker.

4 Add the stock to the frying pan and swirl around to combine all the juicy beef bits left in the pan with the stock. Pour over the beef in the slow cooker, then add the Worcestershire and brown sauces, stir again and cover with the lid.

5 Leave the setting on high or turn it down to low, then leave the beef to cook on high for 6–8 hours, or on low for 8–10 hours.

> **Tip**
> The beef can also be cooked in a large, ovenproof casserole dish. Follow the instructions above for preparing the dish, and then cook in a preheated oven at 180°C/160°C fan/Gas 4 for 3 hours.

For the root veg mash

400g carrots, peeled and
  roughly chopped

400g parsnips, peeled and
  roughly chopped

400g swede, peeled and
  roughly chopped

50g butter

bunch of chives, finely
  snipped

6   When the beef is nearly cooked, make the root veg mash. Put all the chopped veg into a large saucepan and cover with water. Cover with a lid, bring to the boil, then reduce the heat and simmer for 20 minutes until tender. Drain, then return to the pan and heat for 1 minute, shaking the pan to drive off any excess moisture. Remove from the heat, add the butter and plenty of black pepper, then mash with a potato masher until smooth. Stir in half of the chives.

7   Once the beef is cooked, remove the lid and lift the beef out onto a board. Pull it apart into pieces using two forks, then return the meat to the slow cooker to mix with the sauce/juices. Spoon the shredded beef onto plates and serve with the root veg mash alongside. Scatter over the remaining chives to finish.

Spiced Ham and Black Bean Stew with Rice

This delicious stew is packed with vegetables and plenty of spice, making it a hearty everyday meal. It's perfect with rice, but is just as good served on its own for a lower carbohydrate option, or why not try it with jacket potatoes or even crusty bread?

Serves 6

1 tbsp vegetable oil

2 onions, roughly chopped

2 large leeks, washed and roughly chopped

3 large carrots, peeled and roughly chopped

450g long grain white rice

4 garlic cloves, crushed or finely grated

2 tbsp ground cumin

2 tbsp ground coriander

1 tbsp coarsely ground black pepper

1 tsp dried thyme

4 heaped tbsp tomato purée

2 x 400g tins chopped tomatoes

300g lean cooked ham, roughly chopped

½ reduced-salt chicken stock cube

2 x 400g tins black beans, drained and rinsed

small bunch of coriander, roughly chopped

finely grated zest of 2 limes

2 red chillies, deseeded and roughly chopped (optional)

1 Heat a large saucepan over a medium heat. Add the vegetable oil, onions, leeks and carrots and stir to combine, then cover and cook gently for 10 minutes until just softening.

2 Tip the rice into a large saucepan, add 900ml of cold water and stir. Cover with a lid and bring to the boil, then reduce the heat to low and simmer for about 15 minutes until the rice is just tender and has absorbed all the water (leave it undisturbed during cooking). Without stirring, turn the heat off and leave the rice to steam until the stew is ready.

3 Meanwhile, add the garlic, cumin, ground coriander, black pepper and thyme to the pan of onions, stir well and cook for 2 minutes. Stir in the tomato purée, then add the tomatoes, ham and crumbled stock cube.

4 Fill both the empty tomato tins with water, swirl around and add to the pan. Bring to the boil, then reduce the heat to a simmer, cover and cook for 15 minutes until the vegetables are just tender, stirring occasionally.

5 Add the black beans to the pan and cook for a further 5 minutes until hot through.

6 Stir in half of the chopped coriander and all the lime zest, then serve the stew with the rice. Scatter the remaining coriander over the top, and a little red chilli too, if you like it hot!

Sausage and Lentil Stew
with Carrot and Swede Mash

Here's how to make two meals out of one – the lentil stew is simmered with vegetarian sausages in it for the vegetarians in your family and then the meat sausages are roasted separately alongside. So it's all ready together to be served with a tasty carrot and swede mash.

Serves 4

(2 veggie and 2 non-veggie portions)

2 tsp rapeseed oil

4 vegetarian sausages

1 onion, roughly chopped

6 carrots, peeled, 2 roughly chopped and 4 cut into small chunks

2 garlic cloves, roughly chopped

2½ tsp smoked paprika

½ tsp dried thyme

1 tbsp tomato purée

200g dried green lentils, rinsed and drained

600ml vegetable stock

500g passata

4 pork sausages

350g swede, peeled and cut into small chunks

10g butter

50g fresh wholemeal breadcrumbs

½ small bunch of flat-leaf parsley, leaves picked and roughly chopped

sea salt and freshly ground black pepper, to taste

1   Preheat the oven to 200°C/180°C fan/Gas 6.

2   Heat a large sauté pan until hot, then add 1 teaspoon of the rapeseed oil and the vegetarian sausages. Fry over a high heat for 30–45 seconds until brown all over, then remove to a plate and set aside.

3   Add the onion to the pan, fry over a medium heat for 2–3 minutes until just softening, then add the two chopped carrots and fry for another minute. Stir in the garlic, 2 teaspoons of the smoked paprika, the thyme and tomato purée and fry for a further minute, stirring all the time.

4   Add the green lentils, vegetable stock and passata and mix through, then bring to the boil. Add the vegetarian sausages, then reduce the heat, cover and simmer for 30 minutes until the lentils are tender and the sausages are cooked through, stirring occasionally.

5   Meanwhile, place the pork sausages on a baking tray and roast in the oven for 25 minutes, turning them over after 10 minutes.

6   While the stew and sausages cook, prepare the mash. Place the carrot chunks in a large saucepan with the swede and cover with water. Cover with a lid, bring to the boil, then reduce the heat and simmer for 15 minutes until tender.

7   Drain, then return to the pan and heat for 1 minute, shaking the pan to drive off any excess moisture. Remove from the heat, mash with a potato masher until smooth, then season with salt and black pepper. Set aside and keep warm.

8   Heat a frying pan over a medium heat, then add the butter and remaining rapeseed oil and when the butter is foaming, add the breadcrumbs and remaining smoked paprika. Stir well and fry for a couple of minutes until golden brown and crunchy. Season with a little salt, then tip out onto a kitchen paper-lined plate.

9   Check that both types of sausages are cooked through and the lentils are tender, then stir the parsley into the stew. Serve the meat or vegetarian sausages with some of the lentil stew (serving two portions with the veggie sausages and two portions with the pork sausages), with the carrot and swede mash alongside, topped with the crunchy breadcrumbs.

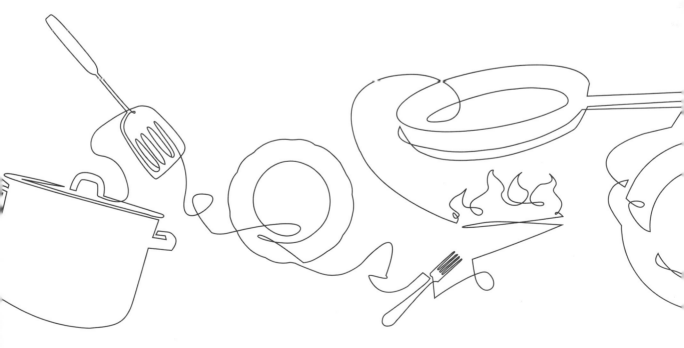

Greek-style Pork, Lentil and Potato Casserole

This is one of those 'throw it all together, then walk away dishes' – ideal for a winter's day. The pork is cooked until it's nearly falling apart and the sauce is thickened with the combination of the lentils and potatoes, making it a perfect one-pot dish.

Serves 4

2 tsp olive oil

500g diced pork shoulder

2 onions, sliced

2 tbsp dried oregano

1 tbsp ground cinnamon

1 tbsp mild chilli powder (if you like a kick, use hot chilli powder)

1 reduced-salt chicken stock cube

2 x 400g tins chopped tomatoes

200g dried green lentils, rinsed and drained

500g potatoes, peeled and cut into small chunks

small bunch of parsley, roughly chopped

100g stoned green olives (optional)

freshly ground black pepper, to taste

1 Preheat the oven to 170°C/150°C fan/Gas 3.

2 Heat a large, flameproof casserole dish over a medium heat. Add the olive oil and pork and fry until golden brown all over, stirring occasionally, about 3–4 minutes.

3 Add the onions, stir well, then cover and cook for 5 minutes until just softened, stirring once or twice to ensure the onions aren't catching. Stir in the dried oregano, cinnamon, chilli powder and plenty of black pepper and cook for 1 minute.

4 Crumble the stock cube into the mixture, then stir in the tomatoes. Fill both the empty tomato tins with water, swirl around and add to the mixture. Fill one tin once more with water and add to the casserole (you should have added three full tins of water), then stir really well.

5 Add the lentils and potatoes, stir well, then bring to a simmer. Cover, then transfer to the oven and cook for 3 hours until the pork and lentils are really tender, and the sauce is just reduced.

6 Stir in the parsley and green olives (if using). Divide between serving plates and serve immediately.

> **Tip**
> Any leftovers will keep in an airtight container in the fridge for up to 3 days or in the freezer for up to 1 month. If frozen, defrost fully in the fridge overnight. To serve, tip the casserole into a saucepan and reheat gently, stirring occasionally, until piping hot throughout.

Lamb Shwarma
with Couscous and Raita

An ideal dish for the weekend, this lamb shawarma gives you plenty of leftover lamb to use during the week. Turn it into a flavoursome shepherd's pie, or simply heat a portion and stir through some cooked rice with a little chopped tomato and red onion for a quick pilau. The spice mixture can be used on chicken, fish or even beef, and if you like it hot, use hot chilli powder or add some dried chilli flakes.

Serves 4

For the spice mix (this makes enough for 4 shoulders of lamb – see Tips)
4 tbsp ground cumin
4 tbsp ground coriander
2 tbsp smoked paprika
2 tbsp medium chilli powder (or use mild or hot, if you prefer)
2 tbsp freshly ground black pepper
4 tsp garlic powder
4 tsp ground ginger
2 tsp freshly grated or ground nutmeg
2 tsp garam masala
1 tsp ground turmeric

For the lamb (serves 8 once cooked – use half in recipe, save half for later – see Tips)
2 tbsp olive oil
finely grated zest and juice of 2 lemons
1 onion, quartered
1.5–1.6kg lamb shoulder
4 wholemeal pitta breads, to serve

1   Preheat the oven to 170°C/150°C fan/Gas 3.

2   For the spice mix, tip all the spices into a clean, medium-sized jam jar, cover with the lid and shake together. Set aside.

3   For the lamb, place the olive oil and lemon zest and juice in a bowl, add 4 tablespoons of the spice mix and mix together really well. Reserve the remaining spice mix for use another time (see Tips).

4   Place the onion quarters in a medium, deep-sided roasting tray and place the lamb on top (you want it to fit snugly so don't use a roasting tray that is too big). Make several incisions in the lamb. Spread the spice mixture all over the lamb, rubbing it well into the incisions. Pour 300ml of cold water into the bottom of the tray, then cover the whole thing with foil. Roast in the oven for 3¼ hours until the meat is tender and falling off the bone.

5   Meanwhile, prepare the couscous. Tip the couscous into a large, heatproof bowl, add the lemon zest and juice, then pour in the boiling water and stir really well. Cover with clingfilm and set aside for about 10 minutes to allow the couscous to absorb the liquid. Drag a fork through the couscous to separate the grains.

6   Stir in the yellow peppers and sweetcorn and mix really well, then stir in the chilli and coriander (if using). Stir once more, then cover and chill in the fridge until you are ready to serve.

7   Finally, prepare the raita. Coarsely grate the cucumber onto a clean tea towel, then gather the tea towel up and hold it over the sink. Twist it until all the liquid comes out of the cucumber. Tip the squeezed cucumber into a separate bowl, then add the yoghurt. Finely grate the garlic over the top and season with the ground coriander, a little salt and some black pepper. Stir well to combine, then cover and chill in the fridge until needed.

For the couscous

320g wholewheat couscous

finely grated zest and juice of
  1 lemon

400ml boiling water

2 yellow peppers, deseeded
  and roughly chopped

320g frozen sweetcorn,
  defrosted

1 red chilli, deseeded and
  finely chopped (optional)

3 tbsp roughly chopped
  coriander (optional)

For the raita

1 cucumber

320g 0%-fat Greek-style
  yoghurt

2 garlic cloves

1 tsp ground coriander

sea salt and freshly ground
  black pepper, to taste

8 Remove the foil from the lamb and baste with any juices at the bottom of the tray. Return to the oven for another 15 minutes until just browned around the edges.

9 To serve, lay the pitta breads on a baking tray and cover with foil. Heat through in the oven for 5 minutes while carving the lamb. Remove the lamb from the tray and pull the meat from the bone, shredding the lamb into small pieces. Mix the shredded lamb back into the cooking juices and onion, stirring until combined.

10 Divide the couscous between serving plates, top with half of the shredded lamb and cooking juices, then serve a warmed pitta bread and a dollop of the raita alongside each portion. Serve immediately.

11 Tip the remaining lamb (four portions) into an airtight container and leave to cool, then transfer to the fridge – this will keep for up to 3 days. The leftovers can be eaten cold or reheated in a microwave oven (see Tips).

Tips

- Any leftover spice mix will keep in the covered jar in a cupboard for up to 1 month. Use it for future lamb joints as above or for marinating chicken.

- To reheat the cold cooked lamb in a microwave oven, place one portion in a suitable heatproof bowl, cover with a piece of kitchen paper and heat on high for 2 minutes until hot through. If not piping hot, heat on high for a further 30 seconds at a time until hot through, then serve.

Grilled Cod Tikka
with Cucumber Yoghurt

Cod is a good, meaty fish that takes on flavours really well. However, don't marinate it for too long in advance as the paste will draw out all the moisture from the fish. A great one to make in advance, this will keep well in the fridge, then can be reheated in a microwave oven when needed (see Tip).

Serves 5

5 x 150g boneless skinless cod fillets

5 tsp tikka masala spice paste

1 cucumber

350g 0%-fat Greek-style yoghurt

5 tsp mint sauce

5 wholemeal pitta breads

3 Little Gem lettuces, leaves separated

1 Preheat the grill to medium and line the grill tray with foil.

2 Place the cod fillets in a large bowl, add the tikka masala spice paste and stir until the cod is completely coated.

3 Transfer the cod tikka fillets to the foil-lined tray. Grill for 4 minutes, then turn over and grill for a further 4 minutes until slightly charred and cooked through. The fish will flake easily when it is cooked; if not, return it to the grill for another minute and check again.

4 Meanwhile, coarsely grate the cucumber onto a clean tea towel, then gather the tea towel up and hold it over the sink. Twist it until all the liquid comes out of the cucumber. Tip the squeezed cucumber into a separate bowl, then add the yoghurt and mint sauce. Stir well to combine.

5 When the cod is ready, remove from the grill tray and set aside while you lightly toast the pitta breads under the grill.

6 Divide the pitta breads between serving plates, top with the Little Gem leaves, a dollop of the cucumber yoghurt and then the cod tikka, and serve immediately.

Tip

If there is any cod leftover, leave it to cool, then transfer to an airtight container and store in the fridge for up to 3 days. To reheat in a microwave oven, place a cod fillet (one at a time) on a suitable heatproof plate and cover with a piece of kitchen paper. Heat on high for 40 seconds until hot through. If not piping hot, heat on high for another 10 seconds at a time until hot through, then serve.

Skinny Smoked Mackerel Carbonara

This interesting twist on a classic carbonara, combining smoked mackerel with courgettes and spinach, means that you get one portion of your 5 a day per serving in this dish, while the fat content is reduced right down by using 0%-fat Greek-style yoghurt.

Serves 6

450g dried spaghetti

400g 0%-fat Greek-style
  yoghurt

4 eggs

60g Parmesan cheese, finely
  grated

1 tsp rapeseed oil

2 courgettes, coarsely grated

350g boneless smoked
  mackerel fillets, skinned
  and flaked

240g baby spinach

small bunch of flat-leaf
  parsley, roughly chopped

sea salt and freshly ground
  black pepper, to taste

1 Bring a large saucepan of salted water to the boil, then add the spaghetti and cook according to the packet instructions until al dente.

2 Meanwhile, prepare the sauce. Tip the yoghurt, eggs and Parmesan into a medium bowl and whisk together until combined. Season with plenty of black pepper, whisk once more, then set aside.

3 Heat a large, deep-sided sauté pan over a medium heat, add the rapeseed oil and grated courgette and stir-fry for 2 minutes until the water has evaporated and the courgette has started to soften. Add the smoked mackerel and mix well, then fry for another minute until the mackerel is hot through and the courgette is softened. Stir in the spinach and cook for another couple of minutes until wilted down.

4 Tip the yoghurt mixture into the sauté pan and stir really quickly over the heat until it's mixed throughout the courgette and mackerel. Turn the heat off – you don't want the eggs to curdle.

5 Drain the pasta, reserving about 100ml of the cooking water, then tip the pasta and reserved cooking water straight into the sauté pan, and stir until the spaghetti is completely covered in the sauce.

6 Serve immediately with the parsley scattered over to finish.

Fakeaway Fish and Chips
with Mushy Peas

Cornflakes are not just for breakfast time! Here, they're bashed up and used to coat fish fillets to make a crunchy coating to go alongside thick, oven-roasted healthier chips and home-made mushy peas. Ready in under 45 minutes, and not a deep fryer or takeaway in sight!

Serves 5

3 eggs

750g frozen skinless white
    fish fillets

150g cornflakes

5 large potatoes, peeled and
    cut into 1cm-thick long
    chips (see Tips)

1 tbsp rapeseed oil

400g frozen peas

50g half fat crème fraîche

small bunch of chives, finely
    snipped

sea salt and freshly ground
    black pepper, to taste

1   Preheat the oven to 210°C/190°C fan/Gas 6½. Line two large baking trays with baking parchment.

2   Crack the eggs into a large, shallow bowl, then season with salt and black pepper and beat well. Add the frozen fish fillets and swirl around until coated all over.

3   Tip the cornflakes into a large, resealable food bag, then seal and bash with a rolling pin until crushed. Open the bag, then add an egg-coated fish fillet (one at a time), turning it until coated all over. Lift out and place on one of the lined baking trays, then repeat with the remaining fish fillets. Set aside.

4   Place the chips (see Tips) on the second lined baking tray, drizzle with the rapeseed oil and season with salt and black pepper. Toss well to coat, then shuffle the tray around until the chips are in a single layer.

5   Place both trays in the oven and bake for 15 minutes, then turn the chips over. Bake for a further 10–15 minutes until the fish is cooked through and the chips are cooked and golden brown.

6   A few minutes before the fish and chips are ready, cook the peas in a pan of boiling water for 2–3 minutes until hot through. Drain, tip back into the saucepan, then add the crème fraîche and crush with a potato masher until the peas are quite broken down. Stir in the chives and mix once more.

7   Serve the fish and chips with a dollop of the mushy peas.

Tips

- To make the chips, cut each potato in half lengthways so you have two long oval halves. Place the halves, flat-side down, on the chopping board, then cut each half into 1cm-thick slices along the length of the potato. Repeat with all the potatoes. Turn the slices so that they are flat, widest side on the board, stack one on top of each other, then cut into 1cm-thick chips, again along the length of the potato. You will now have 1cm-thick long chips.
- If your baking tray isn't big enough, you may need to use two medium baking trays instead to cook the chips.

Herb-crusted Fish
with Roasted Veg Traybake

Keeping a bag of frozen fish fillets in the freezer is a smart thing to do – you can create a healthy, tasty meal in under 45 minutes using the fish straight from the freezer. Topped with orange-infused crispy breadcrumbs, and roasted alongside a mixture of carrots, sweet potatoes and onions, this is an easy weekday meal.

Serves 4

4 carrots, peeled and cut into small chunks

400g sweet potatoes, scrubbed and cut into small chunks

1 red onion, cut into small wedges

1 tbsp rapeseed oil

4 x 150g frozen skinless white fish fillets

40g panko breadcrumbs

2 tbsp roughly chopped flat-leaf parsley

1 orange

160g spinach, roughly chopped

sea salt and freshly ground black pepper, to taste

1   Preheat the oven to 220°C/200°C fan/Gas 7. Line two large baking trays with baking parchment.

2   Tip the carrots, sweet potatoes and red onion onto one of the lined baking trays, add half of the rapeseed oil, season with salt and black pepper and toss well to coat, then spread out in a single layer. Roast in the oven for 15 minutes.

3   Place the frozen fish fillets on the second lined baking tray, drizzle with the remaining oil and season with a little salt and some black pepper. Tip the panko breadcrumbs and parsley into a small bowl and combine. Finely grate the orange zest over the breadcrumbs and mix well, then divide the mixture between the seasoned fish, patting it gently onto the top of each fillet.

4   Bake the fish in the oven with the veg for a further 10 minutes. Remove the veg tray from the oven, turn the veg over, then lay the spinach on top and squeeze the orange juice over. Return to the oven for another 5 minutes until the fish is cooked through, the vegetables are tender and the spinach is wilted.

5   Remove both trays from the oven and stir all the vegetables together. Serve the fish fillets with the roasted veg alongside.

Fishcakes Three Ways

Making one base for these fishcakes means that you can then add a variety of fish to create a selection of tasty fishcakes to suit the whole family. Fresh white fish fillets, tinned tuna and smoked mackerel are the options we include here, but try using other fish of your choice, if you prefer.

Serves 6
(makes 12 fishcakes,
4 of each variation)

For the fishcake base
540g floury potatoes, peeled
   and cut into chunks
15g butter
6 spring onions, trimmed and
   thinly sliced
½ small bunch of flat-leaf
   parsley, leaves picked and
   roughly chopped
finely grated zest of 1 lemon
   and juice of ½
2 tbsp plain flour
3 tsp rapeseed oil
sea salt and freshly ground
   black pepper, to taste

For the fish variations
160g boneless white fish
   fillets, skinned, then diced
   into 1cm pieces
160g tin tuna in spring water,
   drained and flaked
160g boneless smoked
   mackerel fillets, skinned
   and flaked

1   Preheat the oven to 200°C/180°C fan/Gas 6.
2   Put the potatoes into a saucepan and cover with water. Cover with a lid, bring to the boil, then reduce the heat and cook for 15–18 minutes until tender. Drain, then return to the pan and heat for 1 minute, shaking the pan to drive off any excess moisture.
3   Remove from the heat, add the butter and mash with a potato masher until really smooth. Stir in the spring onions, parsley, lemon zest and juice and some salt and black pepper and mix well.
4   Divide the mash into three separate bowls. Add one type of fish to each bowl of mash and mix well. Divide each bowlful of mixture into four and form each portion into a ball, then press gently to flatten into a round patty about 2cm thick. Dust all the fishcakes in the flour to coat all over.
5   Heat a large frying pan over a medium heat, then add 1 teaspoon of the rapeseed oil for each batch. Add the fishcakes in batches of four and fry for 1 minute on each side until lightly browned and crusted. Transfer to a baking tray and repeat with the remaining fishcakes. When they are all done, bake in the oven for 5–8 minutes until hot through, golden brown and just crispy. Insert a knife into the centre to check that the fishcakes are hot through. Serve immediately (see Tip).

Tip
These fishcakes are ideal for a light lunch served with a green salad or the Chinese Leaf Salad on page 126.

Teriyaki Salmon with Noodles

A super-quick lunch or evening meal and ready in under 20 minutes, teriyaki salmon is a delicious healthy dish packed full of veg. The noodles and vegetables cook while the salmon is grilling. You can swap the veg to whatever you fancy – green beans and baby corn make a great alternative, or asparagus and peas when in season.

Serves 2

For the teriyaki sauce
4 tsp reduced-salt soy sauce
2 tsp light soft brown sugar
2 tsp rice vinegar
4 tsp mirin
½ tsp ground ginger

For the salmon
2 x 150g skinless salmon fillets
100g dried egg noodles
160g sugar snap peas
160g broccoli, cut into florets
2 spring onions, trimmed and finely sliced
½ small bunch of coriander, roughly chopped
1 lime, cut into quarters
1 tsp chilli oil (optional)
freshly ground black pepper, to taste

1 Tip all the ingredients for the teriyaki sauce into a small pan and bring to the boil, stirring occasionally. Simmer for 1 minute until all the sugar has dissolved and the sauce has thickened slightly. Stir well, then remove the pan from the heat. Pour half of the sauce into a small, heatproof bowl and set aside to cool for about 5 minutes. Reserve the remaining sauce in the pan for serving.

2 Preheat the grill to high. Line a small baking tray with foil. Bring a medium saucepan of water to the boil (for the noodles).

3 Add the salmon fillets to the bowl of cooled teriyaki sauce, turning them over to coat completely. Transfer the salmon fillets to the lined baking tray and spoon any residual sauce over the top.

4 Cook the salmon under the grill for 5 minutes until lightly charred and cooked through. The salmon will flake when pressed gently. Remove the salmon from the grill, cover loosely with foil and leave it to rest while you cook the noodles and veg.

5 Add the egg noodles to the pan of boiling water and return to the boil, then reduce the heat and simmer for 2 minutes. Add the sugar snap peas and broccoli, stir well and simmer for a further 4 minutes until the noodles are cooked and the vegetables just tender.

6 Drain the noodles and veg, then return to the pan with the spring onions and coriander and toss to combine. Squeeze in the juice from two of the lime quarters and toss once more, then add the chilli oil (if using) and season to taste with black pepper.

7 Divide the vegetables and noodles between two serving plates, top each portion with a salmon fillet, then spoon over any cooking juices and the reserved warm teriyaki sauce. Serve immediately with the remaining lime quarters.

Cheat's Bouillabaisse

Using a frozen fish pie mix is a cheat's way of making a quick bouillabaisse that is just as flavoursome as a more traditional one, and perfect for an everyday family meal.

Serves 3

¼ quantity of cold Tomato and Veg Sauce (see page 96)

½ tsp mild chilli powder

300g frozen fish pie mix

finely grated zest of ½ lemon

2 tbsp roughly chopped flat-leaf parsley

1 medium baguette, thickly sliced

1 Tip the tomato and veg sauce into a saucepan, stir in the chilli powder, add 200ml of cold water and bring to the boil.

2 Add the frozen mixed fish, stir gently and return to a simmer, then cover and cook for 15 minutes until the fish is cooked through – the fish should flake easily when pressed gently.

3 Stir in the lemon zest and half of the parsley. Transfer to serving bowls, scatter the remaining parsley over the top, and serve with the baguette slices alongside.

Super-quick Stir-fry

Stir-fries might take a little time to prepare, but then they are the simplest of things to cook. Follow the order for putting the vegetables in and you end up with a perfectly cooked stir-fry with plenty of protein, plus over three portions of your 5 a day per serving!

Serves 5

300g brown basmati rice

3 tsp groundnut oil

125g unsalted cashew nuts

3 garlic cloves, finely sliced

7cm piece of fresh root
    ginger, peeled and finely
    chopped

2 red onions, finely sliced

3 peppers (mixed colours),
    deseeded and finely sliced

240g broccoli, central stalk
    thinly sliced, then the
    remainder cut into small
    florets

240g green beans, cut into
    3cm-length pieces

400g frozen raw peeled king
    prawns, defrosted

3 carrots, peeled lengthways
    into long, thin ribbons
    (using a speedy/veg
    peeler)

240g frozen sweetcorn

3 tbsp teriyaki sauce

1 tbsp toasted sesame oil

finely grated zest and juice of
    1 lime

2 red or green chillies,
    deseeded and finely
    chopped (optional)

sea salt, to taste

1   Bring a large saucepan of salted water to the boil, add the basmati rice, stir well, then return to the boil. Reduce the heat to a simmer and cook for 25 minutes until tender. Drain and return to the pan.

2   Meanwhile, prepare all the vegetables so that the stir-fry and rice will be ready at the same time (see Tip).

3   Heat a large wok until hot. Add 1 teaspoon of the groundnut oil and the cashews and stir-fry over a high heat for 1–2 minutes until golden brown. Tip out onto a kitchen paper-lined plate and set aside.

4   Add the remaining oil to the wok. Add the garlic and ginger and stir-fry over a high heat for 1 minute, then add the red onions and peppers and stir-fry for 2 minutes.

5   Add the broccoli and green beans, then add 200ml of cold water, stir well, cover with a lid and steam for 1 minute.

6   Stir in the prawns, cover and cook for 1 minute until just turning pink, then add the carrot strips, sweetcorn, teriyaki sauce and another 100ml of cold water. Stir-fry for a further 2 minutes until the veg are just tender and the prawns are pink and cooked through.

7   Return the toasted cashews to the pan, along with the toasted sesame oil and lime zest and juice and stir through.

8   Divide the cooked rice between serving plates and top with the stir-fry. Scatter over the chillies to finish, if you like.

Tip
Don't start cooking the stir-fry until all the veg are chopped and the rice is about 10 minutes away from being cooked, to ensure that the stir-fry and rice are ready together. Have a timer nearby, it really does help with stir-fries!

Spanish Fish Stew

Taking inspiration from sunny Spain, this one-pot fish stew is packed with flavour, using fennel, chilli, smoked paprika and saffron for an authentic flavour. The addition of potatoes makes it a substantial meal and you can use whatever white fish you like – cod, pollock, hake or haddock go really well with these strong flavours.

Serves 6

4 tsp olive oil

3 small onions, sliced

3 small or 2 medium fennel bulbs, thickly sliced

6 garlic cloves, crushed

1½ tsp dried chilli flakes

1½ tsp fennel seeds, crushed

1½ tsp smoked paprika

½ tsp saffron strands

600g potatoes, peeled, quartered and cut into 5mm-thick slices

300ml dry or medium white wine (Spanish, if possible)

2 x 400g tins chopped tomatoes

1 vegetable stock cube

600g frozen white fish fillets, defrosted and cut into 4cm chunks

500g fresh mussels, scrubbed and de-bearded (discard any with broken shells or ones that don't close when tapped sharply)

4 tbsp roughly chopped flat-leaf parsley

1 Heat a large sauté pan or saucepan over a medium heat. Add the olive oil, onions and fennel and cook for 10 minutes until softened but not coloured, stirring occasionally.

2 Add the garlic and cook for another 1 minute, then stir in the chilli flakes, fennel seeds, smoked paprika and saffron strands. Cook for 1 minute, stirring constantly, then add the potatoes. Stir well, then add the white wine and bubble rapidly over a high heat until reduced by half, about 3–4 minutes. Stir in the chopped tomatoes and bring to a simmer.

3 Fill one of the empty tomato tins with cold water, swirl around and add to the pan, along with the crumbled stock cube. Bring to the boil, then reduce the heat, cover and simmer for 20 minutes until the potatoes are just tender and the liquid slightly reduced.

4 Stir in the fish chunks and simmer for 2 minutes until nearly cooked through, then add the mussels, cover and simmer for a further 3 minutes until the mussels open (discard any that remain closed).

5 Remove from the heat and leave to rest (with the lid still on) for 5 minutes – the fish will finish cooking through in the residual heat.

6 Divide the stew between serving bowls, then top with the parsley and serve.

Bakes & Puddings

Mini Baked Lemon Cheesecakes

An oaty mixture gives these healthier cheesecakes an unusual base, but they are still classic in flavour, if not in fat and sugar levels, though you'll be hard-pushed to tell the difference!

Makes 12

1 tbsp rapeseed oil, plus extra for greasing

60g clear honey

120g porridge oats

½ heaped tsp ground mixed spice

300g 0%-fat Greek-style yoghurt

300g half fat soft cheese

2 tsp vanilla extract

finely grated zest of ½ lemon

1 tbsp stevia (or sweetener, to taste)

1 tbsp light soft brown sugar

1 tbsp cornflour

2 eggs

120g strawberries, hulled and sliced

1   Preheat the oven to 170°C/150°C fan/Gas 3. Lightly grease a 12-hole muffin tray with a little rapeseed oil, brushing it up the sides of the holes.

2   Heat the measured rapeseed oil and the honey in a medium saucepan until runny (see Tip). Stir to combine, then add the oats and mixed spice and stir well until completely coated in the honey mixture. Divide evenly between the prepared muffin tray and press down well to give an even layer across the bottom of each hole. Set aside.

3   Tip the yoghurt, soft cheese, vanilla extract, lemon zest, stevia, sugar and cornflour into a bowl and mix together really well. Crack the eggs into the mixture and mix again until smooth.

4   Spoon the mixture over the cheesecake bases, dividing it evenly between them. Bake in the oven for 15 minutes until just set and lightly golden – there will still be a little wobble in the middle of each one.

5   Remove from the oven and leave the cheesecakes to cool to room temperature in the tin, about 1 hour. Once they are cool, carefully remove the cheesecakes from the tin and serve immediately topped with the sliced strawberries.

6   Alternatively, transfer the cheesecakes (minus the strawberry slices) to an airtight container (in a single layer) and store in the fridge for up to 3 days. Eat from chilled and top with the strawberry slices just before serving.

Tip
Alternatively, put the rapeseed oil and honey into a suitable heatproof bowl and heat in a microwave oven on high for about 30 seconds, until runny, then continue as above.

Greek-style Yoghurt Eton Mess

A clever but delectable twist on a popular classic dessert, this uses 0%-fat Greek-style yoghurt instead of cream, and provides one portion of your 5 a day per serving, making it an equally delicious, low fat, high protein alternative.

Serves 5

500g 0%-fat Greek-style yoghurt

3 ready-made meringue nests

400g prepared mixed frozen fruit (such as blueberries, raspberries, cherries, mango, pineapple)

25g dark chocolate (70% cocoa solids), coarsely grated

1 Spoon the Greek-style yoghurt into a large bowl and stir until smooth.

2 Crumble in the meringue nests, then scatter the frozen fruit over the top and mix together really well.

3 Add two-thirds of the grated chocolate and fold through.

4 Divide the mixture between five serving glasses, then scatter the remaining chocolate over the top.

5 Serve immediately, or if you prefer a softer eat, chill in the fridge for up to 1 hour before serving.

Baked Almond and Oat Topped Peaches

Tinned peaches are so versatile. Here, they're topped with a spiced fruit, nut and oat combination and baked in the oven. You can mix and match with different combos – try tinned apricots with a pistachio and sour cherry topping, or tinned pears with a walnut, cinnamon and sultana topping. Keep the quantities the same and just change the components until you find your favourite.

Serves 3

400g tin peach halves in fruit juice, drained

45g porridge oats

45g flaked almonds

15g dried cranberries

½ tsp ground cinnamon

1 orange

150g 0%-fat Greek-style yoghurt

1   Preheat the oven to 220°C/200°C fan/Gas 7.

2   Place the peach halves, cut-side up, on a baking tray.

3   Tip the oats, flaked almonds, cranberries and cinnamon into a bowl and toss together. Zest the orange over the top, then squeeze in the juice from the orange and mix together really well.

4   Spoon the mixture onto the cut sides of the peaches, leaving it slightly higgledy piggledy.

5   Bake in the oven for 10 minutes until the peaches are tender and the oat mixture is slightly crispy around the edges.

6   Serve hot or warm with dollops of the yoghurt.

Mini Key Lime Pie Cheesecakes

Cheesecakes don't always need to be packed full of fat and sugar. This recipe creates individual lighter baked lime cheesecakes made using 0%-fat Greek-style yoghurt – simple to make and quick to bake. Serve with berries of your choice on top for extra flavour and appeal.

Makes 8

8 reduced-fat digestive biscuits

50g butter

250g 0%-fat Greek-style yoghurt

350g half fat soft cheese

1 tsp vanilla extract

finely grated zest and juice of 1 lime

2 tbsp caster sugar

1 tbsp stevia (or sweetener, to taste)

2 eggs

1   Preheat the oven to 170°C/150°C fan/Gas 3. Place eight small glass ramekins (each about 8.5 x 4cm) into a large, deep-sided roasting tray and set a kettle on to boil.

2   Put the digestive biscuits into a resealable food bag and bash with a rolling pin until they turn into fine crumbs.

3   Melt the butter in a small saucepan over a medium heat. Remove from the heat, tip in the biscuit crumbs and mix really well until coated in the butter.

4   Divide the buttered crumb mixture evenly between the ramekins and press down well with the back of a spoon to give an even layer across the bottom of each ramekin. Set aside in the fridge while you make the topping.

5   Tip the yoghurt, soft cheese, vanilla extract, lime zest and juice, sugar and stevia into a large bowl and mix together really well. Crack the eggs into the mixture and mix again until smooth.

6   Spoon the mixture over the cheesecake bases, dividing it evenly between them. Carefully pour enough boiling water into the roasting tray so that it comes halfway up the sides of the ramekins. Transfer the roasting tray to the oven and bake for 15 minutes until the cheesecakes are just set and lightly golden – there will still be a little wobble in the middle of each one.

7   Remove from the oven and transfer the ramekins to a wire rack. Leave to cool to room temperature, about 1 hour. Once they are cool, serve immediately. Alternatively, transfer the cooled cheesecakes to a tray or plate, cover with clingfilm and chill in the fridge until needed – they will keep for up to 3 days. Eat from chilled.

Lighter Rocky Road

Sometimes all you want is something chocolatey, and with this, a little goes a long way – a perfect cross between a crispie cake and a rocky road bar! Chocolate is combined with puffed rice and dried cranberries, but mix and match – if you have other dried fruit, try adding it in instead, just keep the quantities the same.

Makes 20 pieces

vegetable oil, for greasing

100g dark chocolate (70% cocoa solids), roughly chopped

100g puffed rice

50g dried cranberries, finely chopped

3 tbsp date syrup

1 Grease and line a 20cm square cake tin with greaseproof paper.

2 Place the chocolate in a heatproof bowl set over a pan of barely simmering water (ensuring the base of the bowl doesn't touch the water underneath) until melted. Try not to stir until you can see it's all nearly melted.

3 Remove from the heat, then stir in all the other ingredients, ensuring everything is evenly mixed.

4 Tip the mixture into the lined cake tin and squish down using the back of the spoon until the mixture is spread evenly across the tin. Chill in the fridge for at least 1 hour until firm.

5 Once ready, slide the paper and rocky road out of the tin, then use a sharp knife to cut the rocky road into 20 even squares, and serve.

6 Transfer any leftovers to an airtight container and store in the fridge for up to 5 days.

Rhubarb Fool

A classic rhubarb fool takes a little while to make and is full of sugar and cream – a delicious combination. However, it is possible to make a quick and healthy alternative. Tinned rhubarb is combined with 0%-fat Greek-style yoghurt to give a tart yet luxurious-tasting fool. If you like tart, substitute the same quantity of fruit for tinned gooseberries, or for a slightly sweeter version, use tinned mango, cherries, apricots or pineapple. For a little extra treat, serve with shortbread fingers.

Serves 4

560g tin rhubarb in light syrup
500g 0%-fat Greek-style yoghurt
40g (shelled) pistachios (see Tips), crushed with the side of a knife

1   Drain the rhubarb, discarding the syrup (see Tips). Place the fruit in a blender or food-processor with the yoghurt and blitz briefly until the fruit is just broken down and the yoghurt and fruit are combined.

2   Divide the fool mixture between four serving glasses and top with the crushed pistachios.

3   Serve immediately, or cover and chill for at least 30 minutes before serving. This dessert will keep (covered) in the fridge for up to 3 days.

Tip
- Try swapping the pistachios for unsalted cashew nuts.
- Reserve the rhubarb syrup and pour it over muesli for breakfast, or over natural yoghurt for a speedy dessert.

Iced Chocolate Berries

Having some frozen mixed berries in the freezer is a wise choice. It will always give you the opportunity to have a little sweet treat – simply grab a small handful and top with a drizzle of melted dark chocolate, then scatter over some chopped mixed nuts and you have created a perfect sweet and crunchy dessert.

Serves 8

320g frozen mixed berries

100g dark chocolate (70% cocoa solids), roughly chopped

4 tbsp toasted chopped mixed nuts (optional)

1   Divide the frozen berries between eight serving bowls.

2   Tip the dark chocolate into a suitable heatproof bowl, place in a microwave oven and heat on high in 30-second bursts until the chocolate has melted, then stir. Alternatively, place the bowl over a pan of barely simmering water (ensuring the base of the bowl doesn't touch the water underneath) until melted, then stir.

3   Drizzle the melted chocolate over the frozen berries, then scatter the nuts (if using) over the top. Leave to set for a couple of minutes – the chocolate will harden quite quickly and the fruit will soften slightly. Serve immediately.

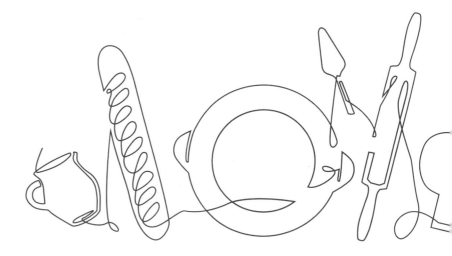

Date and Peanut Butter Butterfly Cakes

Dates have a great natural sweetness and, when combined with peanut butter, they give these cakes a lovely flavour with some added protein to keep you going that bit longer. Perfect with a cup of coffee or for a tasty after-school snack.

Makes 12

For the cakes
200g stoned dates
50g butter
1 tsp vanilla extract
250ml semi-skimmed milk
½ tsp bicarbonate of soda
2 eggs
200g self-raising wholemeal flour
25g brown sugar with stevia (see Tip)
75g smooth peanut butter (no added salt or sugar)

For the topping
60g smooth peanut butter (no added salt or sugar)
finely grated zest of ½ lemon
2 tsp clear honey
120g very low fat soft cheese

1   Preheat the oven to 190°C/170°C fan/Gas 5 and line a 12-hole muffin tin with cupcake cases.

2   For the cakes, tip the dates, butter, vanilla extract and milk into a saucepan and bring to the boil over a medium heat, stirring occasionally, then reduce the heat and simmer for 2 minutes.

3   Meanwhile, place all the remaining cake ingredients in a food-processor.

4   Carefully add the hot date mixture to the food-processor and blitz to a smooth batter, scraping down the sides of the processor bowl a couple of times, if necessary. Divide the mixture evenly between the cupcake cases.

5   Bake in the oven for 12 minutes until golden and just firm to the touch – you don't want to overcook these, otherwise they'll be dry.

6   Remove from the oven and leave to cool in the tin for at least 30 minutes, before transferring to a plate or board for topping.

7   Meanwhile, make the topping. Tip the peanut butter into a bowl, add the lemon zest and honey and beat together until smooth. Add the soft cheese and beat again until smooth.

8   Cut a disc from the top of each cake, then cut each disc in half to create two 'butterfly wings'. Spoon or pipe the topping into the holes left on top of the cakes, then place each pair of 'wings' at an angle on top of each cake, and serve.

9   Store any leftovers in an airtight container in a cool place and eat within 3 days.

Tip
Buying a brown sugar and stevia blend is great if you're trying to cut down on sugar – it's twice as sweet as regular sugar so you only need to use half the amount!

Chocolate and Date Pots

Everyone loves to indulge occasionally, and these chocolate pots feel like a real indulgence, yet they are lower in fat and sugar than a traditional chocolate pot. Ensure that you blitz the mixture until silky smooth for a really luxurious feel.

Serves 8

300ml semi-skimmed milk

1 tbsp vanilla extract

30g cocoa powder

100g stoned dates

75g dark chocolate (70% cocoa solids), roughly chopped

1   Pour the milk into a saucepan, add the vanilla extract, cocoa powder and dates and bring to the boil over a medium heat, stirring frequently, until the cocoa is dissolved, then simmer for 1 minute.

2   Add the chocolate and remove the pan from the heat. Stir well, then pour into a blender and blitz until completely smooth.

3   Pour the chocolate mixture into small serving glasses or egg cups, dividing it evenly, then set aside to cool.

4   Transfer to the fridge and chill for at least 1 hour until just set, before serving. Alternatively, once chilled and set, you can serve these choc pots later – simply cover with clingfilm and keep in the fridge for up to 3 days.

Courgette, Pistachio and Lime Loaf Cake

Courgette might seem an unusual ingredient for a cake but it works beautifully. Paired with a hint of lime and the crunch of pistachios, this makes a really moist cake that you'll be wanting to make again and again.

Serves 12

300g courgettes (about 2 medium courgettes)

125ml sunflower oil, plus extra for greasing

75g white sugar with stevia

2 eggs

250g self-raising wholemeal flour

½ tsp baking powder

finely grated zest and juice of 1 lime

120g (shelled) pistachio nuts

1   Preheat the oven to 180°C/160°C fan/Gas 4. Grease a 1kg loaf tin with a little sunflower oil and line the base with baking parchment.

2   Coarsely grate the courgettes onto a clean tea towel, then gather the tea towel up and hold it over the sink. Twist it until all the excess liquid comes out of the courgettes.

3   Put the sunflower oil, sugar and eggs into a large mixing bowl and beat together until smooth.

4   Stir in the grated courgettes, the flour, baking powder and lime zest, mixing well. Stir in the lime juice and pistachios and mix once more. Transfer to the prepared tin, smoothing to level the surface.

5   Bake in the oven for 45 minutes until risen and light golden brown. Insert a skewer or sharp knife into the centre of the cake – if it comes out clean, the cake is ready; if not, return to the oven and bake for another 5 minutes, then check again.

6   Remove from the oven and leave the cake to cool in the tin for at least 10 minutes, before turning out onto a wire rack to cool completely.

7   Cut into slices to serve. Store any leftovers in an airtight container and eat within 3 days.

Tip
You can slice the cold cake, then transfer to an airtight container and freeze for up to 1 month. Simply remove each slice as needed and allow to defrost fully at room temperature before serving. Alternatively, place a frozen slice on a suitable heatproof plate, cover with kitchen paper and pop in a microwave oven. Heat on high for 30 seconds. Check that the cake is hot through. If not, heat on high for another 10 seconds at a time until hot through, then serve.

Cook's notes

Where we've included salt and pepper for seasoning, we'd suggest using a maximum of ¼ tsp of salt for 2 servings, to make sure you're not eating too much salt.

All herbs are fresh unless stated otherwise.

Cheddar cheese has been used in some of the vegetarian recipes. If you're a strict vegetarian, check the packaging to make sure you're choosing a Cheddar that isn't made using rennet.

All eggs are medium unless stated otherwise.

We've generally used stock pots rather than stock cubes, as these tend to be more flavourful and less salty, but you can substitute stock cubes if you prefer. Also included are 'reduced-salt' stock pots, recommended if trying to lower daily salt intake.

All microwave recipes in this book have been developed/tested using a 1000W microwave oven, so if you're using a lower wattage oven, you'll need to adjust (increase) cooking times accordingly.

To check that chicken is fully cooked through, firstly press it gently with a finger – it should spring back. Then, insert a knife or skewer into the fattest part of the chicken. If the juices run clear, the chicken is cooked through. If any blood comes out, cook it for another 5 minutes, then check again. Alternatively, pierce a piece of chicken with a temperature probe and check the temperature – it should be 75°C.

Spoon measures are level unless stated otherwise.

- 1 teaspoon = 5ml
- 1 tablespoon = 15ml

Menu planners

This new way of shopping and eating is supposed to make your life easier, but if you're not completely confident about getting started, here are two sample weeks laid out for you – complete with shopping list. All of the suggested main meals are recipes from this book, but check the number each recipe serves before you head out to the shops – you might need to double up quantities or reduce them depending on the size of your family. Don't forget, though, doubling up on quantities can give you another meal for the freezer or for another day, with no extra cooking time...

Some of the recipes listed here are good for batch-cooking or make large quantities, and these are marked as such. We've tried to get a good mix of nutritional needs in these plans – some meat, fish, veg, gluten free – but do mix and match according to your family's requirements or preferences. If you crave something sweet in the evening, we've given you some suggestions for healthy, quick and easy desserts that will keep you satisfied. It's always a good idea to have some fresh, frozen or tinned fruit (in natural juice) for emergencies, to chop into a fruit salad, add to some yoghurt or granola, or whip up into a smoothie.

There are a lot of ingredients used in these recipes that you might only need a little of each week, but they are great staples to keep in the store cupboard as they will last for ages – such as dried herbs, sauces and oils – so we've put those in a separate list to make shopping even easier. Some you might already have in your cupboards, so only add them to your weekly list if you need them.

Store cupboard staples

chicken, beef and vegetable stock pots (reduced-salt are good)
cornflour
plain and self-raising flours
cumin seeds and ground cumin
ground coriander
ground cinnamon
ground turmeric
dried oregano
dried thyme
dried chilli flakes
smoked paprika
garlic powder
garam masala
mild chilli powder
medium curry powder
sea salt and black peppercorns
ground ginger
ground nutmeg
tomato purée
baking powder
bicarbonate of soda
caster sugar
cocoa powder
vanilla extract
soy sauce
hot or sweet chilli sauce
clear honey
maple syrup (especially if you have a vegan in the house)
red wine vinegar
balsamic vinegar
reduced-salt and sugar tomato ketchup
Worcestershire sauce
rapeseed oil
vegetable oil
olive oil

Week 1

This week has a variety of recipes to keep veggies and meat-eaters alike happy, with delicious and satisfying suppers. The Tomato and Veg Sauce makes a big batch that can be used in two meals this week, one in Week 2 and still leave plenty to be portioned up and put in the freezer.

Sunday
- One-pan Roasted Chicken Dinner (serves 2)
- Chocolate and Date Pots (serves 8)

Monday
- Tomato and Veg Sauce with pasta (serves 3 – uses ¼ quantity)
- Iced Chocolate Berries (serves 8 – enough ingredients for Week 2 if family of four)

Tuesday
- Beef and Broccoli Stir-fry (serves 6)
- Greek-style Yoghurt Eton Mess (serves 5)

Wednesday
- Gluten Free Chilli Bean Quesadillas (makes 4)
- Yoghurt and fruit

Thursday
- Cheat's Bouillabaisse (serves 3 – uses ¼ quantity Tomato and Veg Sauce)
- Baked Almond and Oat Topped Peaches (serves 3)

Friday
- Chargrilled Steak with Roasted Basil Veg and Chips (serves 4)
- Lighter Rocky Road (makes 20 pieces – enough for Week 2)

Saturday
- Spiced Puffed Rice Chicken Goujons with Sweet Potato Wedges and Green Beans (serves 5)
- Fruit salad with sliced mango

Week 1 Shopping List

Meat, poultry and fish
6 boneless chicken breasts
  (about 800g)
450g frying steak
3 x 225g rib-eye steaks

Veg
300g potatoes
2 parsnips
5 medium sweet potatoes
330–355g broccoli
80g cauliflower
2 onions
4 red onions
2 red/2 yellow peppers
2 bulbs of garlic
4 large carrots
4 celery sticks
4 courgettes
400g fine green beans
2 corn on the cob
160g cherry tomatoes
1 small bunch of spring
  onions
80g mixed chillies
5cm piece of fresh root ginger

Herbs
2 small bunches of basil
  (about 60g)
3 small bunches of coriander
  (about 90g)
Small bunch of flat-leaf
  parsley (about 30g)
thyme leaves

Fruit
1 lime
2 lemons
1 large ripe mango
1 orange
Favourite fresh fruit for the
  week – for fruit salads and
  snacks

Freezer
300g frozen fish pie mix
500g frozen chips
400g mixed frozen fruit
  (blueberries, raspberries,
  cherries, mango,
  pineapple)
320g frozen mixed berries

Dairy
Small packet of vegetarian
  Italian hard cheese
100g light mature Cheddar
  cheese
80ml sour cream
20g butter
2 x 500g pots 0%-fat Greek-
  style yoghurt
300ml semi-skimmed milk

Store cupboard
20g chicken gravy granules
dried garlic granules
4 x 400g tins, 1 x 200g tin
  chopped tomatoes
400g tin cannellini beans
225g dried pasta (whatever
  shape you fancy)
450g brown basmati rice
groundnut oil
oyster sauce
cider vinegar
chipotle chilli paste
8 gluten-free tortilla wraps
puffed rice cereal
3 ready-made meringue nests
200g dark chocolate (70%
  cocoa solids)
400g tin peach halves in fruit
  juice
45g porridge oats
45g flaked almonds
60g chopped mixed nuts
60g unsalted cashew nuts
100g stoned dates
15g dried cranberries

Other
1 medium baguette
2 eggs

Week 2

Last week you will have portioned up your Tomato and Veg Sauce, so a little of this serves as the base for the meatballs recipe here. The roast chicken here serves 8, so can either feed a crowd, or give you lots of leftovers for the week, which can be used to make a speedy supper of One-pot Chicken and Broccoli Pasta Bake. Don't forget to boil up the chicken carcass to make some delicious chicken stock!

Make the lemon cheesecakes on Thursday and they will keep to serve again at the weekend, and last week you will have bought enough ingredients to have the Iced Chocolate Berries again this week, if you are a family of four.

Sunday
- Zero Waste Roasted Chicken (serves 8)
- Rhubarb Fool (serves 4)

Monday
- Herb-crusted Fish with Roasted Veg Traybake (serves 4)
- Lighter Rocky Road (from Week 1)

Tuesday
- One-pot Chicken and Broccoli Pasta Bake (serves 2)
- Greek-style Yoghurt Eton Mess (serves 5)

Wednesday
- Meatballs and Mash (serves 3)
- Yoghurt and fruit

Thursday
- Mexican Tortilla Baskets (serves 4)
- Mini Baked Lemon Cheesecakes (makes 12 – serve the rest on Saturday)

Friday
- Fakeaway Fish and Chips with Mushy Peas (serves 5)
- Iced Chocolate Berries

Saturday
- Sausage and Lentil Stew with Carrot and Swede Mash (serves 4)
- Mini Baked Lemon Cheesecakes

Week 2 Shopping List

Meat, poultry and fish
2kg (extra large) whole
  chicken
300g fresh ready-made beef
  meatballs
4 pork sausages

Veg
650g carrots
400g sweet potatoes
1kg potatoes
350g swede
1 red onion
3 onions
1 bulb of garlic
2 red chillies
160g spinach
160g broccoli
3 large courgettes
2 ripe avocados
1 cos lettuce
4 salad tomatoes

Herbs
Small bunch of flat-leaf
  parsley (about 30g)
Small bunch of coriander
  (about 30g)
Small bunch of basil leaves
  (about 30g)
Small bunch of chives
  (about 20g)

Fruit
1 orange
1 lime
1 lemon
120g strawberries
Favourite fresh fruit for the
  week – for fruit salads
  and snacks

Freezer
1.35kg frozen skinless white
  fish fillets
560g frozen peas
400g prepared mixed frozen
  fruit (such as blueberries,
  raspberries, cherries,
  mango, pineapple)

Dairy
110g light mature Cheddar
  cheese
250ml semi-skimmed milk
3 x 500g pots 0%-fat Greek-
  style yoghurt
40g butter
50g half-fat crème fraîche
300g half-fat soft cheese

Storecupboard
40g panko breadcrumbs
150g dried fusilli pasta
3 ready-made meringue nests
25g dark chocolate (70%
  cocoa solids)
320g dried split red lentils
200g dried green lentils
400g tin black beans or three
  bean salad
4 medium soft wholemeal
  tortilla wraps
1.5kg passata
150g cornflakes
120g porridge oats
40g (shelled) pistachios
ground mixed spice
stevia
light soft brown sugar
560g tin rhubarb in
  light syrup

Other
4 vegetarian sausages
5 eggs
3 slices of brown bread

Index

From top to bottom (left to right):
The Gamblings, The Carters, The Waltons, The Students, The Struthers and The Drews.

Acknowledgements

Here we are with book 4 and in series 6 of *Eat Well For Less?*, and we truly are the sum of a bunch of pretty magnificent and talented people who have worked hard to make it the success that it is – a huge thank you to the dream team! And now to name names…

Our team is led by two incredible women – Fiona Gay and Kate Drysdale. Their creativity and love of a spreadsheet are limitless, and always done whilst keeping perspective and humour. Thank you.

A fantastic casting team led by our yoga-guru Lucy, and more than ably assisted by Sam, Kat and Grace. I really am very proud of you all.

Our shooting teams who spend time working with our families are amazing. They are people that you are always happy to invite into your home. Hard working, talented and always ready for a cuppa. Thank you Nick, Claire, Jack, Heather, Gayle, Hermione, Stephanie, Ben, Charley, Alex, Pete and Grace.

Sophia, Emma, Tom – top foodies who are full of tips and tricks – and huge team support. Thank you for never complaining whatever last-minute curve ball we throw at you.

Our production management team – Laura, Tasha, Caitlin, Talisha and Julia – who will do whatever is needed to support the teams out on the road. Thank you. Carrie and Heather, thank you for making sense with the numbers. Suzanne, thank you for your good advice – and patience.

Our marvellous edit teams – Jo, Jason, Beccy, Tommy, Alex, and Rich. The magic makers, thank you. Also to Charlie and Joe for their support.

A big thank you to Janet, Sam, Phil and Bec for fantastic food and debranded packaging!

Our camera teams who we send far and wide – Jon, Craig, John, Chris, Simon, Paul, Warren, Tim, Nick, Matt, Miles, Paul, Christian, Charlie and Harry.

RDF Television West, my home, with the support of Mark and Angela. And Jim, who is only ever a phone call away. Big thank you.

The BBC and particularly Ricky Cooper, for being such a supporter, and fan, of the series.

Gregg and Chris. May my steps never be too far back from yours! Thank you for believing in us and always being the best. Your jokes may not be, but you are! And Priya, thank you for all your help and great advice.

My last thank you, as always, belongs to those who I hold more dearly than a cheap, healthy, homemade muffin – Mum and Dad (Carol and Ron), thank you for always being there to support us all, and finding great deals when you go shopping! Matty, thank you for making me laugh, keeping me on my toes and only ever making your special stew just the once! Rob, thank you for being my rock and my Rock Star. See, it's in print now, so it's going to happen…

Jo Scarratt-Jones

2

BBC Books, an imprint of Ebury Publishing
20 Vauxhall Bridge Road,
London SW1V 2SA

BBC Books is part of the Penguin Random House
group of companies whose addresses can be
found at global.penguinrandomhouse.com

This book is published to accompany the
television series entitled *Eat Well for Less?* first
broadcast on BBC One in 2015.

Commissioning Editor: Ricky Cooper
Executive Producer: Jo Scarratt-Jones
Series Editor: Fiona Gay
Series Producer: Kate Drysdale

First published by BBC Books in 2019

www.penguin.co.uk

A CIP catalogue record for this book is
available from the British Library

ISBN 9781785944437

Contributing Writer: Helena Caldon
Project Editor: Nell Warner
Design: Gemma Wilson
Food Photography: Andrew Burton
Home Economist: Janet Brinkworth
Assistant: Phil Wells

Printed and bound in China by C&C Offset
Printing Co., Ltd.

Penguin Random House is committed to a
sustainable future for our business, our readers
and our planet. This book is made from Forest
Stewardship Council® certified paper.

Welcome to your BTEC First Certificate or BTEC First Diploma course in Media!

On a BTEC course you will have the chance to put the knowledge and skills that you learn into practice. You will learn to do practical tasks similar to those that take place in the media industry. You will also learn to write reports, draw up plans of action, prepare budgets, write scripts and book people and equipment to be part of your production.

The media industry actually consists of several different sectors: television, film, audio, print, advertising, website design, interactive media and computer game development. To work in any part of the media industry you will need a wide range of skills, some of which appear in more than one sector. These include such skills as photography, writing, animation and graphic design.

You will also need to develop a wide range of research skills, including audience research, and learn to apply them to the production of any media products.

Throughout the book you will find **Try this...** boxes which suggest tasks you might like to try. Some of these will help you directly with creating your products and others will help you to practise your new skills.

Try this ...

Watch a DVD or video and make a note of all the job roles that appear in the credits. Try to identify what each of these job roles involves. Some of the job roles are unusual – 'Best Boy', for example. Find out what a 'Best Boy' does.

When you see a word written in bold, turn to the glossary at the back of the book to find out what it means. You'll also see the appendix there, which has information on media organisations, legal issues in the media and what to do next if you want to take your learning further.

Look at ...

News Corporation is another example of a cross-media company. Look at the examples of their products on the CD-Rom and see which ones you recognise.

The interactive CD-Rom gives you more examples of products to think about, case studies of professional people and situations, and forms you can use to help create your production documentation.

When you see a CD icon in the book, load up the CD. You will see a screen like the one below. Choose the correct chapter and then click on the document name to open it up.

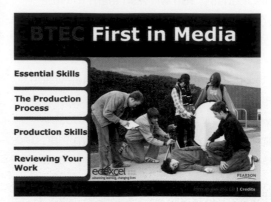

At the end of each chapter you will find a summary box like the one below. This will tell you which BTEC Unit the chapter covers, and all the Learning Outcomes you will achieve by completing it.

Summary

In this chapter you have covered everything you need to know to achieve the three Learning Outcomes relating to Unit 1 of your course. You should now:

- know how the media industry is structured

- understand job rules in a sector of the media industry

- understand how staff are recruited in a sector of the media industry.

Essential Skills

This first section will introduce you to the essential skills you need
to help you to understand the many sectors of the media industries.
You will also learn about what research is, and how to carry it out in
order to make media products. No media product is any good without
an audience, so you will learn about media audiences and how producers
try to make the right products for the wide variety of individuals that
make up media audiences.

1 Introducing the Media Industy

What makes up the media industry?

The media industry covers a wide spectrum of companies that produce media products. These could be radio or television programmes, newspapers or magazines, films, interactive CD-ROMs, pod casts or websites, or even the latest computer game.

Think about the media products that you see and hear every day. All of them have been produced by a media company, and have been commissioned by a client. Look around as you walk through your town or city. You will see billboards, advertisements on the sides of buses, posters and magazines displayed outside newsagents – all of these began as an idea developed by a creative team and then produced by a media company.

The main media industry sectors

The main industry sectors can be categorised as:

- Television
- Radio
- Press
- Music
- Film
- Interactive media
- Photo imaging
- Advertising and marketing

This spider diagram shows how the media products that you see every day fit into these sectors.

Try this ...

On the Media Industry worksheet on the CD-Rom, add the names of some of the products you have seen or heard next to the industry sectors.

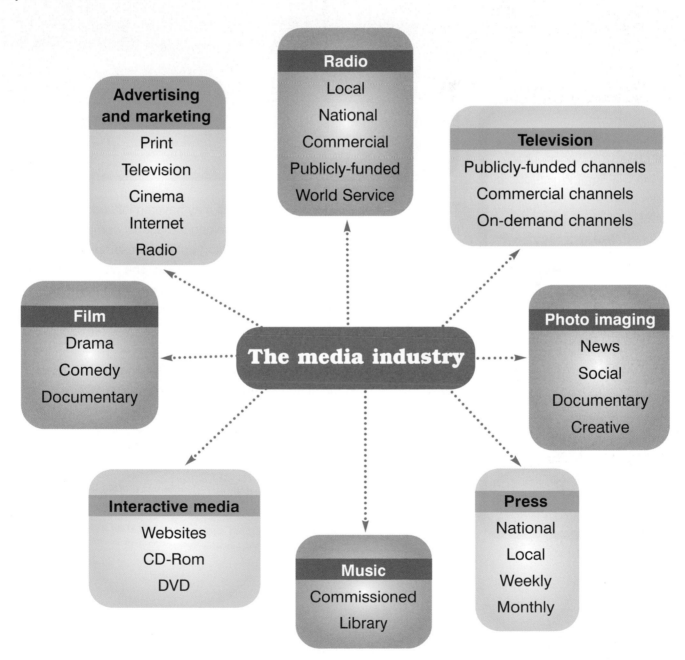

Radio
Local
National
Commercial
Publicly-funded
World Service

Advertising and marketing
Print
Television
Cinema
Internet
Radio

Television
Publicly-funded channels
Commercial channels
On-demand channels

Film
Drama
Comedy
Documentary

The media industry

Photo imaging
News
Social
Documentary
Creative

Interactive media
Websites
CD-Rom
DVD

Music
Commissioned
Library

Press
National
Local
Weekly
Monthly

Size and shape of the media industry

The media industry is not just relevant in one country or one continent but across the whole world. Many media companies operating in the UK are owned by parent companies in other countries. Some media companies that are based in one country own and control media companies in other countries.

Think about the media industry in your local area. What types of media companies can you find? Here are some examples of media companies in Leeds.

Media industry sector	Name of company
Television	Yorkshire Television
Radio	BBC Radio Leeds
Press	Yorkshire Post
Music	Sam Paechter Music
Photo imaging	Andy Smith Photography
Advertising	Gordon Kay Advertising and Design

These media companies based in Leeds may have an influence on other parts of the country, as some of them belong to national companies. Other companies on the list are local. The photographer, for example, is based there and undertakes the majority of his work there. The newspaper is written in Leeds and is distributed across a wide area of the north of England. The radio station is part of a larger organisation that has radio stations both across the country and worldwide.

One of the largest **multinational** media companies is Viacom. They are based in New York and state the following on their website:

> Fuelled by our world-class brands, including BET, Famous Music, MTV Networks – MTV, VH1, Nickelodeon, Nick at Nite, Comedy Central, CMT: Country Music Television, Spike TV, TV Land and more than 120 networks around the world – Paramount Pictures and Paramount Home Entertainment, we are among the world's leading creators of programming and content across all media platforms.

Source www.viacom.com

Look at ...

Have a look at Viacom's brands on the Viacom chart on the CD-Rom. Which of these brands do you know about, and which have you watched, heard or read?

Try this ...

Produce a short illustrated report on the range of products that Viacom produce. Identify what each product is, and if it is available in the UK.

PMH Productions is a media production company based in North Yorkshire. They are an example of a small, **independent** media company. The majority of the media products they produce are made for clients across the UK. They use their website to show clients what they can do.

The Craven Herald and Pioneer is a small, local newspaper based in Skipton in North Yorkshire. The news they report is about the local area, and the newspaper contains advertisements for local companies. It is, however, part of a larger organisation called Newsquest who publish a range of local newspapers across the country. The Craven Herald and Pioneer is small, but it is part of a large media company.

Look at ...

Find the résumé of PMH Productions on the CD-Rom. You will see their mission statement and information about their client base.

Try this ...

Find out about your local media companies in each media sector. What do they produce, who owns them and are they part of a larger media company? Make a list, showing your findings.

| Portfolio | Sales | Factfile | Jobs | History | Roll of Honour | Gannett Foundation | People |

View the latest vacancies across the group...

Newsquest is a subsidiary of Gannett Co., Inc. We serve our customers through:

- our 18 daily titles and almost 300 weekly newspapers
- a weekly readership of more than 13 million
- a weekly circulation of more than 10 million copies
- a digital network which attracts more than 3.5 million unique users
- Nearly 9,500 employees
- 11 newspaper printing sites plus Southernprint
- a network of more than 180 local newspaper and portal websites
- magazine publishing
- heatset magazine printing
- direct marketing and door-to-door delivery

View the latest Gannett share price

Find out about Newsquest's American parent company

Contacts | Diversity statement | Mission statement | Links

Copyright Newsquest Media Group 2006

Structure and ownership of media companies

Media companies can be classified as:

- private companies: in the UK, this is usually a company that is owned by an individual or a group. They need to make available only limited information about their operations to competitors.

- public companies: in the UK, this is usually a company that has shares traded on the stock exchange. They report on their business operations to their shareholders and to Companies House.

- publicly owned companies: these are companies owned by national, regional or local government.

- cross-media companies: these are companies, such as Viacom, that own media operations as well as other diverse companies. You can see in the Viacom chart on the CD-Rom that Viacom have interests in film, music libraries and music programming. They also run cable channels for children's programming. Until recently they owned the Blockbuster chain of video hire shops. They were able to release their films, produced by Paramount Pictures, through this outlet and so saved money on distribution costs.

How could the **ownership** of media products influence how you think about media issues? How might you be influenced to buy a product – or think about the news – if all the information came from just one source? For example, a newspaper is owned by the same person who owns a satellite television company. This person also owns a commercial radio station and has linked these to websites giving 24 hour coverage of news across the world. How much influence do you think this person has if they decide to favour one political party? How much influence do you think they would have on the sales of one brand of a particular product?

Vertical integration is the term applied to companies with a common owner that are linked along the production–distribution chain. The companies can co-operate to produce the materials needed for production, undertake the production process and distribute the end product. This provides a reliable workflow, with increased profits for the company. An example of this is Apple, who design their computer hardware, operating systems and much of the software used in their products. They have recently opened Apple stores for retail sales and Apple iTunes.

Horizontal integration is the term used when media companies own several producers of products in one sector. An example of this is EMI, who are the world's largest independent music company. They own several separate record producers and music publishing companies.

Companies House is an organisation that registers new companies, keeps records of exisiting companies and makes this information available to the public.

 Look at ...

News Corporation is another example of a cross-media company. Look at the examples of their brands on the CD-Rom and identify which products they make.

 Try this ...

Use the Media Industry worksheet on the CD-Rom again to demonstrate that you understand what the sectors are, and what products are produced in each sector. You should provide examples of companies that work in each of the sectors.

BTEC First in Media: A Practical Handbook

Job roles in the media industry

Job roles in the media industry range from technical and creative to administrative and financial. Each job role plays an important part in the production of a successful media product – and ultimately in keeping the media company in business. Media products are generally made by teams of people, and every team member has a role to play.

To understand the variety of roles better, first decide on a sector to investigate. You may have a particular interest in one of the sectors – perhaps you are planning a career in it. You may have already done some in-depth research. Think about the job roles in your chosen sector, such as:

- technical, e.g. camera or sound operator, lighting technician
- creative, e.g. director, lighting cameraperson, journalist
- editorial, e.g. editor, sub-editor, sound or vision editor
- managerial, e.g. producer, location manager
- sales and marketing, e.g. sales manager, telesales
- administration, e.g. production assistant, secretary
- financial, e.g. accountant, payroll clerk.

Try this ...

Watch a DVD or video and make a note of all the job roles that appear in the credits. Try to identify what each of these job roles involves. Some of the job roles are unusual – 'Best Boy', for example. Find out what a 'Best Boy' does.

Professional working practices

People working in the media industry have to work to **professional** standards. These are referred to as **codes of practice**, and though they are not generally compulsory, everyone should follow them.

Here is an example from the press sector's code of practice:

> *The National Union of Journalists' Code of Conduct states that 'a journalist has a duty to maintain the highest professional and ethical standards'. Media organisations subscribing to the UK Press Complaints Commission Code of Practice agree that: 'All members of the press have a duty to maintain the highest professional standards'.*

Source: www.nuj.org.uk

The BBC's editorial guidelines are outlined as:

> *the standards the BBC expects of all BBC content on TV, radio and online. They are designed for everyone who makes content for the BBC, to help them deal with difficult editorial decisions.*

Source: www.bbc.co.uk/guidelines/editorialguidelines/

The advertising code of practice states:

> *The Advertising Standards Authority is the independent body set up by the advertising industry to police the rules laid down in the advertising codes. The strength of the self-regulatory system lies in both the independence of the ASA and the support and commitment of the advertising industry, through the Committee of Advertising Practice (CAP), to the standards of the codes, protecting consumers and creating a level playing field for advertisers.*

Source: www.asa.org.uk

These codes of practice help media practitioners to keep within guidelines of taste, decency and truthfulness.

There are legal restrictions that workers in the media must observe. You cannot simply say what you like, go where you like or record what you like. You must carefully consider the legal issues, such as:

- Libel law: libel is the defamation (damaging) of someone's character, using written words.
- Slander law: slander is the defamation of someone's character, using spoken words.

You will find more information on legal and ethical issues in media in the Appendix.

Race Discrimination Act – these statements are from the Commission for Racial Equality:

> *Racist incidents, ranging from criminal harassment and abuse to physical violence, are offences under the criminal law.*
>
> *Publishing and disseminating materials, such as leaflets and newspapers, that are likely to incite racial hatred is also a criminal offence.*
>
> *Racially offensive material in the media contravenes media codes of practice. Complaints can be made to the Press Complaints Commission or the Broadcasting Standards Authority. Complaints about racially offensive advertisements should be made to the Advertising Standards Authority.*

Source: www.cre.gov.uk

Other legal restrictions you will encounter are:

- Copyright: you must not use other people's work and claim it as your own. If you want to use someone else's work, you must ask for written permission. You always need to be aware of the issue of copyright, and how it impacts on the working life of a media professional.

- Censorship: you have to abide by decisions of government on what you can print or report about certain sensitive issues.

Try this ...

You have been asked by your manager to secretly record an interview and broadcast it on your radio programme. The interview is with the leader of a group of extremists. What legal issues should you consider?

Contracts, conditions and pay

There are a number of different types of contract offered to people working in the media industry:

- Full-time permanent: this type of contract provides work on a full-time basis, with benefits, which could include a pension scheme, sick pay, holiday entitlement or bonuses.

- Part-time permanent: this contract provides part-time working to an agreed work pattern, with benefits, which may be the same as those in a full-time permanent contract.

- Fixed-term: a worker is hired to work on a particular project that lasts for a limited time. For example, you might be hired as a lighting technician for a television drama being shot on location over three months.

- Stringer: this is where you are contracted on the basis of being available at short notice to cover emerging stories. This might be an article for a local newspaper, filming a local football match or recording an interview for radio.

- Freelance: this is one of the most common contracts in the media industry. A freelancer works on a project in a role, such as a journalist, for a contracted amount of time. Freelancers can be working on a number of projects at the same time for different clients.

The term 'stringer' originated in the newspaper industry, where journalists were employed to 'string words together'. They were paid according to the length of the articles they produced – as measured, some claim, by a piece of string.

Working on a permanent contract provides stability for media workers. A fixed-term contract allows them to experience working for different clients, with guaranteed work for a fixed term. The stringer is only given work when there is no one else available, so this is not regular employment. Many stringers do this role as well as other jobs, which might not be in the media. The freelance role is becoming the standard in the media industry. Freelancers have to find their own work, control their own budgets and pay their own tax and national insurance. There is generally no holiday entitlement or sick pay, so they only get paid when they are actually working. Freelancers can be out of work for long periods, so they must maintain a wide circle of contacts, to use when searching for work.

Work patterns in the media industry vary greatly. Sometimes you simply have to work until the job is done. Some administrative jobs follow office hours, but a production assistant will be working alongside a production crew, and will follow their work pattern. Location work, recording interviews, reporting ongoing news and preparing advertising material may require long, unsocial hours. However, the rewards of seeing your work in print, on the television or hearing your work on the radio are well worth the long hours.

A media worker may be on an **annual salary**, paid hourly as a stringer, or paid at the end of a freelance period.

Hospital radio is a radio station for a hospital, or group of hospitals, using a closed loop system. Generally, volunteers run the station, produce the radio shows, visit patients to generate requests and raise funds to buy new equipment. Many well-known radio presenters started their careers by volunteering in hospital radio.

Student newspapers are run by students in schools, colleges and universities. They write the copy, take photographs and edit the material of interest to other students. Again, many well-known journalists became interested in journalism by working on a student newspaper.

Getting a job in a media sector

Skills and qualifications

Many employers in the media industry look for people with **formal qualifications**. These are not always qualifications in a media subject, though they could be in a related subject, such as English Literature if they are looking for writers or journalists. Potential employees with experience of using media equipment as part of their course are more likely to be shortlisted for an interview. Experience of working in a **voluntary** capacity, such as for a hospital radio or student newspaper, could be seen by a potential employer as an example of good skills development and commitment.

Employers understand the value of part-time education, and you might be able to attend a local college to gain further qualifications once you are employed.

Some sections of the media industry operate a 'closed shop', so you will need particular qualifications to work in this area. One example is the newspaper industry, where you need a qualification from the National Council for the Training of Journalists to work as a journalist.

Employees in the media industry should also consider ongoing **professional development**. The nature of the industry means there are constant changes to standards, techniques and technology, so even once you have a job, training should not stop. The BBC offers ongoing training to its staff so that they can build new skills and develop into new roles. You may be able to develop some self-training, where you engage in an activity that you enjoy, which also gives you some new skills.

It is unlikely that anyone undertaking a Level 2 qualification (BTEC First Certificate or Diploma or GCSE) would be successful in their application for a senior production or managerial role in the media industry. It would be better to take on a lower level role and then build up their skills in order to progress. Undertaking a Level 3 qualification (National Diploma, BTEC Certificate or Award or A-Level) will provide a higher level of knowledge, understanding and skill, but still may not be appropriate for some media-related jobs.

There are a growing number of colleges and universities offering media qualifications that teach professional work-related media skills. Often, these can also provide learners with valuable work experience or work-related activities, such as being involved in student radio or newspapers.

If you want to work in the media industry you should consider making contact with potential employers to find out what they are looking for in media job applicants. Taking on voluntary media jobs wherever possible will build on and demonstrate your media skills. Don't be put off by initial rejections but use this as an opportunity to review changes you could make in your application letter or CV.

A **Curriculum Vitae** (CV) is a useful marketing tool. A CV can demonstrate your commitment to developing media skills by outlining all the projects you have undertaken. It also gives you an opportunity to sell yourself to a potential employer or client.

Imagine a CV as a brochure all about you and your skills. What can you do that would make you stand out from other candidates? What can you offer an employer? What are your strengths as a potential media employee?

The CV should demonstrate your team-working skills – through your work on a media project or as a member of an organisation, such as the Boys' Brigade or Guides. Employers do not know you or anything about you, so you must tell them what you are good at, and how you can benefit their company.

There are a number of **trade unions** that offer protection and advice to their members. It is no longer necessary to belong to a union to work in any of the media sectors, but it can be beneficial to have the strength of a union behind you when **negotiating** pay and conditions, or when you are in dispute with your employer.

On the CD-Rom you will find details of universities, colleges and private training organisations offering media qualifications and training courses.

Look at ...

You will find an example of a well laid-out CV on the CD-Rom.

Try this ...

Plan and produce a CV that demonstrates your strengths as a media worker.

On the CD-Rom you will find contact details and information about a range of organisations providing advice and support for people working in the media industry.

Transferable skills

People working in the media industry have a wide range of **transferable skills** – knowledge and technical skills, for example, or commitment (as discussed earlier) and efficiency. You will need knowledge and technical skills in media production if you want to make media products, and be committed to making these products in the most efficient and cost-effective way.

It is important to be reliable and punctual. Working in a media team requires you to be at the right place at the right time.

It is important as a potential media worker that you have **self-presentation** skills. You will have to pitch your ideas or discuss the finished product with a client, and you may have to give a presentation in order to win a contract. You will certainly have to 'sell' yourself at an interview. All of these require self-presentation skills. By undertaking this course you will be developing self-presentation skills that will be useful for the rest of your career.

Methods of recruitment

The media industry uses a number of techniques to recruit staff. One technique is to advertise media jobs in the **national press** – the Media section of the *Guardian*, for example, published every Monday. Every week this paper provides several pages of media jobs and includes them on its website.

There are a number of media **trade publications** that have sections for jobs. *Media Week* is a publication that specialises in keeping media professionals informed about events in the media. They have a section of jobs in their magazine and on their website.

Recruitment agencies tend to recruit for specialist areas – the television industry, for example. Inspired Selection is an agency that specialises in recruiting both creative and administrative staff for the publishing industry. The company has a website that includes job vacancies across its offices in London and Oxford.

Media professionals find the Internet is a useful tool for job hunting. It provides instant access to job details, pay and conditions, and job locations. You can quickly contact the recruitment company or the potential employer to ask for further details, using email rather than 'snail mail'.

Sometimes, simply doing a good job will be a recommendation, so that a company might approach a media professional directly. A media professional might also have built up a list of personal contacts that they can refer to when looking for work. These contacts, too, need evidence of projects the media professional has worked on and their standard of work.

Once you have a job in a media company there is always the possibility of internal promotion. The BBC has a policy of advertising internal job opportunities to staff before advertising them externally. You need to show the transferable skills discussed earlier if you are to achieve internal promotion.

Have a look at this example of a media job advertisement from the *Guardian* newspaper's Media pages.

Z FDC Z   Creative and Visual Media Technician

We are looking for a Creative and Visual Media Technician to operate our video facilities. You will join our expanding team of technicians based in Leeds.

The successful candidate will be familiar with any computer-related processes necessary, including: Avid Media Composer, Final Cut Pro editing systems and DVD Studio Pro. They will keep up-to-date with any advances in that area and will suggest appropriate acquisitions and use of other devices where necessary. They will also have experience of operating video in live performance.

The position is offered as a fixed term contract for nine months with a competitive salary. Send a CV and completed application form to helen.williams@fdc.co.uk by 11th May 2007.

For a job description and application form, please visit www.fdc.co.uk, email helen.williams@fdc.co.uk or phone 01242 726343.

Summary

In this chapter you have covered everything you need to know to achieve the three Learning Outcomes relating to Unit 1 of your course. You should now:

- know how the media industry is structured

- understand job roles in a sector of the media industry

- understand how staff are recruited in a sector of the media industry.

Try this ...

Find three examples of advertisements for media jobs, and identify:

- what qualifications you need for the job
- what the job involves
- the contract being offered
- the salary being offered.

Try this ...

Design an advertisement for a media job in your chosen sector. Make sure you include all the details of the job role, the type of contract being offered, expected hours of work, qualifications needed and the skills required.

2 Research for Media Production

What is media research?

This chapter explains how to decide what goes into a media product or artefact, whether it's a television programme, radio show, newspaper, magazine, advertisement, website, interactive CD or computer game. First you need to understand what is meant by 'research'. Research isn't something you can see or touch, it's a process that you go through. The result of research is a list of conclusions and recommendations that can form the basis of a media product. There are different ways of doing research and many things to discover from the results of research. Researching into media products will show you what products have already been made and how they have been made. This will give you a better understanding of what has already been done and may give you an idea of how to produce a new type of product.

Research methods and techniques

You first need to decide what type of research to do and how you are going to do it. There are two main **research methods**: primary and secondary. Searching for the information in appropriate records is **secondary research**, but doing a survey of your own in the street, asking people questions and writing down what they say is **primary research**. Each of these methods can be used to gather **quantitative** or **qualitative** data. The method that you use will depend on what you want to discover. **Quantitative data** is the facts and figures (the quantities) – how many people watched a particular edition of Big Brother, for example. If you wanted to know what people liked about the programme, this would be **qualitative data.**

Research techniques

You will usually start with secondary research, where you look at data that someone else has already gathered and recorded. The **techniques** that you use to find it will vary, depending on what you want to find out and what facilities you have. Secondary research data is often found in libraries and in printed material like books, newspapers, magazines, old census records, indexes of catalogues in archives, audience viewing and circulation figures, web hits and so on. These days one of the main sources of secondary data is the Internet, which you will be familiar with.

Primary research data is information you gather directly from the source, usually by talking to someone or observing a situation, action or event as it happens.

Techniques you would use to gather primary data include:

- carrying out surveys with **questionnaires**
- **observation** (watching what happens)
- interviewing people
- experimenting.

Try this ...

Secondary qualitative research: read two previews, or reviews, of the same **artefact** in different magazines, and make notes on what they have in common and what their differences are.

Try this ...

Primary quantitative research: ask all your classmates which are their five favourite media products, and keep a tally of their responses.

Try this ...

Ask your tutor or an older person you know about their experiences of being at school when they were your age. Record what they say by using a speech recorder or by writing notes. Compare what you have recorded with your own experience of being at school.

Try this ...

Create a table to track your research information trail, as in the example below.

Finding information

Where would you go to find research data on media products? There are libraries that contain periodicals, magazines, books, videos, and audio recordings. You can find information by reading, looking or listening, and then recording what you have experienced by making notes, or using speech (or even video) recorders. You can watch things happen in real time and you can talk to people about their opinions and experiences.

Information trails

While doing your research, you must make sure you can trace where you started from, through to where you finished. To do this, keep records of where the **data** (information) came from. This is the **information trail** and the recording of the information is called the **log**. The table below shows one way to create an information trail.

Source of information: secondary research data	Description of information
Advertising Standards Authority website: http://www.asa.org.uk/asa/codes/cap_code/ShowCode.htm?clause_id=1578	**Advertising and children** 29.1 Special care should be taken when promotions are addressed to children (people under 16) or when products intended for adults may fall into the hands of children. 29.2 Alcoholic drinks should not feature in promotions directed at people under 18.
Press Complaints commission website: http://www.pcc.org.uk/cases/adjudicated.html?article=NDMzMA	**Bindman & Partners** complained to the Press Complaints Commission on behalf of a fourteen-year-old boy that an article published in the *Sunday Times* on 24 September 2006 headlined 'The ultimate sacrifice' was intrusive in breach of Clauses 3 (Privacy), 5 (Intrusion into grief or shock) and 6 (Children) of the Code.
Press report, 22 Feb 2007 page 5	**Advertising restrictions on junk food** New restrictions on the advertising of unhealthy food and drinks are due to be announced. OFCOM curbs will affect TV commercials for products high in fat, salt and sugar (HFSS). The communications regulator will limit the timing and content of the commercials.

Identifying and gathering research material

When doing research, it is important to first **identify** what information (data) you want. It should then be **gathered** in an appropriate form.

Identifying research material

You must first know what purpose your product is going to serve for its audience. Is it going to be educational, entertaining or informative, or is it going to be a combination of two or all of these? Research data must be relevant to what you are doing and it must contribute some information about either your product or its audience. Here are some types of sources for research.

Secondary – other people's work	Primary – your own work
Reports from professional bodies	Interviews
Newspaper stories	Surveys using questionnaires
Magazine articles	Focus groups
Photographs from clip libraries	
Diagrams of other people's results	
Opinion polls	

You need to be sure that the source of the information is **reliable** and **current** (up-to-date). The information then needs **validating** (checking to make sure it's correct) and **analysing** (examining) to decide what it means and how it's going to affect the product. Having decided what it means, you then have to decide whether it's **relevant** to the message that you are trying to put across in your proposed product. You must reach conclusions about the data and whether or not you are going to use, or recommend its use, in the media product.

To ensure that research data is valid, reliable and current you must be aware of where it was found – its source. Some sources are more reliable than others.

Reliable sources of research
- BBC website: content is valid because the source has a good reputation.
- Newspapers: generally 'serious' papers (which used to be called broadsheets) are more reliable than 'popular' papers (which used to be called 'tabloids').
- Regulating bodies: content must be correct because the body makes the rules.
- Government departments: valid because they represent legislation.
- Government bodies: they make policies.
- Trade magazines: generally valid if independent opinion is stated.
- News bulletins: generally reliable as they state the facts but don't discuss them.

Unreliable sources of research
- Wikipedia: able to be updated by anyone, whether qualified or not.
- TV programmes: cannot be considered reliable because the producers have an interest in selling the programme.
- Advertisements in media products: they may not state the whole truth (although the ASA monitors them).

Gathering research material

Research material can be gathered in a number of ways. Gathering secondary data, whether it is quantitative or qualitative, is relatively easy once you have found the source. Probably the easiest – and sometimes the least reliable – source, is the Internet. You need to know which websites can be trusted and which cannot (see the list above). It is recommended that you gather research material from other sources as well as the Internet.

Gathering includes making a note of each source and taking notes from each source. It is sometimes quicker to simply photocopy pages from books, magazines or reports and to download pages from the websites you have found, but you must then read and make notes about your findings from such material. In some instances, a screen dump with your notes written on it could be the best way to store material found on websites. For television programmes, still images in the form of storyboards with written notes about them are useful.

Try this ...

Make a list of six secondary sources of information, other than the Internet, that might be used to gather research for a product of your choice. Explain why you think the sources you have chosen can be trusted.

Primary research gathering usually involves preparing a questionnaire and asking people to complete it. Questionnaires can use different types of question:

- For **closed questions**, the answer will be 'Yes' or 'No', or a choice from a given list, such as 'always', 'usually', 'sometimes', 'never'. The results from closed questions are quantative data and therefore easy to analyse.

- For **open questions**, the answer could be almost anything, e.g. 'What is your favourite TV programme?' The results from open questions are more varied, qualitative data, and therefore more difficult to analyse.

You could gather primary research data simply by observation – watching what happens in a given situation. You could show a product to a sample audience, for example, and watch and note their reactions.

Collating and storing research material

The secret of research is organisation – the way that you organise and store your research material is important. You must be able to find the information you want and cross-reference it back to its source, and to compare different research findings from different sources.

Collating research material

There are a number of ways of recording information, e.g. writing it down in a list, recording it on to a voice recorder, or using graphs and charts. The information then needs to be **collated** (put in order) in a way that makes it easy to use.

Storing research material

One of the most common ways of storing data is in a database. One of the most common database programmes is Microsoft Access, but there are others. To work properly, a storage system or database must be organised according to what you want to find and how quickly you want to find it. There may be a number of ways that you want to search your data to find relevant information about different aspects of the topic. For a media product, there will be contributors who have given information, so a list of names, phone numbers and addresses is useful. Each contributor may have given opinions on a different aspect of the topic, so a list of views is needed. You will have searched a number of data sources, to find the information, so a list of sources with the titles of the documents they contained and the information you found out, would be necessary. The record card on the next page is one example.

Try this ...

Decide which type of question (open or closed) would be most appropriate for:

- asking people what type of media product they prefer

- finding out what they like about the media product.

Try this ...

Think about the type of information you will be gathering. Make a list of ways that you could collate it.

Contributor name	Contact details
Initial contact method	Telephone
Lead source	Tutor
Topic discussed	Violence on television, believes it leads to copycat crime
Sequence of events or experience	Attacked by youth wearing a hoodie
TV Examples	Any violent films
Method of data collection	Interview discussion
Action	Arrange second meeting

Presenting your findings

Part of the process of getting a commission for a media product involves making a presentation and **pitching** your ideas. This starts with the research findings that you have gathered to support your ideas for your product. There are a number of **formats** that you can use to present your findings, including a written report, oral presentation, PowerPoint presentation or video. You might present your findings by yourself, or as a member of a group.

Planning your presentation

Whichever way you choose to present your findings, it must be planned. To do this you should know the purpose of the presentation, the procedures you are going to use, and the **content** (the data and your material). You will also need to decide whether to use graphics, such as charts and tables, photographs and storyboards. You will have to show how you analysed your findings, what the results were, and the conclusions that you came to. You will also need to provide a **bibliography** (summary of your sources).

When planning your presentation, put your ideas into a logical order, with a title and a short summary of what you are going to say. For example:

Order of presentation
- Title
- What you will do
- Step 1 (introduction)
- Step 2
- Step 3
- Step 4
- Summary
- Bibliography

You must also think about:

• the way in which you make your presentation
• your **expression**
• the structure, clarity and **language register**
• whether you have taken account of the audience.

Presentation content

The purpose of your presentation is to persuade your tutor (or client) to agree to the product that you want to make. Their decision will depend on how closely you can make the content of your product match their original brief and the target audience that you were given. The parts of your presentation must be in the correct order and the ideas that you have must be able to be understood by your tutor. You must provide supporting **evidence** of your statements and not simply say that this is what you want to do because you want to do it. The way in which you communicate your content must be clear, and the key is to know what you want to say and to use your research findings to support your views.

Look at ...

On the CD-Rom you will find a presentation to try and convince a producer that there is a market for a TV programme.

Summary

In this chapter you have covered everything you need to know to achieve the four Learning Outcomes relating to Unit 2 of your course. You should now:

   know about research methods and techniques

   be able to identify and gather research material

   be able to collate and store research material

   be able to present the results of your research.

3 Media Audiences and Products

What is an audience?

In order to be successful, all media products (artefacts) need an audience. You could make what you think is the best TV programme, film, radio show, magazine or computer game, but if you are the only person who likes it, you will never make any money from selling it. An audience is the media version of a consumer – someone who consumes (uses) media products, which can include reading, looking at, listening to, watching or interacting with a media product.

People like different things, and part of the skill of making products is to be aware of the differences in the needs of separate audiences. Media companies are commissioned to make products that appeal to a specific type of audience, and if you become a media producer, this is what you will be doing too. It's not possible to just make products that appeal to you. One of the most important issues to understand is the type of audience that you are producing for, which won't be under your control.

How the media matches products to audiences

Classifying audiences

The various sectors of the media use a range of methods to discover what their **audiences** want. All media sectors divide their audiences into categories, according to:

* age
* gender: male or female
* sexual preference: heterosexual or homosexual
* ethnicity: which country they come from
* postcode or geodemographics: where they live
* disposable income: how much money they have to spend after their main bills have been paid
* Standard Occupational Classification (SOC): what their job is.

Some sectors use different terms from others but the object is the same – to find out how many of a particular type of person there is in an audience or consumer group, so that they can make a product that a large enough group will want to consume. The chart below shows how audiences are organised into groups by age.

Group	Age in years
1	0–10
2	11–15
3	16–18
4	19–25
5	26–40
6	41–55
7	56–70

Classification by occupation

The six socio-economic classes, according to the system drawn up by the UK Registrar General for the 1911 Census, are:

A	Upper middle class
B	Middle class
C1	Lower middle class
C2	Skilled working class
D	Semi-skilled and unskilled working class
E	Residual and those at lowest levels of subsistence

The socio-economic classifications have mostly been replaced by new classes according to the system drawn up for the 2001 Census, by the Office for National Statistics and the Economic and Social Research Council.

These Standard Occupational Classifications are:

1	Managers and senior officials
2	Professional occupations
3	Associate professional and technical occupations
4	Administrative and secretarial occupations
5	Skilled trades occupations
6	Personal service occupations
7	Sales and customer service occupations
8	Process, plant and machine operatives
9	Elementary occupations

Even when a media product is targeted at a particular audience group or segment, there will be an overlap and some consumers from outside the target audience group will consume the product. For example, a TV programme aimed at children aged 3 to 6, which is on in the afternoon, may also be watched by a child's mother. In another example, if you are listening to your favourite music track in your bedroom and it's turned up loud, your parents, brothers or sisters may well hear it.

Further examples of products being consumed by people other than their target audiences are the magazines in doctor's surgeries or the discarded newspapers picked up on public transport. In each case the product may not have been targeted at these other consumers – they were simply exposed to it as well. In this way, a product can sometimes break into a new market.

Try this ...

Make a list of three examples each of TV programmes, radio shows, magazines, websites, CD-Roms, music CDs or computer games that appeal to you most. Talk to other members of your class to see if they agree with you. See if there is one media product that has a large number of consumers in your class.

Researching audiences

Having seen that there are lots of diverse audience groups, you might wonder how we find out about the way audiences change over time. There are many audience and consumer research organisations that specialise in finding out about how these groups are changing. This process goes on for everything that we buy or consume, not just media products. The loyalty store card that is swiped each time you go to the supermarket gives information to consumer profile groups, helping them to decide which goods appeal to which sorts of people.

For media products, the Broadcasters' Audience Research Board, **(BARB)** monitors television viewing, Radio Audience Joint Research Limited **(RAJAR)** monitors radio, Verified Free Distribution **(VFD)** monitors free newspaper distribution, and so on (see the Appendix for a full list). These companies classify groups of people into categories to get an idea of how audience groups might consume different media products.

These research companies don't ask everyone in the country, because that would be too difficult and time-consuming. The methods used to get information include asking a representative sample of people to use set-top boxes that list and remember all the TV programmes and channels they watch and all the radio programmes they listen to. These are called focus groups. For other media products, like websites, users may be asked to complete a questionnaire. You may have seen people with clipboards in the street stopping shoppers and asking questions by interviewing them.

The results of all these types of activity are then sorted and analysed to try to discover what media consumption habits people have. Media producers can then make sure that the right content goes into the product in the right way to make it appeal to any particular audience.

Try this ...

On the CD-Rom you will find a research questionnaire. Complete it on your own to find out your media profile, then compare it with the profiles of other members of your class.

Fill all the scores in on the tally sheet and see how many of your classmates share the same consumer profile.

Appealing to the audience

Categorising products

To talk about media products correctly, you need to use the correct terminology. Cars, for instance, can be grouped according to certain characteristics, e.g. hatchback, sports car, saloon, four-wheel drive, etc. In media, products are categorised by **genre** (type). In film, for example, you will find various genres: fantasy, sci-fi (science fiction), horror, etc, which describe the main subject matter being dealt with. In television the genres vary slightly, such as soap opera, sitcom (situation comedy), documentary and reality, which tend to describe the **style** of the programme. In print matter, newspapers, for example, are classified according to their content: 'popular' for lower socio-economic groups and 'serious' for higher socio-economic groups. They are also classified according to their areas of circulation – national, regional or local. Magazines are usually classified by content (which links to the lifestyle of the reader), by age (as with children's comics) and by gender (girls', women's, boys' or men's magazines). Radio programmes are classified in a similar way to TV, with drama, music, documentary, panel game, etc. The chart below shows genres by sector.

Try this ...

Choose ten media products from a variety of genres, some that appeal to you and some that don't. They could be TV programmes, radio shows, magazines, websites, computer games or CD-Roms. Classify them by genre, listing what it is that makes them different. Decide what it is about a particular genre that appeals to you, or what it is that doesn't appeal to you.

Sector	Genres
Film	Comedy, sci-fi, horror, fantasy, detective, romance
Television	Soap opera, sitcom, documentary, news, current affairs, drama, game show, consumer, magazine, music video, natural history
Radio	Soap opera, sitcom, documentary, news, current affairs, drama, game show, consumer, magazine, music
Print	Popular, serious, financial, specialist, magazines, comics
Advertising	Humorous, direct, series, soap opera, serious, fiction, pastiche
Website	Reference, sales, news, fan culture, music, personal
Interactive CD	Product catalogues, databases, directories, educational
Computer games	Driving, strategy, fighting, adventure, puzzle

Elements of media products

Now you have seen some of the genres into which media products are classified, but what makes one product different from another, apart from the content?

Think about films. **Westerns**, for example, often have cowboys and Indians in them, **sci-fi** can be about space ships, aliens and other planets, **horror** might be about frightening people with the supernatural or scaring people with murderers. In sci-fi, electronic music will be played, and there will be things that are not real. In horror the frightening scenes will take place in near-darkness, with scary noises and music playing, and sudden images of frightening monsters or surprise attacks by people with weapons. The particular mood has to be set up for the situation to create the desired effect on the audience.

The way that scenes or **elements** are put together, or the **construction** of elements, is done in such a way that it has a particular effect on the audience. What makes a particular genre of product work, and appeal to a particular audience, is the order and **selection** of the elements, together with the way in which the objects on the screen are arranged, known as the **composition**, and the way in which the images appear. The composition of the scene, using the elements such as background, costumes, props and actors, is known as the **mise-en-scène**.

> Different types of media products contain certain things that cause us to recognise what genre the product belongs to. For example in a western, we see the Colt 45 gun, but a gun also represents the idea of lawlessness. The gun is therefore an **icon** of crime and killing. The use of objects to suggest something more than their immediate meaning is called **iconography**.

Listed below are the features of two main types of newspaper. It is an example of how elements of construction work to help us recognise two different products in the same sector.

Popular	Serious
Red banner title	Plain headline
Short sentences	Complex language
Large fonts	Small fonts
Big headlines	Lots of text on front page
Photos covering most of front page	More serious news stories
Sport on back page	Fewer pictures
Sensation-seeking stories about trivia	Impartial reporting
	Wider range of stories
	Financial news

The following chart lists the elements of construction by media sector. For each genre of product, in each media sector, the elements of construction will vary.

Sector	Element	Description
Television	Photography	Dark, light, studio, location
	Sound	Speech, dialogue, music, sound
	Lighting	Direction, intensity, source
	Framing	Position of subject, composition
	Camera angles	Low-level, high-level, eye-level, slanted
	Shots	Establishing, close-up, medium, long
	Colour	Warm, cold, sepia, black & white
Radio	Dialogue	Interview, phone-in, drama, panel game
	Music	Lyrics, instrumental, background, mood
	Sounds	Ambient background, atmosphere, effects
	Voice	News, results, DJ, actor, entertainer
	Texts and scripts	Plays, documentaries, features, sequences
	Jingles and idents	Fillers, trails, station, presenter, programme
Print	Style	Large or small format, magazine, newspaper comic
	Composition	Number of pages, position of pictures
	Layout	Number and arrangement of columns
	Words, numbers	Font, type, size, colour
	Heading, masthead	Red banners, paragraph headings
	Use of colour	Monochrome, colour
	Anchorage	Photograph–text relationship
	Visual images	Cartoons, illustrations, line drawings, adverts, banners, photos, maps, diagrams
Interactive CDs and websites	Style	Menu, pages, banners, links
	Text	Size, font, readability
	Images	Moving image, still image, image size, colour, black & white
	Sound	Music, speech, voice-over, commentary
	Graphics	Cartoon style, realistic style
	Interactivity	Menu bars, rollovers, hyperlinks
Computer games	Narrative	Action game, role play game, instructional game
	Text	Size, font, readability, instructions
	Images	Moving image, still image, image size, colour, black & white
	Sound	Music, speech, voice-over, commentary
	Graphics	Realistic, non-realist
	Interactivity	Single console, multi-console, Internet-linked, single player, multi-player

Try this ...

Choose three media products from separate genres – one that appeals to you, one that doesn't and one that you feel indifferent to. Make a list of all the elements of construction in each product. Explain what it is about the combination of elements in each product that appeals to you or what it is that doesn't.

Modes of address

The ways we communicate with each other – whether by speech or body language, according to the situation we are in – affect how we are understood. We can talk back to other people, and check that we understand what is being said, but mass media products don't allow us to talk back to them, so the producer has to have an idea or perception about how the audience will understand or interpret the product. The producer will therefore tell the story or narrative in a particular way. This is called the **mode of address**. It is one of the ways used to appeal to, or target, a specific audience.

The four main modes of address are:

- **Voyeur** or **Observer**: most media products place you as the watcher and simply ask you to watch, listen to or read what is happening.
- **Empathiser**: this puts you in the shoes of the main character, so that you experience the feelings that they are having, and associate with them.
- **Direct addressee**: the producer communicates directly with you, by asking your opinion, to vote for a contestant, answer a question or respond in some way to what has happened.
- **Inclusive addressee**: the producer uses unconventional approaches in order to emphasise that their media product is artificial or unreal, and to go against the normal way that media products do things.

The mode of address makes use of media **codes** and **conventions** to address the audience – in a formal manner, in the case of serious news and current affairs content, or in an informal way for light-hearted and comedy material. Media products that are targeted at families can be said to use a 'domestic' mode of address. Advertisements often use a direct mode of address, and magazines that target male or female readers use a mode of address that attracts their specific readers.

Look at ...

On the CD-Rom there are contrasting examples of products from each of the following media sectors: television, radio, newspapers, magazines, websites and CD-Roms. Each example within a sector is targeted at a widely different audience. Work out what the target audiences are, and give your reasons.

Try this ...

Pick two media products, one that appeals to you and one that might appeal to an older person like your parent, aunt or uncle. Make a list of the modes of address that each uses, and decide which modes of address appeal to you and which appeal to the other person you chose. List the modes of address for the content, language, genre and imagery (visual, aural) of each product.

Television uses various conventions to support specific modes – the way the shots are composed and framed, the type of shot or the speed and sequence of editing. For radio, a particular convention might be to use music under the dialogue, with the choice of music being significant, according to the audience being targeted. For a newspaper, the **font** (text size and design), the complexity of the language used and the intellectual level of the content would identify its target audience. These conventions are found in every type of media artefact, in each of the sectors.

Constraints on media content

When you make a media product you must give a lot of thought to the content and the way in which it is presented to the audience. You can't simply include anything you want. There are **codes of practice** and regulations on the content that media producers in all sectors have to know about and follow. In Chapter 1, Introducing the Media Industry, you learnt about the problems involved when using content made and owned by others. This could include music, quotations, photographs, video footage, registered trade marks, logos and icons.

> Codes of practice are produced by **regulatory bodies** and media organisations, also discussed in Chapter 1. There is a whole range of legal restrictions and laws, which can vary according to which country you are working in. For example, you must be careful not to say things that are untrue (about either people or events) and you must not misrepresent opinions, or disclose confidential information about people. The most important points of this **legislation** (laws) can be found in the Appendix.

How audiences make sense of products

Decoding

Think back to the previous section, about how media products are categorised, how the elements of construction make products appeal to different audiences, and how different modes of address keep audiences interested or engaged with media products. This process may seem a little one-sided, as if the responsibility lies with the producer to engage the audience, but the audience is not just a passive object, without any feelings or responses. Audiences have varying levels of intelligence and understanding, and the audience's level of understanding of a media product depends on how intelligent they are and how they relate to what the product is trying to tell them – the **message**.

As we have seen, the devices used to put the message across are called codes and conventions. The way in which the audience understands or interprets the message is called **decoding**.

Try this ...

In the Appendix, find the body that regulates the media sector that you are studying and go to its website. From the codes of practice, make a list of things you will have to consider when making your media products.

Try this ...

Visit the PRS/MCPS Alliance copyright website. Find the cost of music for the product you are making.

What's the difference between a code and a convention?
- A code is a description of a technique which is used in a media product to communicate its meaning, e.g. starting a scene in a film with a wide shot to establish location.
- A convention is an established practice that has become so familiar that it appears natural, e.g. a TV newsreader sitting at a desk in a suit, speaking to a camera.

There are a number of types of codes, depending on the media sector, and depending on the way in which the message is to be put across to the audience. The first are codes, that we are all familiar with, **linguistic** (language) **codes**. Think of English as a method of communication that is understood by people who speak English, and it is easy to see that to someone who doesn't speak English, we are speaking in some sort of code, where sounds represent words, which themselves represent meanings. Written language is also a system of **symbols** that is coded so that only those who understand the symbols know what is being communicated.

Language is one of the **primary codes** and is used in nearly all media products. It doesn't end there, though, because the same English words may be understood differently, depending on the way they are written or spoken. This is why the language used in legal documents (or the terms and conditions for things like credit cards) is so complex and difficult to understand. The writers are trying to take into account every possible misinterpretation of a word.

When you read something, your interpretation will depend on how you visualise the content, because there are no pictures. Most media products, however, include **visual codes** which help to communicate their message more easily. TV and film rely heavily on their visual codes. If you listen to just the sound on a TV programme, for instance, you won't understand the full meaning of what is happening. It is also easier to understand someone when they are speaking to you directly in a one-to-one situation, if they use facial expressions and **body language**, for example waving their hands about.

When we look at comics, read newspapers and magazines, play computer games, listen to radio shows and music, or watch TV programmes and films, we can usually tell very quickly whether we are going to like them or not. What is it about a media product that provides these signs? Media producers invest a great deal of time and effort in ensuring that each distinct type of audience is targeted correctly, making sure that the way in which the various images are packaged appeals to different groups of consumers. Whether it's the language used in the product (written or spoken), the images displayed (moving or still), the sound images, or the order in which the **narrative** (storyline) is constructed, the way in which the product is packaged makes it appeal to its specific audience.

Here are just some of the codes and conventions used in various sectors:

Technical codes and conventions	Description
Code: piece to camera in news and live broadcasting	Hand-held microphone, reporter talking direct to camera
Convention: following the ball or field of play	Use of zoom lens to cover football and other field sports
Code: use of lens filters	Sepia is used to represent 'old film' footage
Convention: use of camera-mounted lights	Electronic News Gathering (ENG) technique to illuminate contributors on location interviews
Convention: paper	Different types of paper are used for a range of publications
Code: glossy paper	Used for magazines, not newspapers
Convention: software icons	Computer software uses icons to represent its functions
Convention: music	Signature tunes for TV and radio programmes
Code: music	Orchestral strings music is used for romance
Convention: lighting	Steep angles for key lights in studio, magazines and news
Code: lighting	Shallow-angled shadowy lighting for film noir, indicating a hidden aspect
Code: camera	Hand-held camera indicates danger
Convention: camera work	Hand-held camera in war zone, location news and 'docusoap' filming
Convention: acting	Actors don't acknowledge the camera or the audience

Try this ...

Select two media products from the same sector, e.g. two TV programmes, radio shows, magazines or newspapers, which target two different audiences. List ways in which the relevant codes from the checklist above are used to help their audiences understand the product. Add as many other relevant codes and conventions as you can think of.

Summary

In this chapter you have covered everything you need to know to achieve the three Learning Outcomes relating to Unit 3 of your course. You should now:

- understand how industries identify audiences for media products.

- understand how media products are created for audiences. .

- be able to show how audiences make sense of media products

The Production Process

When completing the units that form your diploma or certificate course you will be required to make or contribute to the making of media products. When a media product is produced, just as in any other industry, a procedure must be followed. You can't simply take a video camera or audio recorder out into a location and shoot whatever you want in the hope that the result will come together as a product. The first chapter in this section looks at the procedure for making media products, so this is essential reading. The next two chapters cover the units on factual programme making and media projects. Neither of these units is compulsory so you may be studying both, either one, or none. The content of Chapters 5 and 6, however, will inform your knowledge of the production process and provide you with a method of working that will help to keep your project on time, if you follow it. This will give you a clear idea of how the media industry creates products.

4 The Production Process

Introducing the production process

The production of any media artefact must be planned – whether you are making a television programme, promotional or training video, radio programme, film, magazine, newspaper, website or computer game. The process is generally the same whatever the product. First the idea for the product is developed and its viability considered. The commissioning editor (or commissioner – the person who would pay you to make the product) has to be convinced that it's a good product idea and that you have the resources and skills to make it. Having secured the commission, you then have to plan the production in great detail, to make sure you complete every stage at the right time in the schedule and deliver the completed artefact to the client on time and within budget.

Securing a commission

If the demand to make a media product comes from a media sector company, a **commissioner** will 'call for expressions of interest' by sending a **brief** to a number of different production companies. If a non-media sector company wants a media product made – a training video, for example – they become the client and will contact an independent production company and discuss their needs. Alternatively, a company could invite anyone to apply for the commission, rather than selecting a group of particular companies.

The four stages of the production process

In most industries (the car industry, for example) a product is made according to a **production process**. The media industry is no exception, so to produce media **artefacts** you must follow a logical production process. Making a product is a **linear time-based** process, which means that the various stages take place one after another, in succession.

There may be slight variations in this process according to the sector, the type of product being made and the in-house procedures of each media company, but the general media production process has four stages:

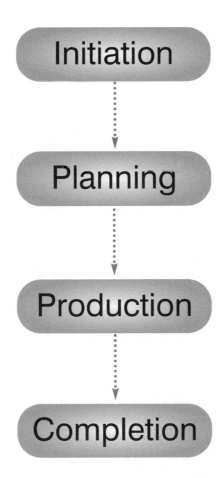

Initiation

When you first think of the idea, you check its **feasibility**, using a **SWOT** analysis, and then turn it into a finished **proposal**. You **pitch** (present) this to your commissioning editor or client (tutor) in, for example, a PowerPoint presentation, in order to be commissioned (get agreement) to make the product. The initiation stage finishes when you get approval to make your product.

See pages 39 and 53 to find out more about SWOT analyses.

Planning

Having been given the approval to make the product, you have to complete all the detailed planning needed to get the product made. It will include preparing a **treatment**: getting **clearances** for **acquisition** and **copyright**, getting **permissions** for use of **locations**, planning how much time will be needed in the production and completion stages, gathering production **personnel**, and preparing production **schedules** and **budgets**. The schedule should show an estimate of how you are going to use your time efficiently.

Production

This stage happens in three parts: pre-production, production (sometimes referred to as **content acquisition**) and post-production.

- Pre-production involves scriptwriting, having pre-interview meetings with contributors, preparing to record, shoot and photograph the images for the production, and creating shot lists and recording lists.

- The production/content acquisition part of the stage may involve shooting footage on location for a television programme, recording sound for a radio programme, writing copy for newspapers, magazines and advertisements, inputting data for websites, drawing animation frames or creating graphic images.

- Post-production is the editing part of the stage, where all the material that has been gathered in the production part is put together in the right order to make the finished product. In many cases it will take place onscreen, on an edit workstation, but there are products that require visual craft skills to edit, so this work will take place in a design studio. An important part of post-production is reviewing material. This may be with a client or an audience. The review will confirm whether or not the finished product is appropriate and changes can be made as a result of the review.

Completion

Your product will probably have been created using an **industry standard** computer application (program) that isn't available generally to the target audience or consumer. During the completion stage the product is turned into a **format** that is compatible with the means of distribution. In the case of a TV programme it is copied onto **Digital Betacam** tape. A programme for BBC radio needs to be sent as a **BWAV** or **Broadcast WAV** data file (they used to accept CDDA discs for programmes). Newspapers and magazines have to be printed and bound to make them available to their readers. An interactive CD must be bulk-copied and put into a case with appropriate inlay cards and instructions. A website must be in a form that can be accessed by users with a basic PC, and a computer game must be capable of being played on a basic computer or on a games console.

When deciding how much time to allocate to the different stages of the production process, you should bear in mind that the initiation and planning stages are probably going to take far longer than the production and completion stages. Within the production stage, it will take longer to write a script than to shoot it, and the content acquisition part (filming, recording, etc.) will take less time than the editing part. In addition, you have to include the amount of time that may be lost by equipment not working properly, people being late, and bad organisation.

Summary

This chapter will be a very valuable reference tool to come back to when you make your products. It represents a general view of the process that must be applied to every product you make.

5 Production Project

Your production project

This chapter will explain how to set about a production project. The result of a project will be a complete media product, for example a newspaper, which would require text produced for Unit 11 (Writing for the media) and photographs for Unit 9 (Photography techniques). These are combined in this production project unit. In Chapter 4 you were introduced to the production process. In this chapter you will learn about applying aspects of the production process when responding to a project brief.

What is a proposal?

A **proposal** is the end result of the first stage in developing of an idea for a media product. The initial process of development could be in the form of a mind map, when you think of several related ideas and then accept or reject them. Here is an example of a mind map for a product, showing ideas for the content of the product.

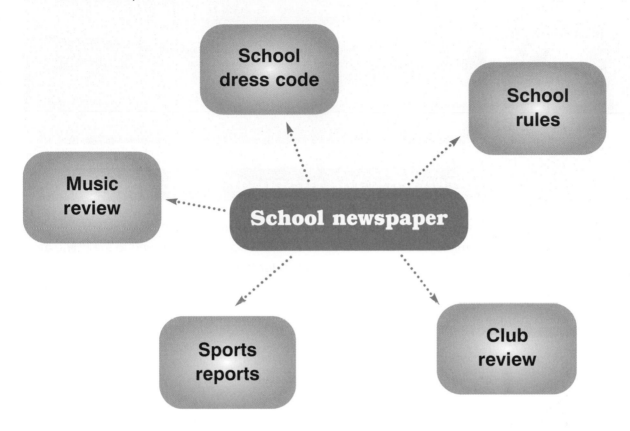

The product is a school newspaper, and the pages that could be included in the newspaper have been identified in the mind-mapping exercise. Each idea is discussed and a final selection is made of the most feasible ideas. In order to make a decision about the best ideas, you should do a **SWOT** analysis.

A SWOT analysis is a professional tool that media producers use to check the **viability** of a product. They consider the strengths and weaknesses of the product, the opportunities for it and the threats against it.

For a school newspaper you would do this analysis by answering the following questions:

- Would this appeal to the audience?
- How easy is to find material for each page?
- Is any page too boring?
- Would each page provide something valuable to the audience? Would it make the newspaper more saleable?
- Is there enough time to find information and produce a page layout?
- Has this already been done before? If so, how successful was it, and why was this?

Try this ...

You have been approached by a client who wants to market a new range of sweets for young children. These sweets contain only natural, fair trade ingredients. They want you to suggest the best way of marketing this product. Your first idea is for a website linked to a video game. Try a SWOT analysis to see if this is a feasible idea.

This is an example of how you might produce your SWOT analysis document.

Strengths	Weaknesses
Will appeal to an audience (pupils at your school). Material is easy to find.	Some pages could be boring. Might take a long time to find the information.
Opportunities	**Threats**
Provides something valuable to audience. Content makes newspaper saleable.	Not enough time. Already been done.

Preparing the proposal document

A proposal is a document that tries to sell an idea to a **client** or **commissioner**. In order to do this, it needs to be clear and to the point, and must provide sufficient information for the client or commissioner to ask for further development of your idea.

A proposal document should be written in an appropriate format, showing:

- working title
- medium to be used, e.g. video, website, etc.
- intended audience
- indication of the style
- summary of the content
- length or size of product.

Look at ...

Look at the example of a professional proposal for a video on the CD-Rom.

Try this ...

Think about how you would pitch your idea for a media product to a client or commissioner. Would you talk through the idea with them, give them samples of your idea, or present your idea using a PowerPoint presentation?

Pitching your proposal

A client or commissioner may ask you to pitch your idea for a media product. This is an opportunity to talk about your idea and expand on it by presenting the information in an appropriate way. You may decide to produce a PowerPoint presentation with a handout. You may be able to talk through your ideas using a range of examples of your page layout or storyboard.

Whatever method you use, you must make sure that your idea is based on appropriate research, that the idea is feasible, that there is a target audience for the product and that it can be delivered on time and within budget.

Legal and ethical issues

When producing a proposal you will have to take into consideration legal and ethical issues. These could be:

- **Privacy**. An individual should be able to keep their private lives out of the public view. Will your product infringe a person's right to privacy?

- **Defamation** is the publishing of untrue statements about a person that damages their reputation. What you say about someone could damage their reputation and you could be sued.

- **Libel law**. Libel is the defamation of a person in print, on television, radio or a website. What you write about someone could have serious implications for your reputation and for your income.

- **Race discrimination laws** protect minority groups from being portrayed in a bad light by the media and by individuals. You need to be careful when representing people and groups.

- **Data protection**. The Data Protection Act requires anyone who handles personal information to follow a number of important principles. It also gives individuals rights over their personal information. You need to ensure that any research material you produce is not openly available to everyone.

- **Copyright**. Using someone else's material without their permission will infringe their copyright. You must not assume that you can simply take material from a website or library without permission from the copyright owner.

- **Codes of practice** are sets of guidelines produced to set standards of professional conduct. Codes of practice should be carefully considered when planning your product (see the Appendix for more details).

When preparing a proposal you must be aware of all these issues.

Developing your proposal

The development of the proposal, once it has been accepted, is called a **treatment**. The treatment is a document that provides evidence of the costs involved in the production, the timescales involved and the crew and talent (actors) that may be used in the production.

A client or commissioner will want to see that you have thought carefully and planned efficiently before any material is recorded.

 Look at ...

On the CD-Rom you will find some examples of legal restrictions from recent media products.

Try this ...

A client wants to market a new range of sweets aimed at young children and you have decided that a TV advert would be the best advertising medium. Find the website giving information on regulations concerning advertising and young children. Make some notes on the restrictions you find.

For more information on research techniques you should look at Chapter 2, Research for Media Production.

Turn the page for more detailed information.

Try this ...

You are going on location to film an essential sequence for your advertisement for a new range of sweets. You have forgotten to ask permission from the owner of the local sweet shop and they do not agree to you filming. You have a crew of six people sitting around waiting to start work. How could you have avoided this situation?

Try this ...

You have interviewed ten people about their thoughts on the fair trade sweets product and recorded their answers on paper. You have given twenty people a questionnaire and received some of these back. You have gathered together twenty people in a room and presented your idea for the product, recording their suggestions on a feedback form.

(a) How would you analyse this material?

(b) How would you store this material?

(c) What would you do with the results of your analysis?

The treatment, which may be created by the producer, could consider:

- All the tasks that need to be completed, e.g. finding locations, finding props, finding resources.

- The roles to be undertaken: the crew required, the talent needed, the support staff required.

- How to manage the team: who will lead the team, how the team will be motivated.

- **Logistics**: where to obtain resources, where to obtain materials.

- **Clearances** and **permissions**, e.g. ensuring that locations will give permission for their use.

- **Health and safety**: Is the location safe? Is the studio safe? Will the crew and talent be safe whilst working?

The actual contents of the treatment will vary according to the product being proposed. Turn the page for more detailed information.

Carrying out further research

In order to produce your treatment you will have to carry out further research. This may be for:

- **Content**: Will the content of the product be appropriate for the intended audience?

- **Viability**: Have you checked that there are no foreseeable problems with the product?

You could do this research using a range of techniques, e.g. using primary sources such as questionnaires, focus groups or interviews.

The information you gather from this research should be analysed and recorded. This analysis will demonstrate that either everything is in place and appropriate or that changes need to be made.

Producing your treatment

The treatment provides an opportunity for you to bring together all the elements you need to start the production process. The treatment is a valuable document and will reassure a client that you have considered all the different phases of production.

The elements that make up any treatment are:

- Research: evidence of appropriate research into content, style and viability.

- **Draft script**: the first version of a script that will be changed to a final script as the production process moves on.

- **Mood board** / **thumbnail** / **storyboard**: the visual representations of the product, used to demonstrate how the product will look.

- **Production schedule**: a timeline for the process, showing the planning for production and post-production. A key part of this is to identify potential health and safety issues. A risk assessment should be done to make sure that the production can be completed safely and on time.

- List of contributors: details of who these people are and how to contact them. The crew will be identified by their roles and the list could include details of who will manage various parts of the production.

- Sources: details of where resources and materials can be found. This might be suppliers of tapes, properties, equipment, crew or talent. It may also include details of clearances and permissions required.

- **Budget**: a comprehensive breakdown of expected costs for the product.

- **Contingency**: a plan for making changes, where necessary, e.g. what would you do if the weather was too bad for filming, or a crew member did not arrive on time?

You will also find some of the following in treatments for particular media products:

- **Shooting script**: a script format that includes camera positions and angles, stage directions and lighting directions. This allows the director and producer to have a clear idea of the final shape of the production.

- **Location recce**: a visit to a location to ensure that it is appropriate and safe. This must be donen early in the planning schedule.

- **Cue sheet**: a list of speech, music and links used when compiling a radio product.

- **Schematic**: a diagram that represents the elements of a website, for example. The schematic demonstrates how pages link together and how links will be put in place to make navigation work.

- **Page layout**: a draft page or front cover of a magazine or newspaper to show how it will look. It is useful for checking margins and gutters, white space and text size.

 **Look at ...**

Look at the example of a professionally produced treatment for a video programme on the CD-Rom.

 Look at ...

You can use the blank templates of the treatment documents on the CD-Rom in your own treatment.

Try this ...

Your proposal and pitch to a client have been successful. They have asked you to develop your idea for the fair trade sweets project. List the documentation you would use to produce a treatment for the client.

Creating your media product

Production

The production process will be the same whichever media form you choose to use for your product. You must:

- monitor: keep careful records and check that the production is on track.
- produce: record visual and audio material for your product.
- review: review this material and, if necessary, produce more material.
- log: note down all the material you have produced.
- paper edit: make decisions on how this material will be linked together to make a finished product.
- edit: shape and manipulate this material in order to produce your finished product.
- present: show your product to an audience and/or a client and obtain feedback on the product.
- alter: make changes to the product in light of their feedback, where necessary.

A chart like this can help you to keep track of your production:

Activity	Date started	Date completed
Produced a cue sheet for the interviews and music tracks for the radio show.	Thursday 1 May	Friday 2 May
Recorded the interviews for the radio commercial.	Monday 5 May	Monday 5 May

You should also keep a production diary. This will help you to demonstrate what roles you undertook and the skills you have developed. Here is an example of a production diary.

Date	Activity	Skills developed/roles undertaken
1 May	Wrote my cue sheet for the radio.	I looked at the examples of cue sheets that my tutor gave me. I then made a list of all the items I wanted in my part of the radio programme. I put this list into a running order and gave copies to my group. We discussed this and between us we made a group cue sheet to use for our finished programme. I made notes about the meeting and gave these out to the group. This will help us to remember what we have to do.

It is important that you understand the production process and follow a plan in order to make your production successful. The flowchart opposite will help you understand the whole production process:

INITIATION

Initial ideas research

Create proposal

PLANNING: TREATMENT PHASE 1

Research style and content

PLANNING: TREATMENT PHASE 2

Create:

mood board

thumbnails

storyboard

PLANNING: TREATMENT PHASE 3

Do location recce

Check resources

Confirm budget and contingency

PLANNING: TREATMENT PHASE 4

Create production schedule

PLANNING: TREATMENT PHASE 5

Create:

shooting script

cue sheet

schematic

page layout

PRE-PRODUCTION

Meet contributors

Create shortlists

Create recording lists

PRODUCTION

Gather content

POST-PRODUCTION: PHASE 1

Edit material

POST-PRODUCTION: PHASE 2

Present to client/audience

COMPLETION

Distribute

How to maintain quality

Throughout the production and post-production process you must think about the technical and aesthetic qualities of your work:

- Have you produced the best images and sound that you can?
- Do the images and sound convey the message that you are hoping for?
- Is the media format you have chosen appropriate for the audience?
- Do all the elements in the product work, e.g. rollovers operate and links are activated?
- Is the product produced in an appropriate genre for the audience?
- Is the narrative structure appropriate for the audience?

As you can see, there is a lot of emphasis on the audience. This is because the majority of media products are produced with an audience in mind, and how well they will sell is determined by the needs of the audience.

The best way to be sure you are producing the correct material is to have an on-going review with your crew and the client. Communication is very important, so you should find a way of showing a client the work in progress to ensure you have not strayed too far from your original idea.

In the film industry there has always been a meeting at the start of the day to review the rushes. Rushes are the sections of the previous day's film material that have been processed overnight, which can be viewed by the director to check there is enough material for a scene. Even though much of the film industry has now moved over to digital film capture, this viewing still takes place at the start of the day.

Reviewing whether your intentions have been met

You must consider how your production process relates to your original proposal. A client will want to be reassured that the idea you proposed at the start of the process is the same as the product you have produced. The client will now have committed money and time to the project, based on your original proposal. You must think about:

- content: does the content match the content in your proposal?
- style: is the style of the product consistent with the style you identified in the proposal?
- audience: will the product meet the needs of the intended audience?
- proposed outlet: will the product be suitable for the market you identified in the proposal?

You need to constantly ask yourself these questions as you go through the production process. If you cannot say yes to each of these points you will need to review the production and see where changes might have taken place, and why.

Throughout the production process, you should record all information accurately because it will help you when you review your own work.

Find out how to review your own work in Chapter 19.

Summary

In this chapter you have covered what you need to know to achieve three of the four Learning Outcomes relating to Unit 17 of your course. You should now:

- be able to prepare a proposal for a media product

- be able to develop a proposal for a media product

- be able to create a media product following a proposal.

When you have finished your product you will need to review it to achieve the final Learning Outcome. To find out how to do this turn to Chapter 19, Reviewing Your Work.

6 Factual Production

What is factual production?

Media products can be fictional, factual or fiction based on fact. Fact is true and fiction is not true. This chapter will investigate factual products and the conventions that are used in making and recognising factual products. These include some television and radio programmes, training videos, printed material like newspapers and some magazines, textbooks and some websites.

Sometimes factual information is changd into a fictional narrative. For example, you can have a film that is based on fact but is adapted to make it more exciting, or a dramatised documentary radio or TV programme, where the characters represent real people but the story is made up.

Types of factual products

The **documentary** is the most obvious form of factual television or radio programme. The **feature** (a self-contained finished item broadcast as a **segment** of a longer programme) is usually factual, though features containing **dramatised** content are not. Television and radio news bulletins are wholly factual, while **current affairs** programmes and **news magazine** programmes can have fictional **embellishments** in the form of personal opinion.

Newspapers that remain committed to reporting news and stories without adding to or taking away from the content are factual, but the **editorial** of a newspaper may be **conjecture** and elaboration that is only based on fact, and so it is questionable. Magazine articles and written interviews that report the interviewee **verbatim** (quoting the actual words said rather than the journalist's interpretation) are factual. Live reporting and reviewing of sport could be considered factual. **Consumer** programmes, magazines and websites are factual products that deal with the truth about finance, holidays, jobs and many other issues.

This table shows some factual products and their equivalent fictional products.

Factual product	Equivalent fictional product
TV documentary TV natural history documentary Radio or TV feature	Dramadoc Docusoap Dramatised radio or TV feature
Consumer radio & TV programmes	Crime reconstruction programmes
Radio news bulletin Television news bulletin	Current affairs, news magazine (contain personal comment that may not be true)
Serious newspaper article	Popular newspaper feature
Investigative documentary	Dramatic reconstruction (based on fact)

Here are some examples of factual products you may already know:

- News 6.00 p.m, Radio 4
- News 10.30 p.m, ITV
- *Natural World*, BBC 2
- *Dispatches*, Channel 4
- *Watchdog*, BBC 1
- *Money Box*, Radio 4
- *Crimewatch*, BBC 1
- *Panorama*, BBC 1
- *Times* newspaper
- *Guardian* newspaper

Try this ...

Get a copy, or visit a website, of a listings magazine (e.g. Radio Times or TV Times) and list the names of some factual radio or television programmes and the channels they are broadcast on. How can you tell that they are factual from the titles?

Try this ...

List as many factual websites as you can. Explain why you think they are factual.

Try this ...

Obtain copies (or go to the websites) of some serious and popular newspapers (formerly broadsheets and tabloids) and some magazines. Highlight which stories are fact and which are either features or fictitious.

Conventions of factual products

Look at Chapter 3, Media Audiences and Products for more information on conventions.

The 'Try this' activities on page 49 asked you to state why you thought a product was factual. Do factual products have characteristics that make them recognisable? Fictional products have characteristics or **conventions** that make them recognisable as fictional products, just as all products have conventions that allow us to classify them by genre (type) and not simply as fiction or fact. The table below shows four common factual products and some of the conventions by which they can each be recognised.

Media product	Convention used
Television news bulletin	• Studio-based newsreader speaks directly to camera • Newsreader uses pre-scripted dialogue • Shot: medium close-up • Language: formal (Standard English) • Each story introduced by piece to camera • Some stories have a videotape (VT) clip • Each story has lip-sync • Each video clip has voice-over (VO) from studio-based newsreader
Radio documentary	• Spoken introduction to programme • Use of narrator to link elements • Formal language used by narrator • Actual words spoken by contributors, using their dialects or slang (called actuality) • Contributors recorded on location • Only contributors' answers heard, the questions have been edited out • Archive material used • Spoken conclusion to programme
Newspaper article	• Main headline for title • Byline for name of writer • Text set in columns • Formal language used • No related picture • Not generally on front page (which tends to be used for breaking news)
Website	• Uniform colour scheme, related to a company's house style and corporate image • Often frame to page • Generally roll-over navigation buttons • More than one way of navigating the site • Banner advertisement • Blocks of colour • Links to other sites • Icons

One convention may be associated with more than one type of product and may well identify another type of product when used in a different combination. The table opposite shows general rules, but it is the combination of conventions used that distinguishes one product from another, whatever genre it belongs to.

In addition to the more obvious conventions listed opposite, the **structure** of each type of product (the way it is put together) will also identify it as a particular type of factual or fictional product. An example of this is a news bulletin on a music radio station. It is introduced by a **jingle**, followed by a new voice reading the headlines. This is followed by each news story read out in greater detail. Many of the news stories will also have a **voice-piece** (a pre-recorded item) delivered by a **contributor**, perhaps a reporter, with a different voice and from a remote location. Between the stories there may be a **sting** (musical phrase) to hold them together. At the end, the newsreader may read the headlines again and then **sign-off** with a standard phrase that includes the name of the radio station. This structure of news programme differentiates them from other programme types. The chart below compares the structure of a radio news bulletin and a documentary TV programme.

Three-minute radio news programme	Documentary TV programme
News jingle	Introduction and menu by narrator
Headlines	First contributor
Newscaster's name	Link voice-piece by narrator
Story 1 Main national story with voice-piece	Second contributor
Sting	Link voice-piece by narrator
Story 2 with voice-piece	Sound effect
Sting	Third contributor
Story 3 with voice-piece	Link voice-piece by narrator
Sting	First contributor
Story 4 Short local story	Sound effect
Sting	Link voice-piece by narrator
Story 5	Third contributor
Sting	Second contributor
Story 6 Curious/amusing story	Closing remarks by narrator
Sign-off	
Jingle, including station name	

Try this ...

Pick one of the factual products you listed in the activities on page 49, and list other conventions that you now recognise make it a factual product. Now look at another product. Identify the most common convention that makes a product factual.

Try this ...

Choose a factual and a fictional media product and write down the component parts to show the two structures.

Initiating and researching ideas for a factual media product

Deciding which factual product to make

Try this ...

With a partner, discuss the type of factual media product you want to make. Draw a spidergram of the possibilities and then decide which medium you will use and which basic type of product you will make.

You can now start to develop your own ideas for a factual media product. First, decide whether it's going to be a television or radio programme, a printed article in a newspaper or magazine, or a factually-based website. Next decide whether it's going to be news or a documentary. You must consider the equipment you will need and the time it will take, which will depend on the sector you are working in. You can draw a **spidergram** of your ideas like this one:

Sport
Running, gymnastics, swimming, off-road bikes

Media
Television, iPods, gameboys, music centres, cinema, films on TV, DVD hires

Music
Listening to and making music, singing, playing an instrument, going to concerts

Youth
What are young people interested in?

Vandalism
Causing damage, harassing people, knife culture

Peer pressure
Conforming, being different, bullying

Fashion
Designer clothes, hoodies, ways of carrying school bags

Developing the idea for your factual product

Having decided what type of factual media product you are going to make, your idea needs to be developed into a viable (practical) proposal. You can use a SWOT analysis to work out the viability of an idea.

Strengths	The strengths of any product should first include the content – otherwise the product will be destined to fail. Other strengths could be the valuable purpose of the idea, whether it is raising awareness about a topical issue, or educating, informing or simply entertaining people. Production strengths might include a relatively low budget, content that is easy to acquire, etc.
Weaknesses	The weaknesses of a product might be that it is not feasible to make, the concept is not quite right or perhaps the content is distasteful to certain audiences. The logistics of a project must be considered. Raising money may be difficult (funding is essential to any project in the real world) or it may not be easy to acquire the content.
Opportunities	The opportunities opened up by a product might include such things as the chance to communicate to the masses, raising awareness, tackling important issues and educating people. A product on sex education, for example, could help reduce teenage pregnancies. Such opportunities depend on the content of the individual product, but they can be a great asset.
Threats	The main threats are the unknown problems that might (and probably will) crop up in the production and post-production stages. Their impact can be greatly reduced if the potential problems can be identified and assessed in the planning stage and, hopefully, eliminated.

See page 39 to find out more about SWOT analyses.

Try this ...

Working with a partner, brainstorm your initial idea, carrying out a SWOT analysis to establish its viability to become a product.

Any of the following could be strengths, weaknesses, opportunities or threats, depending on how much they each impede or support your idea for a product.

- Personal interest
- Knowledge of subject
- Accessibility to contributors
- Availability of primary information
- Availability of secondary information
- Research skills
- Time management
- Contribute to CV/showreel
- Human resources
- Physical resources
- Knowledge of equipment
- Communication skills

- Topicality, currency, relevance
- Access to locations
- Sensitivity of content
- Authorisation
- Copyright
- Budget and costs
- Disclosures/confidentiality
- Access to unconventional sources
- Codes of practice
- Sources of information
- Timescale/availability
- Need to adhere to ethical practices

Try this ...

Produce a **questionnaire** and conduct an audience research survey to confirm the nature of the audience for your product and the means of access (how, when and where the product will be delivered to them). You can use the Audience questionnaire on the CD-Rom to set up your questionnaire for your sector.

Deciding on your audience

Early on in the production process you need to decide who the audience is going to be for your product. You will need to use some of your knowledge from Chapter 3, Media Audiences and Products, to decide this.

Research

You should research how, when and where your audience will access the product and how they will find out about it. Use all the appropriate methods to find the information and don't forget to consider the legal and ethical issues for the audience you identify.

To research the content of your product you will need to apply the primary and secondary research techniques that are covered in Chapter 2, Research for Media Production. Research will involve information searches and interviewing people. You must also consider the relevant legal and ethical issues relating to the type of content that you want to include.

Try this ...

Look back at Chapter 2, Research for Media Production, and then gather the data for your product. Record all your findings, remembering to reference the information correctly so that it can be used in your **proposal**.

Producing a factual product

Recognising media product conventions

It is important to remember that the correct conventions must be used in factual products. The conventions that you use will depend on which media sector you are working in and which genre (type) of product you are going to make, so you will need to have researched your product thoroughly. If you get the conventions wrong, the product won't attract an audience, and will not make money for the company that commissioned it.

Similarly, the structure of the product must follow the conventions of structure for factual products of this genre. This includes the way in which you deliver the narrative, the way you use narration to link the elements of the product, your choice and type of interview and the formal way that you address the audience. You can use your audience research findings to help with this.

Presenting your proposal

Your proposal will need to be **pitched** (presented) to your commissioning editor (this will be your tutor) to persuade them that it is viable. Professionally, this is often done using a PowerPoint presentation, with slides that contain the same main points of information that are in the paper proposal.

Look at ...

Look at the examples of radio and TV proposals on the CD-Rom.

Try this ...

Using your audience research, product research and product ideas, prepare a paper proposal, following the recommended format. Look at Chapter 5, Production Project for help on preparing a proposal.

Try this ...

Prepare a PowerPoint presentation of six slides, similar to the one on the CD-Rom, that covers the main points of your proposal and then pitch it to your tutor.

If the pitch is successful, a contract is prepared by the commissioning agency, the budget for the product is agreed and the two parties sign the contract.

Carrying out pre-production

Once your proposal has been accepted it is necessary to plan the timescale, costs and other production issues in detail to ensure that the budget and deadlines are not exceeded. The detailed planning in the pre-production stage is, often referred to as a **treatment**. There is a copy of a treatment on the CD-ROM. It has ten headings which, when completed, will provide most of the documentation needed to make your product. For **pre-production**, there has to be enough documentation to allow another production team to make the product if you are unable to. In a professional situation, one team may do the research and planning and produce the documentation for another production team to make the product. In a large production company, such as the BBC, one person may only work on a small part of the production.

The sort of pre-production documentation that you need will depend on the media sector you are working in:

Television	Radio	Print	Website	Computer game
Storyboards	Directions	Layout	Navigation	Plan
Scripts	Scripts	Interviews	Text	Text
Crew list	Production team	Staff list	Production team	Production team
Recce list	Recce list	Contact book		
Contact book	Contact book	Schedules		
Equipment	Equipment	Photo-shoot		
Schedules	Schedules			
Set plans	Recording log			
Shot log	Recorded audio			
Shot footage				

Carrying out production

At the production stage you acquire (gather) the content for your product, according to the media sector you are working in. The table below shows what content you will need.

Television	Radio	Print	Website	Computer game
Footage	Audio	Copy	Text	Animations
Music	Music tracks	Photographs	Photographs	Images
Dialogue	Speech		Animations	Graphics
Animations	Sound effects		Graphics	Text
			Sounds	
			Images	

Carrying out post-production

Post-production is the editing part of the production stage, where all the acquired content is fitted together to make the final product. It is important that all the content gathering is complete before you start editing, which means that you must have planned what your product will look like in advance. Going back later for more content will cause delays in editing, and sometimes it is not possible to get exactly what you wanted. For example, in an exterior television or film shoot the weather may not be the same, or one of the contributors may be wearing different clothes or have a different hairstyle to when you first filmed them, making your new shots unusable. In radio you may find that you are in a different ambient environment, where the background noise is not the same as the last time you recorded the contributor's voice. Continuity errors like this are not acceptable for professional media products.

The table below shows what happens, and the order in which it happens, in the post-production stage of each sector

	Television	Radio	Print	Interactive media
Editing process	1. Choose shots	1. Choose clips	1. Place titles	1. Choose content
	2. Decide order of shots	2. Make edit list	2. Columnise	2. Import images
	3. Edit images	3. Edit speech	3. Sub-edit	3. Import text
	4. Add post-sound	4. Add music	4. Add text	4. Edit
	5. Mix music	5. Add sounds	5. Add pictures	5. Beta test
	6. Add titles and credits	6. Mix levels	6. Proofread	
Content into final format	Copy to format	Bounce to format	Print	Upload to server

Summary

In this chapter you have covered what you need to know to achieve three of the four Learning Outcomes relating to Unit 13 of your course. You should now:

- understand conventions of factual media production

- be able to develop and research an idea for a factual media product

- be able to produce a factual media product following appropriate conventions.

When you have finished your factual product you will need to review it to achieve the final Learning Outcome. To find out how to do this, turn to Chapter 19, Reviewing your own work.

Production Skills

This section covers the specialist units that deal with each sector of the media industry. Chapters 7 to 15 will introduce you to the specialist production skills you will use when you make your products. In Chapters 7 to 10 you will meet the video, audio, print and advertising sectors. Chapters 11 and 12 cover the interactive media sector, and Chapters 13 to 15 cover the computer games sector.

The final three chapters introduce you to skills and techniques that are used across several sectors of the media industry. These include photography techniques used in the print, advertising, web authoring and video sectors, animation techniques used in the computer games, web authoring and video sectors, and writing techniques used in the video, audio, web authoring and print sectors. You can choose for yourself which chapters skill be most useful to you, depending on your future career plans.

7 Video Production

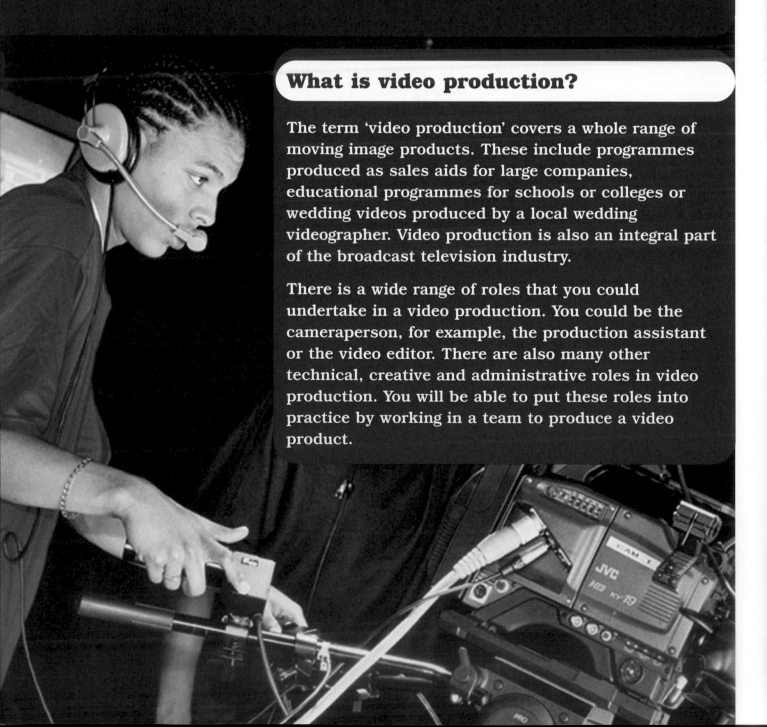

What is video production?

The term 'video production' covers a whole range of moving image products. These include programmes produced as sales aids for large companies, educational programmes for schools or colleges or wedding videos produced by a local wedding videographer. Video production is also an integral part of the broadcast television industry.

There is a wide range of roles that you could undertake in a video production. You could be the cameraperson, for example, the production assistant or the video editor. There are also many other technical, creative and administrative roles in video production. You will be able to put these roles into practice by working in a team to produce a video product.

The production process for video production

Look at Chapter 4, The Production Process, so that you can follow the **production process** to make your video product.

Pre-production

'Pre-production' is the term used for the preparation stage of the production of a media product. You must know about the equipment you will be using and the people you will need to make your product. You will decide what materials, locations and resources are needed for a successful production.

Equipment

There are a variety of recording formats in video:
- VHS: a consumer format that is rapidly being phased out in favour of digital consumer formats.
- Hi-8 video: an analogue recording system (consumer format) with a professional digital sound recording track.
- DV format: a professional digital format using digital video recording on to tape or on to a DVD disk.
- DVCAM: a professional digital video format recorded on to tape.
- HD (High Definition): the latest format that records digitally at a higher resolution to increase the quality of video pictures. Many people can't view this HD image yet as their televisions don't support the higher resolution picture.

You will need the following equipment to make your video product:
- camera support: tripod or mono-pod.
- microphones: rifle mics or radio mics.
- lights: hand-held, stand-mounted or ceiling-mounted.

During the pre-production stage you should make sure that all the equipment you will need for your production will be available for you to use at the time that you will need it. You should do an **audit** of equipment, using a chart like this one:

Equipment needed	Where to find it
Video camera – miniDV	Technician's store – must be booked out at least three days in advance.

Try this ...

Make a list of all the video equipment available in your school or college. Do not forget the lighting and microphones that might be kept in a different department.

Documentation

An important part of pre-production is preparing the documentation you will need for the production process. For video production you will need to create the following documents:

- A production schedule: lists all the requirements for production and a timescale.

- An initial script: the basis of your video product. It includes dialogue for actors and suggestions for the location of each shot.

- A storyboard: the visual representation of your ideas. It also includes suggestions for sound and effects.

- A shooting script: a development of the initial script, and includes camera positions, stage directions, lighting and sound requirements.

- A risk assessment: a document that highlights any potential health and safety issues with your studio or location work.

It is important to understand what each of these documents is for before you start to plan your own production.

Look at ...

Look at the examples of professional pre-production documentation on the CD-Rom.

Production

This is the content acquisition stage. For this stage, you will need to choose how you will be shooting your production. You must consider camera set-up, white balance, shooting techniques, lighting and sound. These are all explained below.

Camera set-up

There are important choices to be made:

- Will the camera be hand-held or on a tripod?

- Will you be shooting all the material on one camera (single camera shoot) or using two or more cameras (multi-camera shoot)?

If you use more than one camera you will have to ensure that they have been set up to produce the same colour balance – otherwise, every time you change the shot from one camera to another, the colours will change. A camera does not automatically know which colour is which, however, so you will need to give it some point of reference. The cameras have to be set up by pointing them all at the same image and then adjusting each one so that they all look the same. They will then have the same colour balance. In a studio, all the cameras are set up using a colour chart and then left in operation mode so that the colours do not change.

White balance

White balance is the system the camera uses to recognise the 'colour' white and then to recognise other colours. This is achieved by pointing the camera at a white source and telling the camera to use this as its white reference signal. White balance is one way of making sure a camera is correctly colour balanced.

Shooting techniques

- Framing: this involves framing the image in a viewfinder to produce the most pleasing image.
- Shot type: there are a variety of shot types, for example:

Long shot

Mid-shot

Close-up

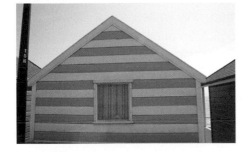

Extreme close-up

- Shot length: the time that the shot you have chosen to use will last. Generally, this is determined by the action taking place in the scene. If it is a scene of someone running through a doorway it may last just a few seconds. If it is a shot of someone running along a pathway and past the camera it may last a minute or more.
- Camera movements: the way that the camera moves during a shot. It might pan left to right to follow the action. It might zoom in to focus on the action or zoom out to give a larger picture of what is happening in the scene.

Lighting

You can use natural light (daylight) to shoot your video or, when shooting indoors or when the natural light is poor, you can use artificial lighting. There are two kinds of artificial lights available:

- 800 watt ('redheads')
- 2000 watt ('blondes')

Both of these lights produce artificial light with a colour temperature of around 3200 degrees K (Kelvin). This is the measurement of the light source that the camera will respond to when filming. Natural daylight is approximately 5600 degrees K. You simply have to ensure that the camera is set up to film using the correct degree K setting. If you film outdoors, using the artificial setting on a camera, your pictures will appear to be yellow. If you film indoors in artificial lighting and use the outdoor setting on the camera, your pictures will appear to be blue. Although this can be adjusted in the edit suite, it is wise to get it right in the first place to save you time in the edit suite.

Sound

A video programme is nothing without a soundtrack, so you must make sure that the microphone is turned on when you record. The sound might be recorded using:

- the camera's onboard microphone (in-camera sound). If the camera is a long way from the subject being filmed, only limited sound will be recorded. The microphone might also pick up unnecessary sounds, such as traffic noise and wind.
- a boom microphone. This is a microphone, usually a rifle microphone, that is mounted on a pole. This means that it can be positioned nearer the subject (but out of camera shot).
- a hand-held microphone, which a presenter or interviewer can hold in front of the interviewee to capture what they say.
- a radio microphone, which can be attached to an actor or interviewee, usually on their lapel or other inconspicuous part of their clothing. The microphone is attached by a wire to a transmitter, worn out of camera shot. The radio signal from this transmitter is picked up by a receiver and fed into the camera. Multiple radio microphones can be used to ensure that all the actors or interviewees can be heard.

Sound effects, such as music or voice-over, can be added at the post-production stage.

Try this ...

Set up a camera and tripod. Plug in a rifle microphone and record an interview with one of your friends. Think about the way you position them in the viewfinder. Have you checked the camera for white balance? Is the sound being recorded? Play back the footage you have recorded and see how you could improve it.

Post-production

You will need to be aware of the processes involved in shaping and editing your recorded material. You should keep a **footage log**, which is a list of the scenes that have been shot. You should include:

- Timecode: where each shot starts and finishes, recorded by a digital video camera on to the tape. The timecode is used by digital editing systems to find scenes. You can enter the timecode and the editing system will find the right place for you. This speeds up the editing process.
- Length of shots: how long each shot or scene lasts.
- Shot description: a brief description of each shot or scene. This will aid you when you are trying to find a particular scene for your programme.
- Audio: a brief description of the audio that has been recorded at the same time as the visuals.
- Suitability of recorded material: your comments on whether or not the particular scene or shot is suitable for your programme.

Here is an example of a tape footage log.

Timecode	Length of shot	Shot description	Audio	Suitability of recorded material
00.10 00.50	40 seconds	Interior of office	Office sounds	Camera shot a little unsteady

Before you start the editing process it is good practice to do a paper edit. This process, sometimes called an 'edit decision list', provides an opportunity to look through the footage log and make decisions about which scenes should go together. This will save time (and money) when you get into an edit suite.

You must always ensure that your tapes or disks are clearly labelled with the name of the production, the name of the crew and the date the material was shot. If the tape has a recording tab, a small removable button, this should be removed to ensure that no one can record over your work. Store your tapes or disks in a secure place.

 **Look at ...**

Look at the examples of professional post-production documentation on the CD-Rom.

Editing techniques

You may have access to a variety of editing equipment to edit your video programme. There are two editing systems – linear and non-linear:

- The linear system uses two (or more) tape-based video recorders to transfer video material. You have to synchronise the two machines to ensure that the material is transferred from one to the other at just the right place. This is the way that analogue footage has traditionally been edited.
- The non-linear system uses digital technology to convert video footage into a form that can be saved as a file on a computer. The computer then uses software to edit together the video footage and output it as a video signal.

In the linear system you have to edit material together in the order in which you want it to appear in the end. The non-linear system allows you to move footage around as you edit it, making it easier to change the order of footage at any time. The development of digital technology has meant that the whole editing process is now more sophisticated.

Video **transitions** can be used to add pace and rhythm to the edited video footage. An editor may use a 'slow fade' to slow down the action or a 'fast fade' to speed up the action. A fade to black followed by a fade up from black is generally used to signify that time has passed. However, overuse of these video effects can make a programme look too flashy and can detract from its message. Sometimes it is better to simply cut between scenes.

You can add new soundtracks to a video using **dubbing** – adding a music track, a voice-over or sound effects, for example, without altering the visual image.

Try this ...

Use the footage you shot of the interview with your friend. Try editing out some of your questions to make the interview shorter.

You will have to decide which delivery format to use for your finished product. Traditionally this would have been on VHS videotape, as this was the format many people had access to. Now this format is dying out and the DVD format has taken over. In order to deliver your finished video on DVD you will have to change the format of the video and audio files and make them compatible with the DVD format. This will involve the use of software, such as DVD Studio Pro, to compress your video footage to an appropriate file size and convert it to MPEG 4 files. You can then use the software to create a DVD menu that allows the viewer to choose how to view your video footage. They might want to see only a part of the video. You can set chapter points on the DVD to allow the viewer to choose what they see.

Contributing to every stage of the production

You must demonstrate that you can make a contribution to the pre-production, production and post-production stages of a finished video. It is useful to keep a production diary that shows just what you have done in this project.

This is a sample of a production diary.

Date	Activity	Roles undertaken and skills developed
21 January	Producing the initial script and storyboard. This will be discussed by the group, who will choose a version to be used in the production.	I have written my version of the script and drawn a simple storyboard, based on the idea that the group decided on. (Hopefully, my version will be chosen for the production.)

Generating ideas

You should undertake a mind-mapping exercise to decide what video product you are going to make. If you are working in a group, then everyone should have an input into the mapping exercise.

Here is an example of a mind map for a professional video product.

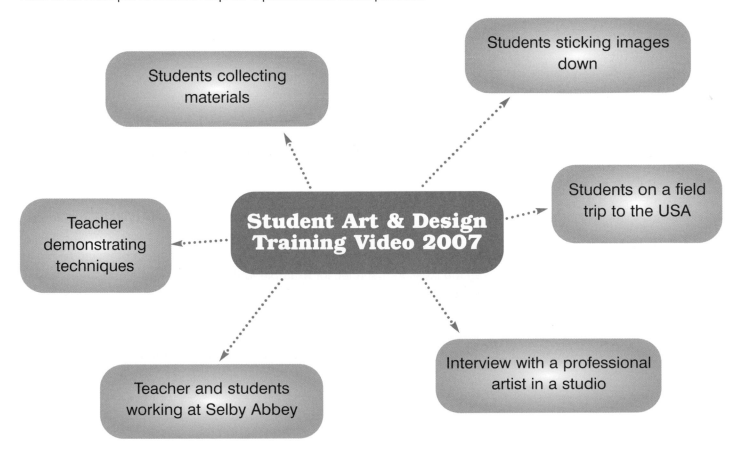

You will need to consider:

- Genre: what genre do you intend to use for your video product? Will it be a documentary, a drama, a horror video, a thriller, a music video or a comedy?
- Content: what do you intend to put into your finished product? Will it be all your own material or do you intend to use found footage? Will it be in colour or black and white? Will there be dialogue and/or music?
- Title: what will be the title of your video product? You should think of a **working title** as soon as you can, so that you can put it on all your pre-production documentation.
- Scope: will this be for one particular audience or for general release? What will be the length of your video product?

Contributing to the pre-production process

You will need to plan carefully for your video product. It can sometimes take more time to plan a production than it does to film and edit it. You must ensure that you provide evidence of your contribution to the planning phase of the production. You should:

- undertake effective research

- devise an appropriate timescale for production

- ensure that any locations and studios have been booked

- book equipment and materials

- communicate effectively with your team

- provide a creative input into the development of the product

- work within the agreed budget.

Contributing to the production process

You must demonstrate your technical competence by using equipment effectively. You should also have a creative input into the production process. For instance, you might suggest what camera angles to use or what sound to record. You should take on one of the roles within the production team – as the location manager, for example, or the camera operator or the sound recordist.

You should carefully record all of the work you do in your production diary, and say how you well think you worked as a team member.

Contributing to the post-production process

You should demonstrate your technical competence in using editing techniques and technology. Editing is not just about storing files and joining them together. It is a creative process, involving the pace and timing of your shots and making the story flow. Your input should be about using the post-production process creatively to produce a good finished video product.

Remember that you must carefully record all the work you undertake in post-production.

Summary

In this chapter you have covered what you need to know to achieve two of the three Learning Outcomes relating to Unit 4 of your course. You should now:

- understand pre-production, production and post-production techniques

- be able to contribute to each stage of the creation of a finished video product.

When you have finished your video product you will need to review it to achieve the final Learning Outcome. To find out how to do this, turn to Chapter 19, Reviewing Your Work.

8 Audio Production

What is audio production?

Audio is anything that we can hear, which includes speech, dialogue, voices, animal noises, sound effects and music.

When we make recordings of audio – for radio, television, film, the Internet, computer games or demo tapes for bands – the process is known as production. Audio can be recorded under controlled conditions in recording studios or in radio broadcast studios. These have been designed specially to keep out any unwanted noise and background sound. There are times, however, when audio has to be recorded or broadcast live from a location other than a studio.

In this chapter you will find out about how this is achieved, about the nature of recording technology, and how to record and edit digital audio for use in broadcast and non-broadcast situations.

Broadcast and non-broadcast audio products and formats

Broadcast audio

There are many types of broadcast audio product, also called radio programmes or radio shows. They may be pre-recorded for later broadcast or they may be live. Some programmes are pre-recorded to their intended broadcast running time as though they were live, and are then broadcast at a later date, without any editing. Other programmes may be recorded at the time that they are broadcast live and then re-broadcast on another day. Different types of programme are recognisable both by their content and by the style and form in which they are made.

Music radio

You may be familiar with radio **breakfast shows**. This **genre** (type) is called a **music sequence** and usually lasts for three or four hours. Its brash **style** is taken from American **format radio**, which means that the show always follows a set format. It plays a specific type of music linked by DJ chat, plus news, competitions, phone-ins, weather forecasts, traffic information, DJ jingles, **stings** and commercials, together with presenter, station and programme **idents** and **sweepers**. In a BBC music sequence there will not be any commercials because the BBC is funded from the licence fee from the government.

The **structure** of format radio is built around a single hour of air time. This structure is repeated every hour and follows the same format every day. The style will differ according to the audience that the show is targeting but it will mainly be music.

Speech radio

At the other end of the scale there is the programme that is all speech, sometimes referred to as **intelligent speech radio**. On speech radio there is a range of genres of programme similar to those found on television. The most serious are political discussion programmes, in which current issues are debated by politicians and experienced political broadcasters and journalists. This genre usually starts with a **presenter**, **chair** or **anchor** introducing the topic for discussion. The chair first introduces each contributor taking part in the programme and then starts the discussion by outlining an opening issue relating to the topic. Each contributor is given an equal amount of time to state their particular opinion before the chair moves the discussion on to the next point. At the end, the chair will allow each contributor to sum up their opinion and then they will **sign-off**. The programme doesn't usually have any music.

Try this ...

Use the 'Listen Again' function on the BBC website to listen to the breakfast show from each of the following radio stations: Radio 1, Radio 2, Radio 3 and your local BBC radio station. Compare the different styles of presentation, genres of music and other content, and see if there are differences in the formats.

Try this ...

Record or listen to clips from the websites of national commercial stations (e.g. Classic FM and Virgin Radio), regional stations (e.g. Galaxy) and your local commercial station. Compare the different styles of presentation, genres of music and other content, and see if there are differences in the formats.

Examples of typical programmes broadcast on intelligent speech radio include:

Name of programme	Genre	Format
The Today Programme	News and current affairs	Magazine
The Archers	Soap opera	Scenes
Analysis	Current affairs	Discussion
6 o'clock News	News	Bulletin
Afternoon Play	Drama	Scenes
Woman's Hour	Issues relevant to women	Magazine
You and Yours	Consumer	Magazine
File on Four	Investigative factual	Interviews
The Now Show	Comedy	Sketches
Claire in the Community	Sitcom	Scenes
News Quiz	Panel game show	Rounds of questions
Today in Parliament	Politics/current affairs	Interviews
The Write Stuff	Quiz	Question and answer
Go 4 It	Children's programme	Magazine
Beyond Belief	Religion	Discussion
Book at Bedtime	Fiction	Reading
The Archive Hour	Historic archive	Narrated documentary

Try this ...

Go to the 'Listen Again' website for BBC Radio 4 and listen to a clip from its breakfast show equivalent, *The Today Programme*. How does its format differ from that of a music station breakfast show?

Try this ...

Listen to a music track that you like. Which radio stations would play it and on which programmes would it be played? Find out by listening to music shows on a range of radio stations.

Try this ...

Go to the websites for national stations TalkSPORT and BBC Radio Five Live and listen to clips from their respective breakfast shows. How do the formats of these programmes differ, and how does each differ from the BBC Radio 4 breakfast programme, *The Today Programme*?

Non-broadcast audio

Some audio products might be heard on radio but originate elsewhere. They may be listened to in their own right using other technologies. The main example is music, which originates as a CD track or a music video track. Music is now also available to download legally from the Internet, and much music is copied (illegally) to personal listening devices, such as iPods.

Audio books

Audio books are also heard on the radio but are not always made specifically for radio. They are recordings of someone reading a conventional book out loud, which are then copied on to CD and tape cassette for sale in bookshops and record shops. Audio books are used by a range of people, particularly those with impaired sight who can't read books, but there is also a large market of sighted people who just prefer to listen rather than read. It is a popular programme type on radio as well.

In-store radio

When you visit some supermarkets or clothes shops, e.g. ASDA or Topshop, you will usually hear their in-store audio, now becoming known as in-store radio. It is distributed from a common source to each shop or branch in the group. Arguably this is a form of broadcast radio since the same content is being distributed to a large number of people simultaneously, and the style and format is recognisable as a radio form, but in some cases it is still referred to as in-store audio. One hour of audio can be repeated frequently during the day, as a customer is unlikely to spend more than an hour in any shop. Any shop that plays its own choice of music, e.g. a charity shop, is playing real audio.

Soundtracks

When you see a film you are hearing another audio form – the film soundtrack. Soundtracks are produced in a distinct way – quite different from a CD music track, for example. A soundtrack consists of dialogue, sound effects, **ambience** and music, mixed in a way that the different elements complement each other to provide the context for the moving image on the screen. The audio without the images would be hard to understand, and vice versa. Another audio form that can be included in this group of products is computer game soundtracks. They use a range of audio material such as dialogue, sound effects, music and various beeps, bells and horns to indicate scoring points, etc. As with films, the audio is meaningless without the visual images.

Try this ...

Visit your school or local library and borrow one or two audio books. Listen to them and then listen to *Afternoon Reading* or *Book at Bedtime* on BBC Radio 4. Think about how they are similar and how they are different.

Try this ...

Listen to and record examples of in-store music (some can be found on the Internet at the stores' websites). What do these audio products have in common with a radio music sequence?

Try this ...

Play a film clip that you have never seen before, first with the picture off, then with the sound off. Decide whether the picture or the sound provides the better means of telling you what is happening.

Audio formats

The way in which you purchase audio recordings will probably have changed during your lifetime. Perhaps you remember audio cassette tapes, one of the main formats in which domestic recordings were sold for many years. Your parents probably collected their music as vinyl records, but at the moment music sold in music stores is usually on CD. Then there are MiniDiscs, and the ability to download music files from websites to iPod in MP3 format. We know that television is due to switch totally to digital soon, and radio broadcasting will also be going completely digital eventually.

'Digital' is obviously the future – but what does it mean? You first need to know that audio signals can be recorded and stored on media in two forms – **analogue** and **digital**.

Analogue recording

Analogue is the original way of recording an audio signal. When sound waves are picked up by a microphone, the microphone generates a small electrical voltage that is proportional to the loudness and the note of the sound wave. This diagram shows a signal being generated.

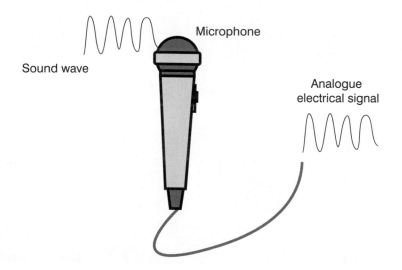

Sound wave

Microphone

Analogue electrical signal

If this varying electrical signal is fed through a preamplifier that is connected to a recorder, the magnetic signal that is recorded on to the recording medium (disc or tape) is proportional to the loudness and tone of the original sound.

This diagram shows the record signal path when an electrical wave is being recorded.

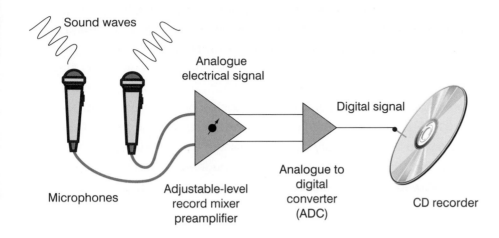

To hear the sound we must reverse the above process. The recorded magnetic signal is picked up from the recording medium (disc or tape) by a preamplifier, which turns it back into an electrical signal and amplifies it through a power amplifier. This feeds a loudspeaker, which turns the electrical signal back into a sound wave that we can hear. This diagram shows the replay signal path when a CD plays from Preamp to Pamp LS.

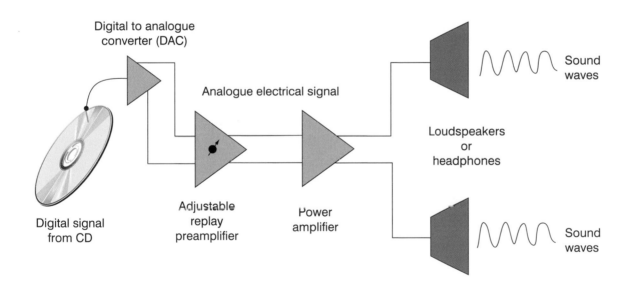

If sound is simply amplified, e.g. at a concert, it remains analogue, and works very well, but analogue sound recording has its own problems. The media that were traditionally used for storing sound (tape and vinyl) were not good at recording accurate analogue signals, and problems arose when people tried to copy from one tape to another, as the electrical circuits and the recording medium itself contributed background noise to the recorded signal. The lower the background noise, the better the recording, and a system's efficiency was measured by its 'signal-to-noise ratio'.

Digital recording

As long ago as the 1930s a system was invented to solve the problem, but the technology wasn't available to put it into practice. The system was called 'pulse code modulation' (PCM) and is the basis of all digital recording today. Each part of the varying electrical signal that represents the sound waves is converted into a series of electrical pulses just before the recording stage, using an 'analogue to digital converter' (ADC). These pulses represent different values in binary code – which consists of just zeros and ones, e.g. 1101010. The pulses are the ones, and the spaces are the zeros. If you know how to count in binary code you will know that 1010 represents the number 9 (counting in base 10) so, in the loudness part of the signal, a pulse followed by a space followed by a pulse followed by a space represents a sound loudness of 9, and so on.

If the recorded signal is simply represented by pulses in binary code, it is less likely to be corrupted with background noise than the original analogue signals. When a digital signal, the pulses are changed back into an electrical signal by the preamplifier, using a 'digital to analogue converter' (DAC). The power amplifier then makes the electrical signal big enough to be heard through loudspeakers.

In this chain of sound reproduction, the microphone and the loudspeaker are both analogue devices (transducers) and only handle analogue signals, so even now there is no such thing as a wholly digital system. The only part that is digital is the signal storage method.

Audio storage formats can be classified in three groups:

Digital storage media, uncompressed
- BWAV – Broadcast WAV (BBC)
- WAV – PC IBM Audio format
- AIFF – Audio interlaced file format
- DAT – Digital audio tape
- CDDA – Compact disc digital audio
- DVD – Digital versatile disc (domestic format)
- HDD – Hard disc drive (on a computer)

Digital storage media, compressed (domestic – not for broadcast)
- ATRAC – MiniDisc
- MP3

Analogue storage media
- Vinyl
- Reel-to-reel tape (no longer used)
- Cassette tape (domestic format)
- VHS videotape (domestic format)
- SVHS videotape (domestic format)

Linear or non-linear access?

The storage media in the list on page 76 can be further divided into two groups: those that can be accessed at any point instantly, called non-linear, and those that have to be played for a time to access any given point, known as linear. This is the difference between linear and non-linear access. For example, an analogue vinyl disc can have its stylus put onto any groove to find any part of an audio track instantly, without playing it from the beginning. A WAV file that is opened on a PC audio application can also do this, by moving the timeline marker anywhere on the timeline and pressing play. A CD or a DVD can be accessed at certain points – the starts of the various tracks or chapters. A videotape or a cassette tape, on the other hand, must be searched by fast wind or rewind to find the place required. The following list categorises media as linear or non-linear.

Linear access
- Reel-to-reel tape
- Cassette tape
- VHS videotape
- SVHS videotape
- DAT – Digital audio tape

Limited non-linear access (to track or chapter only)
- CDDA – Compact disc digital audio
- DVD – Digital versatile disc
- ATRAC – MiniDisc
- MP3

Total non-linear access
- Vinyl
- BWAV
- WAV
- AIFF

Recording and editing technology and techniques

Recording technology

There are two technical processes in making a pre-recorded radio programme. The recording of the dialogue, often gathered on location, is the first process. The second process involves this audio content being uploaded (transferred) to a workstation, edited and mixed with music and other sound effects and then balanced into a final programme.

There is a variety of portable digital audio recorders for gathering speech dialogue. Those that are suitable for radio broadcast work are known as professional recorders. The others are known as domestic recorders. The difference may be in the quality of the microphone or, more likely, the way in which the audio is recorded to file.

Professional audio recorders	Recording format
Hard disk recorders	WAV or BWAV
Flash drive recorders	WAV
SD recorders	WAV
DAT recorders	Helical scan
Domestic audio recorders	**Recording format**
iPod listening/Internet format only	MP3 compressed audio
MiniDisc MD (no longer a broadcast format)	ATRAC compressed audio

Compression

One of the main differences between professional and domestic recorders is the file format used when the audio is recorded. The demand for ever greater quantities of storage space on domestic recorders has resulted in audio files being compressed (made smaller). This is a technique where all surplus digital audio information is removed from the audio file, leaving only the essential material to make it recognisable when replayed. There are two disadvantages to this technique. First, compressed audio files cannot be **fine edited** in the same way as uncompressed files. Secondly, some forms of compression, known as **lossy** compressions, can't be reversed without losing some of the original data. A **lossless** compression, on the other hand, can be reversed perfectly. You will see from the table above that iPod and MiniDisc both use compressed audio file formats and are therefore not suitable for professional radio work, although MiniDisc is a good way to learn how to record on location.

Professional portable audio recorders can **upload** (transfer) their files much faster than **real time** and sound files can often be 'dragged' from the drive or memory card straight to the workstation. MiniDisc files, however, can only be uploaded in real time.

Editing technology

Editing of audio takes place on a PC or Mac workstation, using a variety of specially produced software applications. There are two main tasks to complete when editing. First, the dialogue must be edited to get it to the agreed running time and in the correct order. Then the other sounds must be mixed and balanced with the dialogue to produce a finished programme.

A programme must be edited to
- make the audio fit the time available
- remove any unwanted sounds, words or speech errors
- put the audio into the correct order to shape the programme
- insert retakes and re-recordings.

Two distinct types of editing software are used. The first type edits a single stereo speech channel and the second mixes and balances a number of speech channels. To complicate matters further, there are different applications for PC and for Mac, although some editing software functions on both platforms ('cross-platform'). Some are more appropriate for music recording studios and some for radio studios.

The following is a list of workstation software applications, grouped by function:

Single-track editors

- Cool Edit 96
- Soundforge
- PEAK (bias)
- Audacity
- WAVLAB
- WAVPAD

Multi-track mixers

- Cakewalk (music)
- Cubase (music)
- PROTOOLS
- Audacity
- Soundstudio Gold (music)
- Audiodesk (music)

Combined systems

- Cool Edit PRO
- SaDie

A multi-track editor:

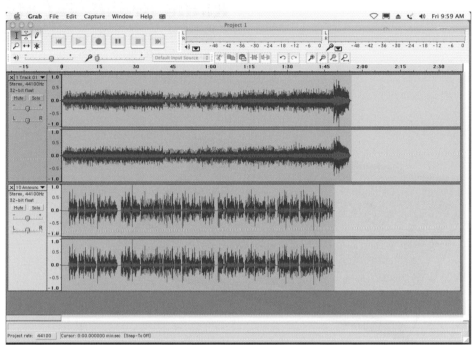

A single-track editor:

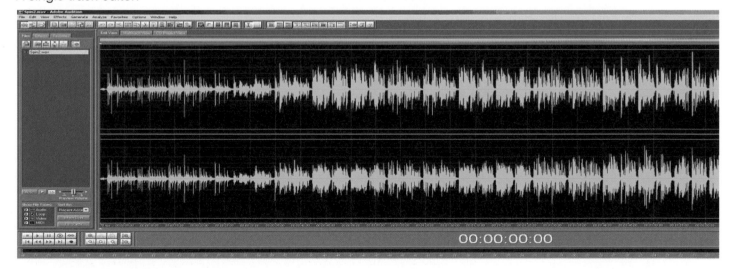

Play-out, trafficking and billing systems

In the radio industry it is necessary to control other aspects of broadcasting using a computer, and here the PC towers head and shoulders above the Mac. All UK radio stations, and most others across the world, use PC-based technology in their play-out, trafficking and billing systems. Play-out is the means by which all audio music, speech and sound is managed for broadcast by a radio station. Trafficking is the name given to the process that stores, selects and plays radio commercials on air at the time required by the client. It also sends out the accounts for billing.

Radio broadcast studios

The heart of a radio broadcast studio is the mixing console, more commonly referred to as the radio desk. For most live radio broadcasts it is 'driven' (operated) by the disc jockey or presenter of the programme.

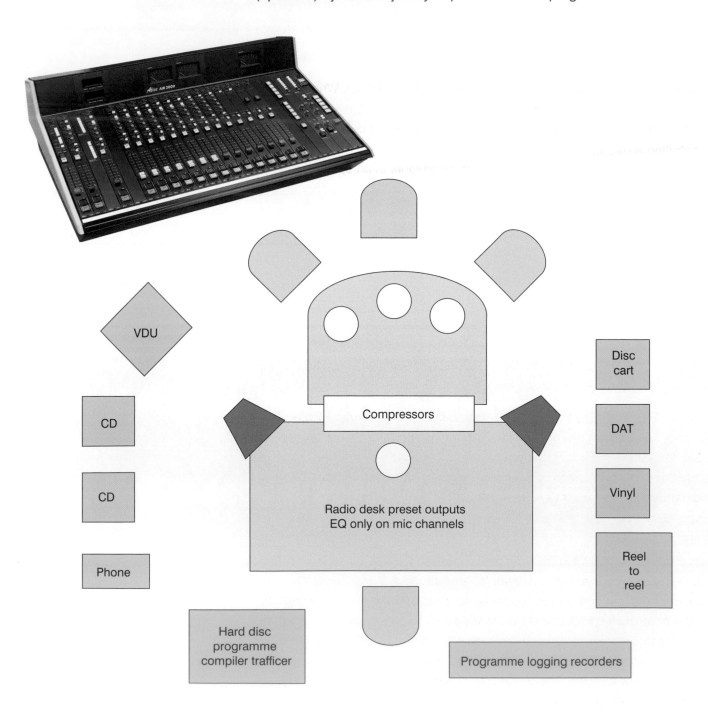

VDU

Disc cart

CD

Compressors

DAT

CD

Vinyl

Radio desk preset outputs
EQ only on mic channels

Phone

Reel to reel

Hard disc programme compiler trafficer

Programme logging recorders

Recording situations

Recorded dialogue (speech) is required for a wide variety of purposes, whether as lyrics for a music track, a voice for an audio book or an interview for a radio programme. The table below shows some locations where dialogue may be recorded for different radio applications.

Type of dialogue used in radio	Location of recording
Reading a story	Recording studio
Commentary on an event	Exterior stadium location
Narration for a documentary	Voice booth
Discussion programme	Radio broadcast studio
Debate with an audience	Theatre auditorium
News bulletin reading	Radio news studio
Interviews with the public ('vox pop')	Exterior street location
Interview with a contributor	Interior office location

Audio products can be recorded live, **as-live** or pre-recorded. When making a live broadcast there must be no mistakes and the organisation of the event must be flawless. If a live programme takes place in the controlled environment of a studio there are fewer chances for things to go wrong. A live outside broadcast, however, whether in an open air location like a stadium for a sporting event, or in an auditorium with an audience, will present many problems that need to be anticipated and overcome. Pre-recorded programmes are easier to produce because there is always a chance to retake a particular scene if it goes wrong the first time. In any professional situation, however, time is costly and so a radio producer can't afford the time and cost of things going wrong. The more controlled a location is, the easier it will be to produce the content.

Producing your audio product

Look at Chapter 4, The Production Process, so that you can follow the **production process** when you make your audio product. The headings used below are similar to those in Chapter 4, because you will need to apply the same principles and tasks to make your product. When making radio products you will always start with a brief, because you are responding to a client who wants a specific product.

Pre-production

The first task here is to think of ideas for your product. If you follow the example brief on page 82 you will make an insert or sequence for a finished programme. Many programmes are made up of a number of self-contained speech items known as **speech packages** produced by different members of the production team to a pre-defined brief, for example an interview, voiced piece or a review. The running time is pre-set and the general style and form of the programme has been decided.

Consider a programme for 9 to 14 year-olds like *Go 4 It* on BBC Radio 4. Listen to an edition of the programme to get a feel for the style and the audience that it is aimed at.

- Find someone to interview, who knows about the effect computer games have on children and can talk about it. Persuade them to give you an interview.
- Have a preliminary chat with them to find out their views on the topic. Keep notes to help you form the questions you are going to ask.
- Start to write your questions based on your notes.
- Next to each question, write the general answer that you would expect your interviewee to give, based on the opinions they gave in your pre-interview chat. This will act as your script during the interview.
- Before the interview, time how long it takes you to ask the questions so that you can make a **running order** of the whole interview package. This will ensure it lasts long enough to get a 3:00-minute final edited recording.
- Keep a record of what you did and the date and time when you did it. This will contribute to your **production diary**.
- With practice you will be able to write down in advance all the things you need to do to produce the interview. This is called a **production schedule** and you should follow it as closely as you can.
- Agree a time and date for the interview to take place.
- Make a budget sheet to show how much it would cost to complete.
- It may be appropriate to have a music track playing while the interview is being conducted, bearing in mind that speech with music accompaniment tends to hold the attention of younger listeners more than speech on its own. This must be planned in advance and found from a production music library. You should choose a suitable music track with no lyrics and it must have a running time in excess of the time required.
- Track details and 'in' and 'out' cues should be noted if the interview is going to be broadcast on radio. (Your product probably won't be broadcast, but you should follow professional practice.)

This is an example of a running order for an interview:

Description of item	Time	Total time	Number of words
Introduction to package	0 15	0 15	45
Question 1	0 10	0 25	30
Answer 1	0 15	0 40	45
Question 2	0 05	0 45	15
Answer 2	0 20	1 05	60
Question 3	0 10	1 15	30
Answer 3	0 20	1 35	60
Question 4	0 10	1 45	30
Answer 4	0 20	2 05	60
Question 5	0 10	2 15	30
Answer 5	0 20	2 35	60
Question 6	0 05	2 40	15
Answer 6	0 15	2 55	45
Conclusion and thanks	0 05	3 00	15

Production

You are now ready to conduct the interview and record it on a portable recorder.

- Check that the batteries are charged, there is sufficient disc space, the recorder works and you know how to use it.
- At the agreed time, meet your interviewee.
- Make sure you are in a quiet place to record.
- Make sure the microphone is in the correct place to record the voice of your interviewee by doing a test question and answer.
- Monitor the sound level using the **record level display** and, using headphones, monitor the sound balance between your two voices.
- Conduct the interview.
- If your voice hasn't recorded as loud as it should be, you could re-record your questions to get a better signal. You just need to ask the questions, one after the other, with a short pause between. Make sure that you do this at the same location, immediately after the interview, to maintain the same **ambient background**. Your questions can then be edited into the interview in the editing stage.
- When you have finished you can record your introduction and conclusion to the speech package.

Post-production

The next stage is to upload the recorded interview to the workstation. The example shown on the CD-Rom is a single-track edit on the free editing software Audacity.

Single-track stereo speech editing

When the audio track is in the edit screen the different parts of the interview can be edited into the correct order. Any parts that are of poor quality need to be deleted and the re-recorded questions (at the end of the interview) need to be inserted into the right places just before the answers. Don't edit the questions and answers too tightly together or they won't sound natural. There should be a slight pause between each question and response to enable the participants to breathe. You need to ensure that the questions and answers are all at the same playback levels. This can be done by highlighting any speech clips that are low, one by one, and using the **Amplify** option in the Effects dropdown menu to get the clips up to the same level as the rest of the dialogue. When all levels are similar the **waveform** will be the same height throughout.

Single-track stereo music editing

You can now import the music track to another audio track in Audacity so you have the two tracks running together on the workstation. You may need to edit the music track to fit the running time of the interview. This should be done with care, and you should try to edit to the beat of the music track so that it runs smoothly.

Mixing and balancing

When the running time is correct you are ready to mix and balance the two tracks. Use the level controls to make sure that the speech can be heard clearly above the music. Ask someone else to test this as your sample audience. There must not be too much music, but just enough to engage the listener and make the interview interesting. The overall sound level, as shown by the replay level indicators, should be close to maximum but not in the red 'Clipping' area. This may mean increasing both speech and music.

Bouncing or exporting

When you are satisfied that the interview is as good as you can get it, you should export it as a WAV file so it can be burned to disc and played. In some applications this process is called bouncing to disc. You should also save your project as an Audacity '.aup' file so you can come back to it if necessary. In any case your tutor will want to see how you arrived at the final mix.

Summary

In this chapter you have covered what you need to know to achieve three of the four Learning Outcomes relating to Unit 5 of your course. You should now:

- know about broadcast and non-broadcast audio products and audio formats

- understand audio recording and editing technology and techniques

- be able to produce an audio product

When you have finished your audio product you will need to review it to achieve the final Learning Outcome. To find out how to do this, turn to Chapter 19, Reviewing Your Work.

9 Print Production

What is print production?

The print industry covers a wide range of products. This includes conventional products like books, magazines and comics, but also the large advertisements in bus shelters and on hoardings and the packaging in which things are wrapped. The industry uses techniques that are either craft-based and require high levels of skill, or are repetitive processes that involve monitoring machines. Over the years the processes have changed, and mass printing is now done very quickly.

This chapter will give you an insight into the techniques used – both past and present – in the production of print for publication. You will also learn how to develop ideas for print products and convert those ideas into a print product.

Understanding print production techniques and technology

Over the years, printing processes have evolved from manual techniques through mechanical techniques to the digital techniques that are used today:

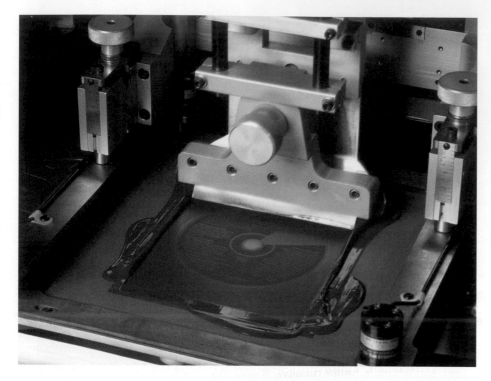

Manual techniques
- Etching
- Linocut
- Screen printing
- Woodcut
- Lithograph

Mechanical techniques
- Letterpress
- Gravure
- Screen process
- Hot metal
- Spirit duplicating
- Offset litho

Digital techniques
- Desktop publishing
- Photocopy
- Laser print
- Inkjet

Manual techniques

One of the earliest manual printing techniques involved carving or etching the image onto a master block made from a hard material to which ink was then applied by hand. The inked surface was then pressed, again by hand, onto successive pieces of paper. A range of materials have been used to make blocks, including wood, metal, linoleum and glass. Another method, using silk fabric stretched across a rectangular frame, required the use of a blocking-out medium to block up the fabric to prevent ink from passing through any parts of the silk that weren't part of the image.

Manual techniques for duplicating the same text or image usually required a high degree of practical skill from the person making the block or original plate from which the copies were to be stamped. They were not, however, expected to be able to read or write, simply to be able to carve or etch the shapes of letters or pictures accurately onto the material of which the stamp, die or block was made. A high degree of practical, rather than academic, skill was required to print using mechanical techniques. This was a time-consuming, slow and costly task. There were also many opportunities for things to go wrong if the skills of the printer were not good. Prior to the introduction of the printing press to England by William Caxton (1422–1492) books were very expensive and few people had enough money to buy them.

Mechanical techniques

There were two main mechanical printing techniques. One process took various versions of the pre-formed blocks used in the manual technique, or individual letters fixed together in rows with image blocks, and mechanised the application of ink to the blocks and the method of bringing the ink-charged blocks into contact with the paper. In the second, the silk screen process, the application of the ink to the skin (porous fabric) was mechanised, along with the application of successive sheets of paper to the ink-charged skin.

The mechanisation of the printing process meant that many more prints could be produced quickly by one operator than before. This put many people out of jobs but also drove down the cost of production, so over time books became cheaper and more readily available, meaning that more people could afford them. This led to an increase in the number of people who wanted to learn to read.

Digital techniques

Digital printing techniques were made possible by the invention of the personal computer. This allowed the writer to input the text directly, produce a page layout and transfer it all to the printer, which produced a hard copy. A variety of techniques are used to print from a computer – the most popular are the inkjet printer and the laser printer (which is better quality). Laser technology is also used in photocopies, which can produce cheaper copies than printers.

Desktop publishing software

Desktop publishing (DTP) uses **word processing**, **photo-image manipulation** and **page-assembly** software. These are distinct and different in how they function. Word processing software is used to generate the text, which is saved as '.txt' or '.rtf' files. It is usually unformatted and contains instructions to the typesetters who will assemble it using a DTP application. Any illustrations, charts, diagrams or photographs are kept separate as **JPEG** files (.jpg) and are processed using a photo-image manipulation application before they are imported into the DTP application. The DTP application allows the typesetter to arrange the text and images in an appropriate way to make the publication look good.

Some images are sourced as hard copy (paper or card) and have to be turned into electronic images by using a scanner. The electronic image is saved as a JPEG file and can be imported into a suitable image-manipulation application (e.g. Adobe Photoshop) to be cropped and retouched (modifying details) prior to being imported into an assembly application (e.g. Adobe InDesign) for laying out.

Typical computer applications used by the print industry include:

Word processing
- Microsoft Word (PC or Mac)
- Word for Works (PC)
- Claris Word (Mac)
- Corel Wordperfect (PC)
- AbiWord (Linux)
- iwork (Mac)

Image manipulation
- Adobe Photoshop (PC or Mac)
- Digital Image Suite (Mac)
- PhotoImpact (Ulead) (PC)

DTP packages
- Adobe InDesign (PC,or Mac)
- Quark Express (PC)
- Microsoft Publisher (PC)
- Print Explosion deluxe (Mac)
- Print Shop deluxe (PC)
- Scribus (free) (Mac)

Adobe Acrobat PDF files

The Internet has provided a means of distribution for electronic publications. One of the most common forms of electronic publication is the Adobe Acrobat **PDF** file. One of the problems with making publications available on the Internet is copyright theft. If the author is trying to make a living from publishing printed texts, people must pay for what they read. The PDF document file is an attempt to offer for sale on the Internet secure documents that can't be **plagiarised**. However, it is possible (but nevertheless illegal) to highlight text in a PDF file and copy it into a Word document. In doing so the text looses its formatting and any layout. The only way to manipulate a PDF file fully is to purchase, at considerable cost, a full copy of the Adobe Acrobat distiller software.

Digitisation of texts means that books can be shared electronically and the Internet is the biggest means of distribution of electronic media. This process has the advantage that costs are driven down even further, making publications more readily available than ever. There are, however, financial disadvantages for owners of the work, as copyright theft is relatively easy.

The development of digital printing techniques has meant that many skilled manual workers have found themselves without a job because they could only do the practical process, not create the original text. One of the most significant and recent examples of this was in 1986 when the newspaper industry moved from using mechanical printing techniques to producing newspapers using computers. This was brought about by Rupert Murdoch, owner of News International which publishes the *Times*, *Sunday Times*, *Sun* and *News of the World*, when he moved production of his newspapers in London from Fleet Street to Wapping, causing a major industrial incident that made many printers redundant.

Developing ideas for your printed product

Look at Chapter 4, The Production Process, so that you can follow the **production process** when you make your print product. When making print products you will always start with a brief, because you are responding to a client who wants a specific product.

Example brief

Design the front page and a double page spread of a school or college magazine. The magazine format will be A3, folded to A4, with a page count of 16 (or one page for each member of your class). You should decide what the magazine should be called, the **typeface** and font size, the title design and layout. Everyone in class could think of a title and design a front page, and you could hold a competition to choose the best one. If your front page is not chosen, you will be responsible for producing an inside double page spread, in pairs, for the finished magazine.

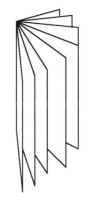

16 page magazine

Generating your ideas

This is the **initiation stage** of the production process where you have to come up with the initial ideas for the magazine. The first question to think about is 'Who is the magazine targeting?' Will it be students the same age as you, will it be older or younger students, or will it be your tutors or parents? When you have decided the target audience you can start brainstorming how the magazine will look and what content it will have in it.

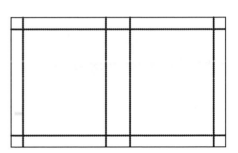

A3 Sheet layout with text boundaries
Fold 8 of these to make a 16 page magazine

- Brainstorm ideas for how it will look. This will include the layout of the front and back pages and the general layout of the inner pages. Will the title be a banner, spread across the top of the front page, or will it be in one corner? What colour will it be? How many columns will the pages contain, should pictures go across columns, what typeface and how big? To decide on these matters you should collect magazines that target the same group as your intended audience and look at them to get ideas.
- Brainstorm ideas for content. What sort of articles will your magazine contain? Make a list of topics that could be the subject of articles and a list of contributors and sources that you could consult for material. Some articles are produced as a result of conducting an interview with a contributor, or a discussion between two people with different views on a topic. Everyone in the class will write something for the magazine. It is best to plan to produce more articles than you actually need to allow the editor to make changes and fit them in the final magazine.
- Make notes about the sort of photographs you would want for each article.
- Would you want to include advertisements (which can be produced by following the advertising production unit)? If so, you will need to allow sufficient space to include them and to decide how many. The inclusion of advertisements will affect the style of the magazine, and the audience will dictate which products and services are advertised.

89.

Originating your design

Based on the information that you gathered in the brainstorming sessions, start to design your idea for a front page (A4) and your idea for a layout for the inner double page spread (A3). This will start as initial drafts with appropriate text boxes and layout guidelines, either on a workstation or using pieces cut from magazines, and pasted onto layout pages as a **mock-up**. You will need to show examples of titles, pictures and headlines for the front page and use **body type** and picture blanks for the inner pages, which you should show as a double page spread. You will write the articles when the design is agreed.

Some things you must consider

While you are designing the magazine you will have to consider a number of different factors that affect the production of a magazine commercially. The first and most significant consideration is that the content should not infringe **copyright** by publishing the work of others without their permission. Similarly, all writing and photographs must be **ethically** correct. They should not be in bad taste, for example, or **defamatory** (writing bad things about people that are not true). **Expletives** (swear words) must not be used in the text and what people say should never be **misquoted** or quoted out of context.

You should keep notes on the amount of time it takes you to work through each stage, because in the print industry people are paid for doing these jobs. If you were designing for a real commission there would be significant costs involved and you should be aware of this. What resources are you using? Computers, premises, lighting and heating all cost money and would have to be paid for. The materials that are used when the magazine is printed have to be purchased, so how much paper and how much ink for the copiers? How many copies of the magazine are you going to produce and how much are you going to sell them for? Is it going to be possible to sell advertising space in your magazine to help pay for publishing it, allowing you to keep the selling price low?

Producing your print product

Now that the design has been agreed, you are ready to produce your individual pages for the magazine, focusing your attention on writing the articles and either finding or photographing the images to accompany them. (To learn more about producing photographic images read Chapter 17.) You may be producing the magazine on a computer, or you may be doing a manual **paste-up** where you type the text, find hard copy photographic images, cut them out and stick them to a layout sheet in the order you want them to appear. This was the way it was done before computers existed.

If you decided to include advertisements, you would have agreed which pages they should appear on, so this will affect how much text and graphics you can include. Now is the time to write the text. If you are interviewing anyone, this should be done and notes taken – then you can start writing. When you have completed the articles, remembering to produce more than you need, and produced the images, you should see how they fit into the page layout. The method of production will dictate how you do this, either using the cut-and-paste technique, or by importing each graphic as an image and each article as a text file into your assembly application and arranging them on the layout page, using the text boundaries to position them.

When your page is complete you will need to get your tutor to act as the editor and to **proofread** it. After any alterations, it will be ready to join the other pages.

Other possible products

This chapter has shown you the processes involved in producing a school magazine, but there are a wide range of print products you could produce as an alternative. You could, for example, produce a magazine for a local church, your village or another school. Alternatively you could produce a newspaper for your school or another school, or for an organisation like the Guides or Scouts. Fliers, car stickers, posters, leaflets and other single-sheet publications that are not simply advertisements are good choices. Whatever you decide to produce, it should be as professional as possible.

Summary

In this chapter you have covered what you need to know to achieve three of the four Learning Outcomes relating to Unit 6 of your course. You should now:

- understand print production techniques and technology

- be able to develop ideas for printed material

- be able to produce print products.

When you have finished your print product you will need to review it to achieve the final Learning Outcome. To find out how to do this, turn to Chapter 19, Reviewing Your Work.

10 Advertising Production

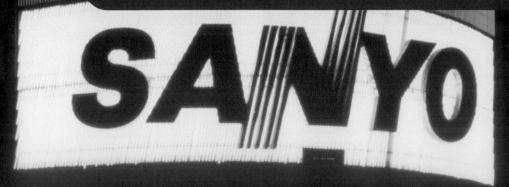

What is advertising production?

Advertising exists in some shape or form in every medium – television, film, radio, newspapers, magazines, periodicals, on the Internet, and in the street on **hoardings**, bus shelters and on public transport. It is used by the manufacturers of products and the providers of services to increase their market share and their sales. Advertising is big business, and represents a significant proportion of any company's budget.

Independent media companies generate much of their income by broadcasting or including commercial advertising in their products. The fees from the advertisers pay some or all of the costs of generating and distributing the media products. As a result, most audiences and consumers of media products only pay only a fraction of the real cost of producing them.

Constructing adverts

The **structure** of an advertisement depends on the medium in which it is used. An advertisement can consist of moving images with sound in television and cinema and on the Internet. It can have sound only on the radio, or still images only in magazines, newspapers, periodicals and hoardings.

Moving image advertisements

Moving image advertisements are mainly in colour and have sound (although there have been some notable exceptions). A moving image advertisement happens over time and will often tell a short **narrative** (story) with an introduction, development and a conclusion, like an essay. This is known as the **narrative structure** and is applicable to most media products that are time-based. Moving image advertisements also tend to have a still image or caption of the product and the logo as the final shot. Cinema advertisements tend to be similar to TV advertisements for national products, but simpler (and cheaper) for local products and services. Some Internet advertisements are moving image, for example those on the homepages of MSN and Yahoo. They are structured in the same way as TV adverts although they tend to be longer. Moving images are convincing but not permanent, so they must be creative to leave a lasting impression.

Some moving image advertisements are like a mini-series or a serial and follow an individual through a number of experiences. A very famous 'series ad' was for Nescafé and depicted a man and a woman meeting and falling in love.

Audio advertisements

Like moving image advertisements, radio adverts are time-based and they can have similar narrative structures, but on radio they can only use voices, sound effects, music and silence. Radio adverts can take advantage of the 'stereo image' that many FM and digital stations broadcast in order to get voices and sounds appearing to come from different directions. A common structure is two voices discussing a problem and then identifying the advertised product as the solution. This is often followed by a third voice giving the details of where to find the product or service. This is called the **tag line**. Many radio advertisements also have music playing in the background. In radio, any music that accompanies speech delivery is called a **music bed**.

Try this ...

Gather a range of advertisements from the media sector you are working in.

Try this ...

Gather some advertisements appropriate to your chosen media sector and identify the narrative structure.

The BBC doesn't broadcast commercial advertisements – its programme-making activities are funded by an annual licence fee from the government. But it does advertise its own programmes and its print products on its radio stations and television channels. The BBC also indirectly advertises other products when it broadcasts images of sporting events that display sponsors' logos.

Try this ...

If you are making a broadcast advert, record and time a range of radio adverts. See how close they are to multiples of ten seconds.

On TV and radio, advertising space is sold in slots that are multiples of ten seconds (the average being a 30-second advertisement) which means that all advertising production has to be very tightly structured. Advertisers want to get as much as they can into the slot they have bought.

At the beginning of a radio commercial there will usually be an upbeat musical phrase to grab the attention and at the end there will often be another pounding musical phrase or sting that is there to motivate the listener to buy the product.

Print advertisements

Print images appear in everyday reading material and, in public places, on any surface on which an advertiser can get permission to stick an advert. Print adverts are not time-based (although in comic strip advertising a story or narrative is told through a series of images, the last one carrying the product or service logo). Colour and black and white images are both commonly used, and usually a single image must tell the whole story and sell the product. The still image adverts found everywhere on the Internet are called **banner ads**. Print adverts tend to consist mostly of significant images, with few words other than the logo or a selling statement. Still images are more permanent than moving images or sound images, so they can be continual reminders, particularly on public transport and on hoardings.

See Chapter 3 for more on targeting audiences.

The **style** of an advertisement depends very much on the product or service and the target audience. There are many ways of identifying the target audience. Specialist companies gather data on lifestyles and sell their findings to manufacturers so that their products can be targeted more specifically at an identified market.

Try this ...

Gather a range of advertisements in as many different styles as possible. See if you can identify the target audience from the style, regardless of the product.

Advertisers make sure that they only place their adverts in the appropriate print products – those whose target audience might buy their particular product or service. The adverts themselves will be styled to suit the print product and its audience. If advertisers don't use the correct magazine, newspaper or website to target their users properly, or if they place an inappropriate advert, there is a chance that the consumer will be put off buying the print product itself. If that happens, both the publisher of the print product and the manufacturer of the product being advertised would lose money.

Advertising techniques: persuasion

Product information

The task of the advertising agency is to produce an advertisement that persuades people to spend their money on a product or service. This includes convincing the potential purchaser that the product is the best available, by telling them about the product's features, what it can do that other similar products can't and the benefits of buying this product rather than other products. Some products or services may have some features that other products of its type don't have. The Dyson cyclone vacuum cleaner, for example, works in a different way to conventional vacuum cleaners. This is known as a **USP** (unique selling proposition or unique selling point).

Emotional manipulation

While some products or services may be sold on their reputation (e.g. the Apple iPod) others are sold by playing on people's emotions. For example, advertising junk food during children's TV programmes (now banned) played on the emotions of children and used emotional blackmail to persuade parents to buy the products for their children. Other examples are the advertising of alcohol during football matches, the suggestion that certain foods keep you slim and the idea that some brands of makeup are going to make you look more attractive than others.

Identification with brands

Professional sporting personalities often sponsor brands, from sports clothes and watches to health drinks and holidays. Many people aspire to be like such personalities and famous people. The press constantly reports the fashions these people are wearing and the hairstyles they have, because they know that consumers will buy the newspapers and magazines and watch the TV programmes that feature them. It's big business for the fashion houses and cosmetics manufacturers to advertise that their products are used by the famous people, in the hope that consumers will buy them. If a celebrity endorses a product, for example Nike trainers, then you can be sure that many fans of the celebrity will want to purchase and wear Nike trainers, although a different product may well be better value or quality. In such cases the consumer is paying extra money for the 'famous' label.

Try this ...

Make a list of ten products that you are interested in advertising and list them by type, e.g. clothing, game, food, etc.

Try this ...

Make a list of all the product types that you believe are advertised by emotional manipulation.

Try this ...

Make a list of all the product names that you think are bought for the name rather than the product.

Try this ...

In groups of two or three, brainstorm some ideas for an advertisement. Write up your version of the results and explain the conclusions that you have reached.

Generating ideas

This is the **initiation stage** of the production process when you come up with your initial ideas for an advertisement. The type of advertisement will depend on which medium you choose, but the processes will be the same. It is usual in the advertising world for the **client** (the person or company that wants the advertisement made) to contact the advertising **agency** (the company that will plan, produce and place the advertisement), so it's not normal for someone who makes adverts for a living to choose the product or service themselves. This part of the process is called **commissioning**. Your tutor, who will represent the client, may give you some choice of which product or service you can make your ad about. You should first hold a **brainstorming** session with other members of your class. Think of all the possibilities that you can together and write them down in your own **spidergram**. It will help if you first collect as many advertisements of different styles and products as possible in the chosen medium. Radio and TV commercials can be recorded and print adverts can be cut out and collected in a portfolio. You should classify them by product and method of persuasion:

Advertisement	Persuasion technique
Nike	Celebrity endorsement
Red Bull	Peer group
McDonald's	Emotional manipulation

Client requirements

The client (your teacher) will specify some of the **parameters** – the limitations within which you must work. For print, these will be cost, size and circulation, for TV and radio it will be running time, for websites it will be the period of time the advert will run, its size and prominence on the screen. If it were a real commission, the parameters would be based on the amount the client wanted to spend and the production costs. There wouldn't be a bottomless pit of money and there would have to be compromises between potential increased sales of the product and the cost of the advertising campaign. For your advertisement, you will have to decide which is going to be the best outlet, in terms of radio, TV station, newspaper, magazine, website, location or billboard. Next you will need to decide how to target your specific audience. Advertisements can't simply be put out on every channel at all times of day and night, or printed every day in every magazine and newspaper until successful. That would be far too costly, so you have to do some audience research to find out when is the best time of day, day of the week or season of the year to screen, broadcast or publish your advertisement. For a start, you could look at how products similar to the one you are advertising are treated.

Try this ...

Imagine you own a manufacturing company and you want four of your products to be advertised. Decide what the products might be, and what different ways you would want each of them advertised. Think about how you would want each one to be represented to the consumer.

Treatment

In order to persuade the client that you can do the job, and to give them an idea of how you will do it, you need to produce a **treatment**. The form that the treatment will take will vary according to the medium in which you are working:

Medium	Treatment
Television	Storyboard
Cinema	Storyboard
Radio	Script
Print	Visualisation
Website	Moodboard

The treatment will show the **content** and **style** of the advertisement and will usually be visual, except in the case of radio when it will be a script with technical directions included.

The marketing **strategy** and the **budget** for a project are part of the overall advertising campaign, and will need to be decided as part of the brief. If the advertising is for a nationally known product (like a Ford car), it may be that a 'bi-media' or 'tri-media' campaign is appropriate, with advertisements running on radio, television and in the newspapers at the same time. On the other hand, if it is for a local car sales company, a single radio ad or a run in the local paper could be most effective at reaching the target audience. Research should always be done to establish the most appropriate medium for your advert.

Regulations and codes of practice

Advertising is tightly regulated by the **ASA** (Advertising Standards Authority) and there are codes of practice that all advertisers must follow. For example, an advertisement must be in good taste, and it must not claim that the product or service can do things that it can't. It also can't say that competing products or services are worse. For example, while McDonald's could claim that they probably make the best burgers in the world, they couldn't be defamatory and claim that Burger King's burgers were worse. On the other hand, a mobile phone company can claim in its adverts that its text prices are cheaper than another named company's, if they are actually cheaper. The broadcasting industry has it's own regulatory body called **Ofcom**, which publishes its own codes of practice about when and how products and services can be advertised in broadcasts. It is Ofcom that banned the advertising of junk food during children's TV programmes.

Try this ...

Create a treatment for your advertisement, based on one of the examples of treatments on the CD-Rom.

See Chapter 5, Production Project for more on producing a treatment.

Try this ...

Visit the ASA website and find their code of advertising practice for the product type that you intend to advertise and the medium that you intend to use. Make notes on the restrictions and limitations that apply.

Try this ...

If you are making a radio or TV commercial, visit the Ofcom website and find the relevant codes of practice. Make notes about the restrictions and limitations on what and when you can broadcast.

Pre-production

It is now time to make the advertisement. Refer to the production process section for further details on how to complete the production process. The nature of the pre-production stage will depend on the medium. You will need to plan any content acquisition, get locations permission, find the contributors (who may be classmates), make a production schedule and produce all the appropriate documentation.

Tasks for completion during pre-production stage include:

Moving image	Audio	Print	Interactive media
• Prepare schedule and shooting script	• Prepare schedule and recording log	• Prepare schedule	• Prepare schedule
• Draw storyboard	• Write scripts	• Produce first draft	• Draw mood boards
• Draw ground plans	• Confirm voice actors	• Draw mood boards	• Design graphics
• Write scripts	vClear music	• Prepare visuals	• Agree colour scheme
• Confirm talent	• Clear sound effects	• Agree layout sheets	
• Agree crew list	• Agree crew list	• Produce overlays	
• Get permissions			
• Clear music			
• Prepare stills			

Content acquisition

This is when the content of the advertisement is gathered. Look at Chapter 4, The Production Process, for more detailed information on how to do this. In advertising it is often a good idea to gather material to provide variations on the style and alternative storylines to present to the client. This makes the whole project easier (and cheaper) because it avoids the need to go through the content acquisition process again if the client wants something that is different to the idea originally agreed.

Tasks for completion during the content acquisition stage include:

Moving image	Audio	Print	Interactive media
• Shoot footage	• Record dialogue	• Produce final graphics	• Produce graphics
• Log footage	• Review takes	• Write copy	• Write content
• Review takes	• Select final music and FX	• Agree final layouts	• Acquire images
• Mark good takes			

Post-production

The content has been gathered and it is time to edit it together into a final advertisement. If there is enough material, a range of options can be tried and presented to the client for final approval.

Tasks for completion during post-production include:

Moving image	Audio	Print	Interactive media
• Batch capture clips • Colour match clips • Prepare paper edit • Decision list • Edit images • Make final changes • Add post-production audio • Complete fine edit	• Prepare edit list • Adjust levels • Mix and balance sounds • Make final changes • Adjust final levels	• Typeset images and text • Proofread • Review	• Add graphics • Add text • Add images • Test navigation

The completion stage should now be carried out as stated in Chapter 4, The Production Process so that the product can be distributed.

Summary

In this chapter you have covered what you need to know to achieve three of the four Learning Outcomes relating to Unit 7 of your course. You should now:

- understanding advertising techniques

- be able to develop ideas for an advertisement

- be able to create an advertisement.

When you have finished your advertising product you will need to review it to achieve the final Learning Outcome. To find out how to do this, turn to Chapter 19, Reviewing Your Work.

11 Interactive Media Production

What is interactive media production?

Interactive media products are websites, CD-Roms or DVD-Roms that allow people to interact with the data they contain. They include websites that you use to order goods or services online. Many companies that previously used paper catalogues to distribute their product information to the public have now set up interactive websites. These not only display all the information, but also allow customers to order the products direct. Other forms of interactive media include games CD-Roms, played for enjoyment, or educational CD-Roms, used to widen your knowledge.

Producing interactive media requires the use of specialist authoring software. Interactive media products function on different computer platforms, on mobile phones and on personal assistants with varying technology specifications.

Understanding interactive media production technology and techniques

Hardware

Computers are not all the same: some are more powerful than others, and the way an interactive media programme responds will depend on the end user's computer. There are three major platforms (types of computer) in general use – the PC (personal computer) popularised by IBM; the Mac (Macintosh) developed by Apple; and the UNIX, developed as a free platform by a group of individuals to make computers freely available without serious cost implications.

At the heart of a typical computer is the **CPU** (central processing unit). It is the speed of this device that dictates how fast your computer can process data. The size of the **RAM** (random access memory) determines how much data your computer can work with at any time.

This table explains the function of the most common hardware found in all computers.

Try this …

Find out what hardware there is in the workstation that you normally use. On a PC, this can be found in the 'Add/remove hardware' menu within the control panel. On a Mac, it can be found in the 'About this Mac' dialog box. Also find the CPU speed, the amount of memory, and the size of the hard drive. Make notes so that you can compare the specification with your classmates.

Device	Function
CPU (central processing unit) Speed measured in GHz (gigahertz)	Governs processing speed of computer. Doesn't hold any data when not powered up.
RAM (random access memory) Capacity measured in Mb (megabytes)	Controls the amount of data that can be processed. Doesn't hold data when not powered up.
HDD (hard disc drive) storage capacity measured in Gb (gigabytes)	Magnetic disc to which all programmes and data are written and saved.
Virtual memory	Part of hard drive used to operate as RAM.
VDU (video display unit), also known as the monitor	Shows the content of the computer on a screen so that it can be read.
GUI (graphical user interface)	The operating system that makes the computer understandable to users.
Graphics card	Interface used to allow the computer to connect to a VDU.
Peripheral devices	External components that are plugged into the main computer (printer, scanner, digital camera, webcam, microphone, video camera, etc.)
CD-Rom (or DVD-Rom) drive	Device that allows the computer to read compact (or digital versatile) discs.
CD-RW (or DVD-RW) drive	Device that allows the computer to read and write compact (or digital versatile) discs.
Floppy disc drive	Device that allows the computer to read and write floppy discs.

Software

Computers can't work without software, also known as programs or applications. Programs are classified by type, according to their generic function, as shown in the table below:

Program/software/application	Function
Word for Windows	Word processing
Access (Windows)	Database
Excel (Windows)	Spreadsheet
PowerPoint (Windows)	Presentation tool
Photoshop (Adobe)	Digital graphics editor
Audition (Adobe)	Audio editing and mixing
Final Cut Studio (Mac)	Video editing tool
Dreamweaver (Adobe)	HTML editor with visual and code support
Flash (Adobe)	Animation tool for rich web content
Shockwave (Adobe)	Media player for Director
Director (Adobe)	HTML authoring tool
Fireworks (Adobe)	Graphics editor
Freehand (Adobe)	Multimedia web authoring tool
FrontPage (Microsoft)	Web page creation tool

Note the spelling of the word 'program' for computer software. This is different to the word 'programme' used for media products in radio and TV.

Try this ...

List all the software on the workstation that you normally use. On a PC, this can be found in the 'Add/remove programs' menu of the control panel. On a Mac, it's in the 'Applications' folder, found by clicking on the hard disc icon. List the software that can be used for making websites and assembling content for websites. Compare your list with those of your classmates.

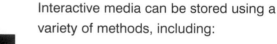

Storage and access

Interactive media can be stored using a variety of methods, including:

* remote Internet server
* local intranet server
* local hard disc drive
* CD-Rom
* DVD

They can be accessed by a variety of **end user devices** (workstations) including:

* Interactive television
* PC
* Mac
* mobile phone (limited)
* laptop
* PDA (personal digital assistant).

Distribution of content

The way an end user accesses the interactive content of a website will depend on what type of device they have and the location and method of storage of the content data. There are a number of options for distributing interactive content, for example:

- dial-up narrow band (slow)
- broadband (at least 10 x dial-up speed)
- satellite link (5 x dial-up speed)
- WiFi wireless (3 x dial-up speed)
- bluetooth (short distance).

Limitations of interactive content

A whole range of factors – which might limit the end user's experience – have to be taken into account when designing interactive media. These are:

- the size of the files that make up the interactive content
- the form in which they are stored
- their location relative to the **point of use**
- the speed of the connection between files and the end user's device
- the reliability of the software used to access the interactive content
- the specification of the end user's device.

The following specification details of the end user interface must be considered when designing interactive media:

- display resolution
- quality of graphics card
- screen size
- Internet connection speed
- CPU speed
- amount of RAM.

You will find a list of specification requirements like this in the material accompanying most CD-Roms:

Hardware requirements: PC
- Operating system: Windows 95(OS R2), 98, ME, 2000, NT, XP or Vista
- Pentium 400 (IBM Compatible PC) or equivalent PC
- 128MB of RAM or higher
- 16 bit graphics card
- CD-ROM drive (minimum 16 speed recommended)
- SVGA colour monitor and 1024/768 resolution
- Sound card
- At least 100MB free hard disk space

Hardware requirements: Mac
- Operating system: X 10.1.5 or higher
- 500MHz G4 processor
- 256MB of RAM or higher
- 450MB of free hard disk space
- 16 speed CD-ROM drive
- 16 bit colour monitor set at 1024/768 600 resolution

Try this ...

Check the resolution of the display on your workstation. On a PC you will find the display information in the control panel, and on a Mac it will be in 'System preferences'. Check the Internet connection speed of your workstation.

Ideally, the file size will be small, files will be downloadable to a local drive, the speed of the connection will be fast, the software will be reliable and the end user device will be high specification. However, this is not always the case.

When designing interactive media products, follow these five basic rules:
1. Don't design a product that will be out of the reach of a large consumer market – by, for example, creating product that only runs on specialist hardware.
2. Work in the most compatible software environment.
3. Assume an end user device with basic specification in terms of: platform (PC, Mac or Linux), screen size and resolution, processor capability, memory and software.
4. If large files are necessary, distribute them to the end user to enable them to be accessed on a local drive.
5. Use a small file application.

Developing your ideas for interactive media products

Ideas development

This is the **initiation stage** of the production process (as described in Chapter 4, The Production Process) when you will have to come up with initial ideas for an interactive media product. The type of interactive product will vary, but the processes will be the same.

There is a wide range of interactive media products available. Some are simply interactive, electronic web-based versions of a product that was available previously in a non-electronic or non-interactive form. This is where it helps to have a broad grasp of the sort of conventional products that can be converted to interactive products. Start with a **brainstorming** session with other members of your class. Think of all the possibilities that you can and write them down in your own **spidergram**. You should make notes of all decisions and discussions.

When you plan an interactive media product you need to map out the different screens, and the links that the user will need to move between them. This is called a **navigation chart**.

Try this ...

Work in pairs to brainstorm some ideas for interactive websites. Pick the two best ideas and find examples of them on the Internet.

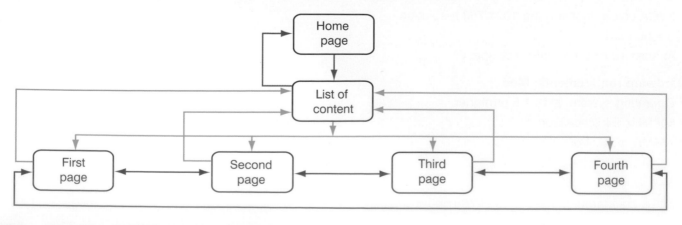

Functions of interactive media products

As part of your **secondary research** you should investigate several examples of interactive media, serving as many different functions as possible. Examples of common interactive media products include:

- electronic photograph album
- electronic presentation
- interactive training
- interactive tutorials
- multimedia encyclopaedia
- electronic publishing
- multimedia documents
- electronic product catalogue.

> **Try this ...**
>
> Find two website examples of each of the interactive media products in this list and make notes on what you find.

Producing your interactive media product

Format

The two main formats are websites and removable media such as CD-Rom and DVD-Rom. The format of your product will depend on what the client wants it to do. A catalogue with continually updated prices and an online order facility will need to be web-based, and its design and construction will be dictated by needing a small file size, which will be easy to use by a customer with a low specification computer. An interactive learning game for primary school children, which uses large files of colourful images but won't need updating, can be produced on a CD-Rom and distributed to the schools by post.

Development

From your initial discussions with your client (tutor) who will provide the **brief** (what the product must do) you will need to decide on the format (website or CD-Rom) and the detailed specification of the interactive product. Technical details such as file size, image quality, speed of interaction and minimum workstation specification must be agreed. Then the initial designs for the product can be created using **mood boards** (storyboards to show how action develops in images), layout and navigation charts to show how the product is structured, and you need to consider whether your interactive product will contain any audio such as speech or music. This should be pitched to your client in the form of a proposal, and then the timescale for the production process must be agreed.

> **Try this ...**
>
> A client wants you to design an interactive album to show their photographs. Sketch a navigation chart of the pages that would be needed, showing how they will be accessed. Use the example of a navigation chart on page 104 as a guide.

Producing or importing assets

When all the planning is complete, you can gather the **assets** (content) for the product by creating them yourself or by finding them from other sources. The table on page 106 shows the sort of content you are likely to need.

Content type	Source
Digital still images images	Scanned hard
	Digital camera
	Mobile phone
Digital video	Webcam
	Video camera
	Mobile phone
Sound	Recorded
	WAV (PC audio file)
	AIF (Mac audio file)
	CD (CDDA)
Text	Word document
	OCR scan
Graphics	Bitmaps
	TIFFs
Animation	Self-created

Production

Look at Chapter 4, The Production Process, so that you can follow the **production process** to produce and assemble your product it in its final form. The stages you must follow include designing and making the interactive media product. You will need to consider style, screen specifications, interaction, navigation and controls, typography, graphics, layout, colour, sound, video and the use of animation.

Summary

In this chapter you have covered what you need to know to achieve three of the four Learning Outcomes relating to Unit 8 of your course. You should now:

- understand interactive media production technology and techniques

- be able to develop ideas for the production of an interactive media product

- be able to produce an interactive media product.

When you have finished your interactive media product you will need to review it to achieve the final Learning Outcome. To find out how to do this, turn to Chapter 19, Reviewing Your Work.

Try this ...

From the websites that you have visited, select three that you consider to be the most attractive and easy to navigate. Rate each website for interactivity, ease of navigation, ease of reading, quality of graphics, layout and use of colour, sound and animation.

12 Web Authoring

What is web authoring?

Web authoring is the name given to the process of producing material to put on a website. This may be text or images, converted to a file format that can be read by a web browser. A web browser is a programme that allows you to view files from the web on a computer or other digital device.

Many companies, both large and small, now have a website. It is a good way of demonstrating (and selling) the goods or the services they offer. You can purchase music using a music website, review the work of a new band or listen to samples of their music. You can have your own website that tells people all about you.

This chapter will help you plan and produce your own website, using software and making decisions about style and content.

The tools for web authoring

The world wide web

Try this ...

Find a range of examples of website home pages – from sales, marketing, schools or colleges, music and information sites – and download them as images. Print these out and make them into a poster. Annotate the poster with details of what each site is, its domain name and a copy of the link.

The Internet is an international network made up of host computers, linked together using digital technology. Information can be requested and passed between these networks. The world wide web contains this information, and is a collection of pages, designed using computer languages such as HTML. The Internet grew out of a US Government-backed project to connect government and academic research institutions.

The Internet is an extremely important tool in business today. Websites are often the main method of communication for business and organisations who want to present their message or product to the public. Currently, around 90% of people in the UK are able to access broadband technology.

An Internet Service Provider (ISP) is a business or organisation that provides access for consumers to the Internet. In the past this was the role of telephone service providers but now there are hundreds of companies offering this service.

Tiscali is one example of an ISP. You can see below that they provide a wide range of services. ISPs can arrange for the registration of a domain name (the name of your own site) and can host your site.

tiscali.broadband

Join online today or call free **0800 107 9000**

- **home**
- **broadband**
  - broadband benefits
  - tv benefits
  - product comparison
  - member rewards
  - business broadband
  - max extra
- **our services**
  - our phone rates
  - installation advice
  - order tracker
  - broadband help
  - broadband faqs
  - ts & cs
  - code of practice
  - fair usage policy
- **other products**
  - dial up products
  - pc security
  - cheap phone calls
  - broadband shop

Welcome to Tiscali

Unlimited Broadband

Up to 2Mb Broadband
£14.99 per month
Join Now!

Up to 8Mb Broadband MAX
£17.99 per month
Join Now!

Unlimited Broadband and Talk

Free weekend calls and up to 1Mb Broadband
£9.99 per month for the first 3 months, £12.99 thereafter
Join Now!

Free anytime calls and up to 8Mb Broadband
Special offer
£17.99 per month
Join Now!

Product Comparison

Tiscali Talk voted No. 1 for home phone customer satisfaction

Great reasons to join

- **FREE** modem and connection
- **FREE** email anti-spam and anti-virus
- 24/7 dedicated customer support
- Always-on connection
- Keeps your phone line free
- Award-winning portal

Tiscali Customers
Change package

Web authoring software and HTML

You will need to use software applications in order to produce your website. You may know how to write your own HTML script for the site, but it will probably be time-consuming. There are a range of software applications available for web authoring including, for example, Adobe Dreamweaver CS3 and Microsoft Frontpage.

HTML is short for Hyper Text Markup Language. Hypertext is ordinary text that has added information such as images, formatting, multimedia and links to other documents. Markup involves taking ordinary text and adding extra command symbols. Each of these symbols is a command to the browser on how to display the text.

HTML is written in the form of labels (known as tags), surrounded by less-than (<) and greater-than signs (>). It resembles old-fashioned typesetting codes, where a block of text is surrounded by codes that indicate how it should appear. HTML allows text to be 'linked' to another file on the Internet.

Developing a plan for your website

You will need to plan carefully when developing a website. You must start by identifying the purpose of the proposed site. Will the website:

- sell a product?
- promote a service?
- provide information?

You must consider the audience for your website. Will it be aimed at:

- businesses?
- young people?
- older people?
- fans or followers?

Whatever the audience, you must make sure that your website will meet their needs. It would not be sensible to develop a website that has an introductory section with rap music when the site is aimed at young children. Equally, a site that has lots of images of furry animals would not be appropriate for heavy metal fans.

Try this ...

Think of an idea for a website. It might be a site that is just about you, a site that gives people information, one that helps a charity or one that promotes your own band. Think about the people who might look at your website. Will it provide them with useful information? Will it make them want to support a charity or encourage them to buy the latest CD? Make a list of all the features you would want to include on the site.

Legal and ethical issues

There are several legal and ethical considerations you will need to take into account when developing your ideas:

- Privacy: Will your website infringe anyone's right to privacy?
- Defamation: What you say about someone on your website could damage their reputation, and you could be sued.
- Libel law: What you write about someone could lead to serious implications for your reputation – and for your income.
- Race discrimination law: You need to be careful when representing people and groups on your website.
- Data protection: If you store information about the people who view your website you would have to register with the Data Commissioner's Office.
- Copyright: You must not assume that you can simply use material on your website without permission from the copyright owner.

You must consider whether your website would be appropriate for any age. Websites can be accessed by anyone (unless you can protect the site with a password). This means you must ensure that offensive material is not easily accessible by children.

Creating a structure

Think about how your website will be structured and how it will function. An important part of any website is the 'home' page – the first page that the viewer sees when they access your site. It should be colourful and exciting, making the viewer want to explore your site further. You should consider:

- Navigation: how will the viewer be able to move between all the different pages of content?
- Page layout: do all the pages on your site have the same design, colour, background and headings?

Try this ...

Consider whether all the features that you would like on your site would be appropriate for your intended audience. Are there any legal or ethical issues you would have to consider? Would there be any violent images that might affect young people? Have you used someone else's work? Is the music fit for the audience or will it put them off?

You should produce a **schematic** diagram to help you to think about how the website might work. Here is an example of a web schematic:

Try this ...

Think about how you will include all the features you considered earlier, and draw a web schematic for your website. What navigation issues will you need to consider? How can you make sure the viewer can find the information they are looking for?

Home Page

Contents Page

Page 1

Page 2

Page 3

Page 4

End Page

Producing content

What kind of content will you put on your website? It could be text you've written yourself, but for variety it is usually preferable to include some imported content (from other sources):

- Text: you may find really interesting text that would be useful for your site in other publications, but be aware of the font support needed to display it.
- Images: these could be your own photographs or drawings. They might need to be manipulated in order to fit on your web pages.
- Animation: you could produce an animated sequence, possibly on your home page, using Adobe Flash technology. It's also possible to 'create' an animation by combining multiple GIF images in one file. The result is multiple images, displayed one after another, which give the appearance of movement.
- Video: you may be able to include some video footage in a small window, but you will need to have the video material in an appropriate file format.
- Sounds: you could add a sound effect that plays when the viewer moves between pages.
- Music: this could be incorporated into the home page, or it could be playing as the viewer moves through the site. It will need to be in an appropriate file format.

You must remember that it is not appropriate to simply use someone else's copyright material on your website. Your site could be shut down if you infringe someone else's copyright. If you want to use copyright material you must obtain permission to do so. Or you could always produce your own material.

Producing your website using web authoring software

File types

There are a variety of file types you could use when developing your website, including:

- HTML (Hypertext Markup Language), which is used for creating web pages, is the authoring software language used on the world wide web.
- JPEG (Joint Photographic Experts Group) is a common image format. Art and photographic pictures are usually encoded as JPEG files.
- GIF (Graphic Interchange Format) is another image format type generated specifically for computer use. Its resolution is usually very low, making it unusable for printing purposes.
- Wav is a digitised sound file format for Microsoft Windows, which has '.wav' as the file name extension. It was developed jointly by Microsoft and IBM as the standard format for sound on PCs.

Page structure and layout

Each page you produce will have a 'header' – the part of the page that identifies to the viewer where they are and what the page is all about. Pages will also have a body containing the bulk of the information. If you were producing a website for a band, for example, the pages might have a header that identifies that this is the band's site and the body text might give information about where the band's next gigs are.

A metatag is an HTML code line that identifies the contents of the web page to search engine indexes, such as Google. This means that the search engine will be able to locate key phrases from your website. In order to increase the number of visitors to the site you should carefully decide what metatags to use. However, the use of these tags is dying out in this fast developing industry. These days, you may simply describe the purpose of your site in the first few lines of your home page. When you register with a search engine it will look at your site and produce a description based on what you say in the first few lines.

You should think carefully about the layout of your pages:

- Background: you might choose to use the same background layout for all your pages. This would give your website a uniform feeling.
- Repeated content: you could have the same basic information on each page to identify it as part of your site. This might include your name, company name, logo and copyright information.
- Template: you might choose to use a design that has been produced by someone else. These templates are made so that you can add your own content to them.
- Style sheet: you can define a consistent look for all your pages by using a style sheet.

Content: what will you put on your website?

Tables

Tables on the site are designed to provide information to the viewer in a way that is easy for them to see. Here is an example of a basic table:

Line one, column one	Line one, column two	Line one, column three
Line two, column one	Line two, column two	Line two, column three
Line three, column one	Line three, column two	Line three, column three

Text

It is important that the font you choose is appropriate for the site. If it is too small then it may not be easily read. If the font is too intricate it may also pose problems for the viewer. The text needs to be carefully aligned to fit with images you may want to place on the page.

You may want to emphasise some key words in bold type or in a different colour. You must be careful to avoid overcrowding of text on a page. A viewer will not want to plough through lots of text to find the information they are looking for.

Images

You will need to use appropriate software to ensure that the resolution of your images is suitable for your website. You will also need to ensure that the image is the right size for the page. Will the image fit with the text you have prepared and is it more appropriate in a **landscape** (horizontal) or **portrait** (vertical) format?

Hyperlinks

Hyperlinks 'link' specific words of the text on one page of a website to other documents. Users can quickly navigate from one related document to another, simply by clicking on the hyperlink. You could link your home page to an image from another site, or you could use a hyperlink to explain in more detail what a word or phrase used in your text means.

Summary

In this chapter you have covered what you need to know to achieve three of the four Learning Outcomes relating to Unit 12 of your course. You should now:

- know about web authoring
- be able to develop a plan for a website
- be able to use web authoring software to produce a website.

When you have finished your website you will need to review it to achieve the final Learning Outcome. To find out how to do this, turn to Chapter 19, Reviewing Your Work.

Try this ...

Design a simple website that is easy to access, and make sure that all the pages, features and links work. You can work on the idea that you developed earlier in this chapter. You will need to consider all the points discussed in this chapter.

13 Reviewing Computer Games

Introducing computer games

You may have played many computer games, but have you ever thought about how they were made? This chapter looks at the history of computer games and then shows you how to analyse them and how to write a review about one.

You will explore the elements that make up a game and analyse why they work for different audiences. You will learn to comment on the style, content and 'playability' of a game. Your analysis of computer games will help you to think about how you might produce your own computer games.

The history of computer games

It is often claimed that that computer games were born in 1962, when a game called *Spacewars!* was developed. This involved two rocket ships travelling round a screen and firing torpedoes to kill their opponents. In fact, a simple game of tennis had been developed four years earlier, but was not widely known about because it was only ever used to entertain people on an annual visitors' day.

From this unpromising start the first video arcade game, called *Pong*, was launched in 1972. This was a success and the company that developed it, Atari, sold many thousands of machines.

The golden age of arcade machines started in 1978, with the release of *Space Invaders*. This spawned a whole raft of manufacturers producing arcade games. This then led to the development of hand-held games and ultimately to the development of complex games that could be played on a computer at home.

Try this ...

Use a search engine to find appropriate websites with more information on the history of computer games. Google's video search function is a good place to start.

The first games were launched in the 1960s and by the 1970s there was a recognised 'games industry' with video arcades and home entertainment consoles. Home computing exploded in the 1980s and brought a period of huge expansion and creative innovation. Games became an established industry, and moved away from the companies where just two or three talented, devoted and creative 'mavericks' were responsible for every aspect of a project.

Developing top-of-the-range computer games now involves large teams of people in national and international organisations, and costs millions of pounds. It begins with widespread market research and development. Teams of people then work to produce design documents that state all the elements that make up the final game, all the possible paths the players can take, and the mechanics of the actual 'gameplay'. If the game has narrative (story) elements, then scripting and storyboarding also take place.

Gaming is now a mainstream leisure activity in the UK. The average age of gamers is in the mid-20s, and it is estimated that over half of all males and a quarter of all females play games regularly. As with other entertainment forms, there are games aimed at consumers of different ages, from the very young to the over-18 market.

The development of technology

Processor technology

The Apple II was the first true 'personal computer'. It was factory-built, inexpensive and easy to learn and use. The mid-1970s Atari models 400 and 800 were considered the best personal computers for games and colour graphics. The Commodore 64 is the best-selling personal computer of all time.

In 1993, Intel brought the PC to a new level with the Pentium processor. Once the first Pentium processor technology became out-dated, the Pentium 2 was introduced. The Celeron processor was introduced by Intel in 1998, and soon after, the Pentium 3 processor, which ran at 450 MHz, replaced the Pentium 2. Both Celeron and the Pentium 3 processors are still in production today.

Try this ...

Make a timeline of processor technology. Use some illustrations of computers and games consoles on the timeline to illustrate how processors have developed.

Display technology

A computer display monitor is a piece of electrical equipment which displays images generated by a computer.

Traditionally, monitors used cathode ray technology to produce an image on the screen. The latest technology uses TFT-LCD (Thin-Film Transistor Liquid Crystal Display) screens which can vary in size from just a few centimetres to cinema screen size.

These days, plasma screens are also available. They use a mixture of gases in a thin sandwich of glass to produce high-quality images. Plasma technology, however, is generally only used for the larger screens that are popular for home entertainment, rather than for computer monitors.
You can, of course, use any of these monitors to view computer games, and technology allows the majority of playing systems to be viewed on any type of monitor.

Data storage technology

1940s:	Data was mostly stored on punched cards and punched paper tape. These punched cards and tape are the distant relatives of the modern CD and DVD disks, which use small punched pits to store information.
Late 1940s:	The first magnetic memory was introduced in the form of an array of magnetic cores, with each core storing one 'bit' of data – the smallest unit of data storage. This memory was reliable and fast, but unfortunately the data was erased every time it was read, requiring an immediate rewrite.
1961:	The first hard disk drive with the air-bearing slider was introduced, advancing hard disk drive technology towards much higher recording densities and reliability.
1962:	The laser diode was invented and became the fundamental technology for read–write optical storage devices.
1967:	The next major achievement was digital audio, demonstrated by NHK (Japan Broadcasting Corporation). The medium used was a 1-inch tape for a helical-scan video tape recorder (VTR). The encoding used for recording was called PCM (Pulse Code Modulation). This first digital sound system is a close relative of the modern computer magnetic tape, the floppy disk and the hard disk drive.
1970:	Portable storage was born with the invention of the floppy disk.
1977:	Three Japanese companies, Sony, Mitsubishi and Hitachi, demonstrated their optical digital audio disk (DAD) systems which used a large disk, about 30 cm in diameter (like LP records).
1982:	SCSI (Small Computer System Interface, pronounced 'scuzzy') was produced. It is a high performance parallel peripheral interface that can independently distribute data among peripherals attached to the PC.
1995:	The first commercial products using Firewire technology were Sony's DCR-VX700 and DCR-VX1000 digital video camcorders.
1998:	The first DVD-ROM drives became available for computer users.
1998:	IBM demonstrated the ability to write 100 GB of data on a single LTO (linear tape open) tape cartridge, the highest tape cartridge capacity in the industry at the time.
2000:	IBM introduced the 1GB microdrive, which was smaller than a matchbook and weighed only 16 grams.
2000:	The first ATA-100 hard disk drive was announced by the Quantum Corporation.

The computer game industry

Games publishers

Video games publishers are companies that publish games developed internally in the company or externally by other companies. Just as in the print publishing world, games publishers will have links with the distribution chain to get the games into people's hands. Eidos and Frontier are examples of games publishers. You will see on this page and the next that both of these companies are also developers. This is quite commonplace in this industry.

Games developers

The following case studies will help you understand what games developers are and what they do.

Eidos

Based in Wimbledon, South London, Eidos Interactive Ltd, part of SCi Entertainment Group Plc (SEG), is one of the world's leading developers of entertainment software. Eidos consists of publishing operations across Europe and the US and several development studios, including Crystal Dynamics, IO Interactive and Pivotal Games, as well as valuable stakes in other studios.

The UK's two largest video games publishers, SCi Games (founded by Jane Cavanagh in 1988) and Eidos Interactive, merged in 2005, resulting in a combined group with a valuable portfolio of intellectual property and a global distribution network.

Frontier

Frontier, based in Cambridge, employs over 100 people and is one of the games industry's leading independent developers, having built upon the innovative creations of founder David Braben, co-author of *Elite* – the 3D game (1984).

Frontier works with a number of top publishers and is currently developing for all major platforms including PlayStation 2, PlayStation Portable (PSP), Xbox, Windows PC, Nintendo Wii, Xbox 360 and PlayStation 3.

Frontier has a proven reputation for original game design and commercial success. It received three BAFTA nominations and several awards for its recent console games *Dog's Life* and *Wallace & Gromit* in Project Zoo and scored a Christmas 2004 No.1 position in the USA with its *RollerCoaster Tycoon 3* PC game.

Frontier holds the publishing rights for Aardman Animations' *Wallace & Gromit* characters on mobile phones. Frontier's game of the Oscar-winning *Wallace & Gromit: Curse of the Were-rabbit* was published by Konami in 2005.

Frontier's development path includes both industry-standard and state-of-the-art in-house tools and technology. This allows the company to deliver industry-leading gameplay innovations, as well as true platform independence.

Try this ...

Make a list of all the games developers you can find. Next to each developer, list the games they have produced.

Games industry associations

Games industry associations represent the interests of games developers and publishers and act as a link to the regulators. They have a committee of members from a representative sample of their member companies, and can speak for all their members when issues arise, for example, the suitability of a game for a particular audience.

TIGA

Tiga is the trade association representing the business and commercial interests of over 150 games developers in the UK and the rest of Europe. It represents the interests of its members by lobbying government bodies and the European Parliament to help create a successful business environment for its members, the majority of whom are independent development companies.

ELSPA

The Entertainment & Leisure Software Publishers Association was founded in 1989 to establish a specific and collective identity for the British computer and video game industry. ELSPA works to protect, promote and provide for the interests of all its members, as well as addressing issues that affect the industry as a whole through:

• industry promotion
• sales charts and reports
• conferences and seminars
• anti-piracy enforcement
• reviewing proposed legislation
• content ratings
• research reports
• careers promotion.

Understanding the elements of computer games

Gameplay

Gameplay is a term used to describe the overall experience of playing the game. This includes all the interaction with the game systems, but may not include the graphics, sound or narrative. Many people think that gameplay is the most important consideration when reviewing a game. The reviewer will give points for gameplay as well as for the quality of the graphics, the soundtrack and the narrative.

Gameplay rules

Gameplay rules are the 'make believe' rules that are put in place to make the world of gameplay work. This includes rules like the ability to make the game harder or easier to play. Rules can determine the choice of game to be played or the handicaps that are included.

In modern games, there is a built-in ability to adapt the game and the gameplaying experience. This might involve building your own track or buildings, choosing to make new objects or changing the game environment.

Recognising game genres

Like all other media forms, computer games can be divided into genres. These can depend on the way in which a game is played, the content of the story involved in the game or the requirements of the player in the game. As the game industry is still relatively young, new genres are being developed all the time. The genres listed below give a basic guide to some of the main ones that exist, but it is not an exhaustive list as new genres are appearing on the market all the time.

Action games

These are like action films, and use weapons, vehicles and physical violence. The games tend to be built around creating tension and can feature a wide range of themes, stories and game styles. This genre is usually mixed with elements of other genres, such as adventure or stealth.

Adventure games

Adventure games are mainly based on exploration – following a path towards a story-led goal. Though they are often crossed with elements of other genres, 'pure' adventure games usually leave the player to discover elements of a story themselves, by investigating a location, observing the scenes around them and interacting with other people and objects. The best-selling *Myst* series, for example, leaves players to investigate and solve a mystery, with no clues or instruments other than their own observation skills.

Point-and-click adventure games, a sub-genre, use a mouse to control a character within a 2D environment, clicking on objects or people to interact with the game world. Examples include the *Broken Sword* series and LucasArts titles such as *Monkey Island*. This genre is seeing a revival on hand-held and mobile platforms.

Driving games

These games, also called racing games, focus on improving a player's success at racing against their opponents by making adjustments to their cars. Players can often choose whether to view the action from a first-person or third-person perspective, and play is usually structured into races, joined together by option screens which allow players to develop their cars. The genre consists of three sub-genres: simulation driving games, arcade driving games and driving adventure games.

Simulation driving games attempt to provide a realistic recreation of a particular driving experience. This includes Formula 1 racing, in games such as the F1 series, or rally driving as found in the *Colin McRae Rally* series.

Arcade driving games try to make it challenging and fun, rather than accurately simulating how a car handles in real life. These games, although visually impressive, are very similar to the first racing games that appeared in arcades. Some – *Ridge Racer 4*, for example – have a story, with short sections of character interaction appearing between races.

Driving adventure games, such as the *Driver* series, use driving as their method of achieving a goal, but also include a story element.

Fighting and beat 'em up games

The fighting genre covers games that use physical violence in battles with other characters. This usually happens as a player progresses through a location, with 'waves' of opponents appearing to challenge the player character. Action usually takes place from a third-person perspective, with the camera fixed behind a character to allow a player to see what is ahead. Examples of this include the *Fantastic Four* game and *Batman*.

Beat 'em up games, which were first seen in arcades, are based on a series of fights between opponents, usually structured into levels where characters fight in an enclosed space, such as an arena or a ring. The levels end when a character is beaten. Players learn a series of button combinations which activate specific 'moves' by the player-controlled character. In 'single-player' mode, the player's opponents are computer-controlled characters who increase in ability through the levels. In 'multi-player' mode, two or more players' characters fight against each other. These games often include some form of oriental martial arts (though wrestling games are now a popular sub-genre). Classic examples of beat 'em up games include the *Tekken* series, WWE *SmackDown!* and *Soul Caliber III*.

First-person shooters (FPS)

These highly popular games involve the use of weapons to fulfil a goal. The onscreen action is viewed from a first-person perspective – through the player-character's eyes. First-person shooters are often crossed with elements of other genres, such as stealth and action, making them hard to categorise. *Metroid*, for example, released in 2001, which had strong elements of the adventure and puzzle genres added to the usual elements of an FPS, was actually categorised as the first 'First-person adventure', a style seen in many other titles since. Some of the most popular FPS games are the *Doom* series, the *Quake* games, *Duke Nukem 3D* and *Goldeneye 007*. It used to be said that FPS games had little or no story, with action being the main focus. However, recently games such as *Half-Life* and *Half-Life 2* have entered the genre, with a much stronger sense of narrative and character development.

God games

These games encourage players to take on a commanding role and control the lives of people or worlds. Usually, the aim is to ensure that an environment is created that will help the people of the virtual world succeed. The player takes on the role of a supreme being, similar to gods or mythological figures, and those in the game world are aware of the player's presence. God games can be played on a large scale, controlling a world, or on a small scale, looking after an individual or a small group of people. Action is usually viewed from above (top-down view), from a third-person perspective. Large-scale God games include *Populous*, *SimCity* and *Black and White*. Small-scale games include *The Sims* and its many sequels.

Light-gun games

These games, which use a light-gun (a peripheral attached to the computer) are often versions of arcade machines, converted for home use. Usually viewed from a first-person perspective, light-gun games test the accuracy and speed with which the player can use the light-gun. Games can be linked by a simple plot, where characters fight their way through groups of enemies, which gets steadily more difficult as the game progresses.

Massively multiplayer online games (MMOGs)

These games are played via the Internet, with a large number of characters controlled by human players. There are also other characters, directed by the computer program, who deliver important information or quests that a player should embark on. Players may be able to group their characters together to progress through the story, working as a team to overcome challenges. The majority of MMOGs are based on a fantasy theme, with the use of magic spells, and settings and characters from the Middle Ages. Objectives may be related to mythological objects or characters. Players usually view MMO games from a top-down, third-person perspective, being able to see their player-character interact with the game world and the other people in it. Players usually buy the game first from a retailer and then connect to the game servers online to play with other people.

Massively Multiplayer Online Role Playing (MMORP) games are a sub-genre of this group, which combines MMO game elements with those from the RPG genre (see pages 126–127). MMORP games usually offer a menu-based character-development system, and the opportunity to interact with large numbers of people online.

Party games

Party games are designed to be played in groups using multiplayer features. They usually involve small individual tasks rather than a story-led structure. The tasks often test players' reactions and dexterity, and pit players against each other. Sometimes games may require peripherals, such as light-guns. The Sony Eye Toy was developed to be used in these games and consists of a small camera which projects images on to the game screen, allowing direct physical interaction with onscreen objects. Party games are usually released on console machines rather than PCs because whole groups of people need to be able to view the action.

Peripheral interactive games

Some of the features of party games apply to this genre, but the key element of these games is their use of a particular device. Items like touch-sensitive floor-mats suitable for dancing games have been released for consoles, along with motion-sensitive game-pads and microphone headsets. The genre is distinct because these peripherals are tied to a particular game, unlike some – steering wheels or light-guns, for example – which may be used for a number of different games.

Platformers (platform games)

Once the most popular form of computer game, particularly on early consoles, platform games were originally in 2D format. They are called platform games because they usually feature characters moving between small platforms whilst collecting certain items and avoiding enemies. Examples of this genre include the original *Super Mario Bros.* and *Sonic the Hedgehog*. These 2D platform games are still common in Internet and mobile gaming because they don't need a lot of processing power to run.

Today, 3D platformers are the more common form, with games such as *Super Mario Sunshine*, *Jak and Daxter* and *Ratchet and Clank* being popular. The new 3D platformers have the same style of gameplay as the original platform games. They tend to be quite 'cartoony', with the lead characters being either caricatures of human beings or creatures with human qualities.

Players of 3D platformers usually view the action from a third-person perspective, with the camera following the action from behind the lead character. The camera position can often be altered by the player to help them move around the levels.

3D platformers are now more commonly referred to as action adventure games, but certain titles still stick to the platformer traditions quite closely.

Puzzle games

These games involve solving puzzles about shapes, colours, words and numbers. Whilst many computer games now include an element of puzzle-solving, this genre focuses on the puzzles themselves. They usually require a player to apply logic and reasoning to a situation, under a time constraint or other pressure, progressing through levels of difficulty to an eventual goal. *Tetris* is probably the most famous puzzle game released for home computers and consoles, with a version existing for almost every single platform. Other popular examples include the *Bust a Move* series, *Pac-Man* and *Snake*.

Role-playing games (RPGs)

Based on pencil-and-paper role-playing games, where players take on the role of a character and the action is determined by throwing dice, RPGs have found a natural home on computer systems. Computer-based RPGs give a visual image of the situations and characters onscreen, along with the ability to make complex calculations and generate more random decisions than was possible by just throwing dice.

In an RPG, players take on the role of a character or group of characters and progress through a story. They develop their skills and abilities, often in the form of magical spells. There is an element of combat with enemies, often using a turn-based system (for more on this see the strategy genre). Often, the player uses a series of menus to decide the attributes of characters within a group and to allocate special skills or 'power-ups' gained from battles or discoveries. These games are usually long and involve epic stories, with many characters. RPGs are usually viewed from a distant, third-person perspective, letting the player see their characters interact with the world and the other characters.

Some of the most popular RPGs are the console-based *Final Fantasy* games and the PC-based *Baldur's Gate* and the *Elder Scrolls* series.

The character-development element of RPGs has also been incorporated into other genres in recent times, including MMO, action and adventure games (the *Zelda* series, for example).

Shoot 'em up games

A favourite of early gaming, shoot 'em up is one of the simplest, but most addictive, genres. Usually the player controls a vehicle and the gameplay involves constant, rapid fire of a weapon, destroying 'waves' of enemies to progress through a level. Action is always seen from a third-person perspective, allowing the player to see any danger their vehicle is in.

Famous examples of shoot 'em up games include *Space Invaders*, *R-Type* and *Tempest*. Although not as popular as they once were, shoot 'em ups can still prove successful, e.g. *R-Type Final*, the recent revision of *R-Type*.

Simulator games (sims)

Simulator games can simulate a variety of different activities. Many games classed as simulators also come under another heading, such as sport or driving. These games attempt to recreate experiences as near to real life as possible and give people a chance to try things they normally wouldn't be able to do. Simulators are usually played from a first-person perspective, to help the player feel that they are experiencing what is happening onscreen. Some simulators encourage players to become as good at the activity as they would need to be in real life. Flight simulator games are one of the most popular of this genre, with the instrument panels of aircraft replicated in a computer form for players to operate. Some simulators are used in professional settings, with commercial flight companies and the military using them as training tools. One of the most popular simulator games is *Microsoft Flight Simulator* for the PC. This game can be played with a force-feedback joystick, which copies the pressure that needs to be applied to real-life flight controls.

Sports games

Sports games give players the chance to play either as an individual competitor or as the controller of a team of sports players. Sports games follow the rules of the sport they are copying and are structured so that a player selects the type of match they wish to play. They also choose the opponents they wish to face and any other details about the upcoming challenge that they can change. Players use the controller/keyboard to control their players. Sports covered in games so far include basketball, American football, soccer, ice hockey, golf, tennis, bowling, rugby, cricket, boxing, horse riding and athletics.

The sub-genre of football management games is an exception to the usual conventions of sports games. These games involve tactical planning and organisation of a football team, rather than controlling the players during a match. In some cases, a player will make many tactical plans before a match and then watch the computer players play the game out, to see if their plans have worked. One of the most popular examples is the *Championship Manager* series.

Stealth games

The gameplay in these games involves moving around a location without being detected. Games such as *Thief: The Dark Project, Splinter Cell* and *Metal Gear Solid* set players story-led challenges which require them to remain unseen and unheard. Most stealth games, however, are mixed with elements of action and adventure games, and are normally, but not always, set in the third person.

Strategy games

Strategy games can be very similar to God games, because they involve managing groups of people, with the player taking an 'all-seeing' position on the action. However, strategy games are usually more biased to the development and control of groups in warlike situations. This genre also shares some similarities with RPG games, but largely titles fall into one category or another, determined by the nature of the story being told and the style it is presented in.

Games of this genre are largely concerned with logical reasoning and decision-making towards a particular goal. They are split into two smaller groups: turn-based and real-time, depending on the way in which players interact with the world. In turn-based games, after each of the player's moves, the computer-controlled characters make a move, effectively taking turns. *Advance Wars 2* and the *Civilization* series of games are turn-based strategy games. Real-time strategy games operate without any 'turns', with the computer and the player making moves all the time, constantly opposing each other, leading to a different style of gameplay. Examples include *Age of Empires III* and *Shogun Warrior*.

Survival horror games

In these games, players have to survive numerous dangers as they progress through frightening or dangerous locations, solving puzzles to achieve an aim. The games, which usually include many supernatural references, are very narrative-based, with the development of characters being a key part of the experience. Usually the gameplay will involve some combat with other people, supernatural creatures or animals. Many of the traditional conventions of horror literature and films are included in these games. Players usually view the action from a third-person perspective, sometimes switching to first-person during combat. Survival horror games usually progress through levels, with the elements of the narrative revealed over the course of the game. Classic examples of the genre include the *Resident Evil* series, *Silent Hill*, *Eternal Darkness* and *Siren*.

Retro games

Many people born in the 1970s and 1980s grew up with computer games as a major form of entertainment. But technology has moved on, and those arcade and early home computer and console games have disappeared. Today, however, there is quite a demand for them be made available again, for today's platforms, and these re-released versions are classed as retro games. There is a strong following amongst the gaming community for retro games and, like the film industry before it, the game industry is starting to see appreciation for things that, on their release, were largely dismissed by mainstream culture.

Try this ...

Using a form like this one, make a list of the major game genres, with an up-to-date example of each.

Game genre	Example of a game
Sports	Wii Sports (for the Nintendo Wii)

Producing a games review

Analysing and comparing games

To analyse a game you will need to look at its elements. You must analyse in-depth its look, playability and difficulty. You should use appropriate language when analysing the game and include illustrative examples in your analysis.

Try this ...

Choose a game that you are familiar with. Write an Internet review, a print-based review and a television-based review of it. Include a comparison of the game with other games that you know. Make sure that you analyse the game in depth and make comparisons such as the playability of each game, the characters and environments used, the level of difficulty, etc. Make sure that you use fluent and correct terminology throughout your three reviews.

You must compare the game you are reviewing with other games of the same or a similar genre. To do this you will need to play these games and then discuss how the games compare. You should use examples from each game to illustrate your review.

The review document

The review document could be produced in a number of ways, for example:

- An Internet review. This could be linked to a review website, and images from the game could be used to illustrate the points you are making in your review.
- A print-based review. This could be a review for a popular gaming magazine. You will have to write the review in an appropriate software application so that a magazine would accept it. Still images from the game could be included.
- A television-based review. This would be a review produced as a voice-over for action shots of the game, or as an interview in a studio situation.

For all of these reviews you will need to write your review clearly, using appropriate technical language. Imagine you are the reader and include information that you would find useful and informative.

In your review you should include:
- the platform the game is played on
- the game genre
- the target audience
- how difficult it is to play (mention and short cuts or cheats)
- how addictive it is
- what you think of the sound (include examples of good or bad sounds)
- what you think of the quality of the graphics (include actual illustrations from the game)
- whether you would choose to play this game and why.

Summary

In this chapter you have covered what you need to know to achieve the four Learning Outcomes relating to Unit 14 of your course. You should now:

- know about the history of computer games
- understand the main game elements
- be able to recognise game genres
- be able to produce a game review.

14 2D Computer Games

What are 2D computer games?

If you are thinking of entering the world of computer games development you will need to know about how 2D games are constructed. 2D games were the first generation of computer games, but they have moved on from very simple arcade games to platform games where characters can run and jump between different levels – all to an accompanying soundtrack.

In this chapter you will learn how a game is constructed and how you can use the techniques and technology, including games engines, to produce a games element. It is important to remember that games are produced by a team, and in this unit you will produce an element of a game that the team could use to make a finished 2D game.

Game Info

2D computer games

In 2D games everything is represented in a two-dimensional (2D) form, viewed from one angle. This means the demands on the player are generally more limited than with 3D games.

Games are driven by a programming core, known as the game's **engine**. An engine is often used in several different games, but each one is distinctive because it has added its own narrative, characters, layouts, weapons, etc. These elements are known as the game's **assets**.

Games platforms

Handheld console platforms

Machines which play games using battery power, allowing them to be played 'on the move', are referred to as handheld console platforms. The most popular handheld console series is the Nintendo Game Boy platform, which continues to be revised and improved. In 2000, Nintendo announced the ten millionth Game Boy sale, making it one of the most successful platforms in

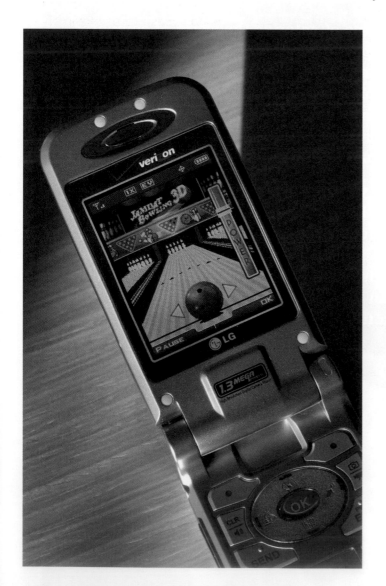

the history of the games industry. Other handheld systems have been developed, but few have had the continued success of Nintendo's machine. The Nintendo DS is a recent development – a dual-screen device operated both by buttons and by a stylus that can be used to 'draw' on the screen to control the action.

Sony's new handheld console, the PSP (PlayStation Portable), provides stiff competition for Nintendo, as it includes new features such as the ability to play movies and MP3s.

The advantage of handheld platforms is that you can take your game wherever you go, without needing a power supply, an external screen or any peripheral devices. The main disadvantages are the smaller screen size and the limited amount of power available (from the batteries) to run games.

Mobile phone platforms

Recently, the development of mobile phones has increased their use as games platforms. The early models were equipped to play simple animated 2D games, but newer models can display more advanced graphics and software, which allows games to be downloaded or bought especially for phones. Some models are now designed to be a cross between a phone and a handheld console. One of the most popular of these was the Nokia NGage, now being replaced by the Smartphone. The Gizmondo is a handheld console which includes the ability to send and receive text messages, along with some multimedia functions.

Mobile phone platforms can function both as communicators and games consoles, but their limited power can be a disadvantage.

Internet-based platforms

Games are also available on the Internet, either as downloadable software that can be played offline, or as an online system, such as online card games. These games can be presented in a variety of ways, but Java animation-based games are the most popular.

Games from other platforms can also be played via the Internet, using online multiplayer modes built into some software. Most PCs and some games consoles can now be connected to the Internet for this purpose. The game software usually provides an interface for the player to use and connects with the Internet, using the platform to make this connection. There is sometimes a charge for this service (in addition to the cost of telephone calls for those using a dial-up Internet service).

Try this ...

Make a list of handheld console platforms, mobile phone platforms and Internet-based platforms. Try to find out the names of some 2D games that are played on them.

Limitations of 2D games

Once 3D games became available, the market for 2D games shrank, because everyone wanted to enjoy the 3D games experience. The original 2D games didn't have the depth of perception and the real depth of colour that can be found in 3D games. This reduced the players' enjoyment.

In general, 2D games are less **immersive** for players. Their lack of 3D realism means that players find it more difficult to engage with the game – to become fully involved and take an active part in gameplay.

Understanding assets of 2D games

Graphical assets

Sprites

A sprite is a two-dimensional image or animation that is part of a larger scene. Sprites were originally used as a way to integrate several images together in 2D games.

Backgrounds

Creating backgrounds for 2D games is relatively easy because backgrounds for a wide range of games can be downloaded from the Internet. This provides the basis on which you can then place your characters and scenes.

Colours

It is important that colours are carefully thought out in 2D games to make sure that characters and objects stand out from the background.

Behavioural assets

Behavioural assets are interactive elements of the programme such as:

- Events: e.g. something falls as the character passes by
- Objects: e.g. a box that opens, as part of an event, to produce the next clue or object
- Scripts: a sequence of events that happen, e.g. something might be triggered by an event or object.

Core mechanics

This is the basic way in which a game will play – how the player's character interacts with the world around it – and you must decide how this will happen early on in the design process. You must first consider whether a character will be able to climb walls, swim, pick up objects, use weapons, destroy things and talk to other characters, at the player's will. These initial decisions affect the rest of the gameplay including the challenges, tests, puzzles, level design, graphical features and sound, which are all part of the core mechanics.

The core mechanics may be introduced to the player with a training or tutorial mode, using a mixture of full motion video (FMV) sequences and player interaction, to help the player learn the basic controls. Alternatively, some games allow players to start the game without training, letting them learn the mechanics and how to operate them through practice and experimentation.

Sound assets

The audio content of a game is one of the most important ways you can achieve a sense of reality and a 'suspension of disbelief' when playing a game. Even in a game with highly effective graphics, if the sound is not convincing, the illusion will be spoiled. The sound within games can be divided into three main groups: music, voice acting and sound effects. While these have separate content, they are often used together throughout a game. The sound may be heard when players start up a game, while they are in the menus (selecting controller options, saving progress, etc.), while the action is happening, and during **cut-scenes** and non-interactive sequences.

Music

The music in a game will add to the atmosphere that you're trying to create. There will usually be a piece of music identified as the theme of the title, which will play on start-up. This theme will be carried throughout the rest of the game in elements of the other music. **Incidental music** is played while the player is in control of the action onscreen and will mirror the nature and theme of a level. It is what you want the player to feel. Upbeat, loud rock music could be appropriate for a high-speed, exciting chase, for example, but a mellow orchestral piece would not.

Voice acting

The way a character sounds is almost as important as how they look. Voice actors have to convey a character using only their delivery of the lines. Designers hold casting sessions, similar to those held for radio, television or film productions. They must choose the right person for a character, and everything about the way the actor delivers their lines must fit with how the designer sees the character.

Some speech may be heard more than once in a game, for example words used in a fighting game as a 'taunt' or in a 'First-person shooter' when an enemy is spotted. You must make sure that this speech doesn't become irritating or comical (unless this is intended) when heard repetitively.

Some voice actors have become well-known in the gaming world for their part as a particular character, such as the actor Simon Templeman, who has played Kain, the vampire lord, in the *Legacy of Kain* series of games, to great acclaim.

135.

Sound effects

To add reality to the events in a game, the sound effects which correspond to actions should always be as convincing as possible. You need to consider things like what a character's footsteps will sound like on different surfaces. The noises that objects make in real life and how sounds behave in certain situations (such as echoing in a tunnel) are important.

Sounds can also add to the sense of achievement a player may feel within the game world. If a long journey and a puzzle has led to the discovery of a key, then the noise of the key unlocking the necessary door should sound momentous and triumphant. As well as using sound effects for emphasis, subtle additions like quiet birdsong or background traffic noise can add 'believability' to the game.

Again, as with the speech samples mentioned above, it is important that the sounds chosen do not start to irritate or lose their impact when heard often.

> Turn to Chapter 8, Audio Production, for more about recording sound and producing sound effects.

Try this ...

Make a list of file formats used for sound, including the ones given here. Identify examples of how these files are used in 2D games.

File types for sound

Two examples of file types used for sound in 2D games are:
- WAV files (wave file audio format or wave file format): a standard format for storing audio files on a variety of computers.
- MIDI files: typically created using desktop/laptop computer-based sequencing software (or sometimes a hardware-based MIDI instrument or workstation) which organises MIDI messages into one or more parallel 'tracks' for independent recording and editing.

The computer games industry

Game engines

When a game is created, there are certain parts of the programmed mechanics that will be the same as others of a similar type or of the same genre. Often, when a games company has designed a particularly innovative way of making a genre or game work, they will sell some of the core programming at the heart of the game to other games producers. This core programming – the game's engine – acts as a base for all the complex calculations and sequences that a game needs to run. Companies that buy an engine will then add their own game assets – the narrative, character designs, level layouts, objects and weapons. Games engines mainly run the graphic element of the game, although they can also be used as a basis for **AI** (artificial intelligence) elements of a game. Engines can provide common game requirements like collision detection (when the game is aware of one object in the game coming into contact with another).

Middleware

The purchase of games engines became so popular that some companies began to build engines specifically to sell to other companies. These soon developed into software suites that provide basic systems for graphics, sound, physics and AI. This type of product is known as **middleware**.

'RenderWare' is one of the most famous examples of middleware. It was designed by Criterion Software as a system which could be used by other developers. Rockstar North used RenderWare to build *Grand Theft Auto: San Andreas*, one of the best-selling titles of recent years.

Mods (modifications)

Mods are the modifications and alterations that can be made to existing game code to change features of the game to a user's requirements. You might expect designers to try to stop people changing their games, but in fact they encourage it. Tool kits, developed by the games companies themselves, help users make these modifications and are often included with the original game.

Counter-Strike, the online, multiplayer First-person shooter, originated as a mod of Valve Software's *Half-Life*. It is now one of the most popular online games of all time, with an estimated 1 million games played every day.

User documentation

The instructions for actually playing the game should be embedded within the game, and accessed via a 'help' system. Printed instructions should only list key uses or give an overview of the menu system. Help should be **context-sensitive**, so that when you ask for help, the first help screen you see is relevant to where you are in the game.

A **readme** file will contain general information, such as how to install the game, configuration instructions and copyright information.

Distribution of games

Traditionally games have been produced and distributed on a CD-Rom, DVD or floppy disk and then loaded into a PC or MAC computer. Now gamers can purchase games over the Internet by paying for a game online and receiving it as an **executable file** or a **zip file**. An executable file is one that is capable of being 'executed' (run) as a program in the computer. Zip files are data compression files. One or more files are compressed into a zip file to reduce their download time.

Constructing your 2D game element

Generating ideas

Narrative structures and story paths

Most computer and video games contain a story. Having a storyline which develops is one of the best ways to capture a player's attention and encourage them to work through the challenges and trials set before them. As game playing is interactive, the story needs to progress in relation to the actions of the players themselves. This is very different from the way a story develops in a book or a film. The story could progress on completion of a level, but it could also be triggered by discovering a clue or solving a puzzle. In books or films, the writer controls exactly what is experienced and when, but in games you must always consider how players will experience the story and when they will discover certain elements of the plot.
In some games – the *Final Fantasy* role-playing games, for example – characters are developed constantly by what they say during conversations and through their actions when not controlled by the player. However, large portions of the actual narrative are told through short full-motion video sequences that are **pre-rendered** – produced and rendered using computer software and then played back like a short film. This allows the player to

control characters whilst finding out small pieces of information about them during gameplay, experiencing battles alongside characters, and journeying with them. It also allows for sections of story to be told under the controlled setting of a short pre-rendered piece, making sure that the player has all the information they need. These short films also act as an incentive to players to continue during difficult parts of the game.

The narrative can also be controlled by making sure that the story's progression is triggered by certain events, such as the discovery of an item, or a character. This means that the narrative, and how it is to be revealed to the player, needs to be thought through very carefully before work begins on a game. Is it best to write a short plot synopsis before planning how your story will be revealed.

Once a basic plot has been written, you must decide how the plot will be discovered by players. Some games work on a linear plot strand structure, which involves one main storyline through which players progress. Other games have multi-strand or multi-path narrative structures which allow players to discover the story in different ways or to make different decisions which lead to different paths through the story. The outcome of some games is determined by ongoing progress but others, such as *The Legacy of Kain*, give players a decision at the end of the game which leads to different resolutions of the story.

Character development in narrative

Like any story, it is important that a game's narrative shows the development of the main character and those around them. A computer game's narrative usually involves the progression of an individual or small group from one point to another, learning something or changing in some way in the process. The first task is to write a short character outline, describing each of the major characters, their nature, their involvement in the story and their motivations.

Once you have decided on the characters, you should write a plan of how they may interact with each other by creating a **character map** or web. By drawing a simple visual plan of how characters feel about each other when they first meet, you will have a clear idea of what the characters need to do within a story and what emotions they need to portray in order to make the story clear.

Planning

Once you have decided the basic plot and characters for your game and how the game will play, you should create a **walkthrough** of the game on paper. This document describes what players will do to advance the story and how the game will be structured. This stage of the process is very creative as you can now see how the game will take shape and develop these ideas further.

A walkthrough sequence should include the objectives and goals for the game as a whole, and for each section of the game. It may be, for example, that a character needs to visit four locations on their journey to find an item. Each of these locations could be a level that they need to progress through, with its own challenges and aims. The player's overall goal will be to find the item, but their objectives within each level may be to survive in order to continue.

A walkthrough should also include details of any optional paths that may be taken by a player and how these link up with the main story. If a player is given the option of visiting the four locations in any order, you must check that the right information will still be learned at the right time, to make sure that the story as a whole still works.

Your schedule

When planning the production of your game it is vital that you produce a schedule that allows you time to:

- think of ideas
- develop these ideas
- book the resources and material
- learn new techniques
- use technology
- produce the game
- test the game.

You should use a scheduling system that will let you make changes as you progress though the process. It is not always possible to keep rigidly to a schedule, because things can change. You might find that there is an updated piece of software that you can use, or you think up another character, background or environment.

Producing a simple chart like the one below will help you keep a note of what you have to do and record any changes you make.

Activity	Finish date	Changes made
Produced a mind map of my ideas	Monday 1 May	Decided that I needed more ideas, so arranged to finish the mind map by Monday 8 May

The schedule will allow you to manage your time effectively. You will also need a clear picture of the whole process, so you should produce a production schedule that clearly indicates deadlines for each stage of the process. You may have a wonderful idea that would sell to millions of gamers across the world and then identify that it will sell best at Christmas. You advertise the game and the release date in the press, but what do you think will happen if the game is not developed in time and is not available on the release date? You can use a chart like this to keep track of your deadlines:

Stage	Start date	Finish date
Pitching of idea to my tutor	Monday 15 May	Monday 15 May

Your team

It is very important that you work as a team member. It may be possible to think of an idea for a game on your own, but you will need to work with other people to develop it. You may need:
- a designer to produce the characters or environments
- a sound person to produce the sound effects
- one or more actors for the voices.

You must always stay in communication with your team. You should let them know how the project is developing, what changes have been made and when they will be required to work on their sections of the game.

Try this ...

Produce a production schedule for your own game element work. Start to put in the key dates after discussing them with your tutor.

Try this ...

Consider how you would keep in touch with your team. Make a list of your team members and decide how you would keep in contact with them.

Producing your game element

You should think carefully about how you will produce an element that contributes to the production of a finished 2D game. Remember that you will be working as part of a team. Will your element be:

- a sprite
- the background
- an event or action
- an object
- a script
- sound effects, music or a voice?

Whatever you produce, consider how it would contribute to a finished 2D game.

Your game specification document

You will need to produce a game specification document that provides:

- a 'layout plan' to give a clear idea of how the game will look
- a 'required asset list' to show the assets you will need to make your 2D game.

Summary

In this chapter you have covered what you need to know to achieve the four Learning Outcomes relating to Unit 15 of your course. You should now:

- know about 2D games

- understand 2D game assets

- understand how 2D game engines are used to produce a game element

- be able to construct a 2D game element.

15 Digital Graphics

What are digital graphics?

If you want to work in the computer games industry, you must understand the graphics required for games. Players constantly expect more realistic images, objects and characters. This means the quality of graphics must improve all the time. In this chapter you will learn about digital image software and the different graphic styles that can be used to suggest moods and themes in a game.

To learn about the range of genres that exist in computer games, turn to pages 122 to 129. This will help you decide what sort of graphics you want to produce.

Graphical themes and styles in computer games

Graphical themes

Computer games, like all media forms, can be divided into genres which each have their own graphical themes. The distinctions between genres depend on the way in which the games are played, the content of their stories or the requirements of their players. You will find a list of current genres in Chapter 13, Reviewing Computer Games, which gives a basic guide to their characteristics. You must remember, though, that the games industry is still relatively young and so new genres are being developed all the time. This list covers:

- action games
- driving games
- first-person shooters (FPS)
- light-gun games
- party games
- platformers (platform games)
- role-playing games (RPG)
- simulator games (sims)
- stealth games
- survival horror games

- adventure games
- fighting and beat 'em up games
- god games
- massively multiplayer online (MMO) games
- peripheral interactive games
- puzzle games
- retro games.
- shoot 'em up games
- sports games
- strategy games

Try this ...

Make a list of graphical styles, with examples of each.

Graphical styles

There are many graphical styles used in games, including:

- cartoon: drawn figures that are exaggerated or caricatures
- photo-realistic: a style where the graphic is a realistic representation
- cel-shaded: a type of non-photo-realistic image that is made to appear to be hand drawn
- exaggeration: where the graphic is made to look totally unrealistic, e.g. an animé image (a form of animation originating in Japan)

Planning your digital image for a game

Freehand drawing

It would not be sensible to start the production of digital images for a game without making some drawings first to see if your ideas will work. It is important to use freehand drawing skills when developing your ideas. You should practise these skills so that you will be able to produce a drawn storyboard that shows your ideas for the finished digital images. This will give your client (or a potential audience) a good idea of what you are planning.

Your images of characters should be drawn to demonstrate their features, style and colours. Objects could be drawn to demonstrate how they will look and operate in the game. Your drawing could also demonstrate the viewpoint you will be using or the scale and perspective of your work.

Characters

In order for a narrative to work within a game, the characters in the story must be ones that the player cares about. Making players feel close to a character or group of characters is sometimes made easier because the player is taking on the role of the main character throughout the game, and so shares their experiences. Unsympathetic or annoying characters will discourage players from progressing through a game, so characters must always be carefully designed. Within a game, a character's persona can only be expressed through their appearance, their voice, what they are given to say and what is said about them. When planning your characters, you must also think about what their weapons will look like and what they will do.

Background

When planning your background, you will need to ask yourself several questions. Will the background be a moving or still image? How will the background sit with the characters being developed? Will the colours of the characters, objects or weapons clash with the background?

Generating ideas

The game concept document

The game concept document contains all of the core details of the game. Within this short written report you must express the idea of the game, including a description of:

- the nature of the game
- the genre that the game will fit into
- the background to the idea
- the platform the game is intended for
- the main features of the game
- the game's USP (unique selling point or unique selling proposition).

A concept document usually begins or ends with a short paragraph, sometimes known as the 'pitching paragraph', describing the proposed game in an exciting and positive way. This allows anyone who reads the document to see the very best elements of the idea.

The design document (concept art)

In order to make an impact, and convey a real sense of what the finished game might look like, it is essential to produce some visual representation of elements of the game. While it may not be possible to build photo-realistic **renders** of game worlds, some sketches and artwork produced using traditional art techniques will work just as well to give the 'feel' of a game. A design document doesn't need to have a full visual representation of everything within the game, but effective, well-presented artwork can make a big difference at this stage to how your project comes across. Most companies employ artists who will sit with the designers and try to capture the look that they have in mind for the game.

Producing your digital image for a game

File types used in image production

Raster files are files made up of grids of pixels, and they are particularly suitable for photo-realistic images. The following are raster files:
- bmp (Bitmap) file, also known as a 'bump' file. This is a Windows/bitmapped graphics file format. It is the Windows native bitmap format, and every Windows application has access to the bmp software routines in Windows that support it.
- JPEG (Joint Photographics Expert Group): a commonly used format for compressing photographic images.
- gif (Graphics Interchange Format) file: a common file format used to store images such as photos, documents and simple animations. The gif file format is widely used on the Internet because it uses compression to reduce the size of the file that contains the images. This allows Internet users to download the file quickly. Files you upload to your website must be stored in a gif or JPEG file and have the file extension of .gif or .jpg.
- tiff (tagged image file format): used for storing images such as photographs. It is a flexible and adaptable file format.

Vector files are files that use geometric principles to join together points. They can produce curves using straight lines, or objects such as polygons. Vector files are ideal for simple drawings that do not require photo-realism. The following are vector files:

- psd: a file format used for saving large Photoshop documents – those over 30,000 x 30,000 pixels in size. It supports images up to 300,000 x 300,000 pixels.
- wmf (Windows Meta File): used specifically on the PC platform. WMF files can contain either pixel-based information or vector information in 16-bit RGB colour space.
- Fla: a source Flash file that contains all animation and graphics. To manage this file you need Macromedia Flash MX 6 or higher installed on your computer.
- ai: a vector graphics file created in Adobe Illustrator.

Using digital tools

Digital tools are the tools you use to construct your digital graphics. These tools might:

- manipulate size and resolution of the graphic
- change the colour of the graphic
- produce layers used in the construction
- crop the size of the image
- select areas of the graphic
- copy the graphic
- paste to another area or page
- undo a previous task
- add effects to the graphic
- save the work to a file.

> **Try this …**
>
> Produce a list of digital tools in the programs available to you and identify what each one is used for.

> **Summary**
>
> In this chapter you have covered what you need to know to achieve three of the four Learning Outcomes relating to Unit 16 of your course. You should now:
>
> - know about the graphic styles used in games
> - be able to plan a digital image for a game
> - be able to produce a digital image for a game.
>
> When you have finished your digital image you will need to review it to achieve the final Learning Outcome. To find out how to do this, turn to Chapter 19, Reviewing Your Work.

16 Writing for the Media

What does 'writing for the media' involve?

In media there is a great deal of material that has to be written. This chapter is concerned with the text or dialogue that is written to be read or heard by an audience. You will also write production documentation to convey your intentions to other members of the production team or the client, but this is not dealt with in this chapter.

The sort of writing you will do in this unit will be for your chosen media sector and is likely to include one or more of the following:

- scripts for television or radio programmes

- articles and stories for newspapers, magazines and periodicals

- text content for websites or interactive CDs.

Types of writing produced in the media industry

Different styles for different media sectors

Different media sectors require different styles of writing, even for the same material. A good example of this in practice is when a news agency sends a multi-skilled journalist to cover a news story and they bring back video footage that they have shot themselves and a shorthand copy of the material. The journalist will then turn this into copy in one style for a news bulletin on television and in another style for a newspaper article.

If you listen to a news story on the radio you will find that the dialogue is much more descriptive than coverage of the same story on television. The reason may seem obvious: in addition to the newsreader's introduction, the television story has moving images – video clips of the relevant content – to illustrate and assist in telling the story. This means that less spoken description is required and the story may be told more quickly (which is useful, as television is a much more expensive medium than radio). Radio, on the other hand, has to describe the scene and convey a picture to the listener in words alone.

A news story in the newspaper is written in a way which would make it difficult to read conversationally. The word order is not the same as it would be if you were speaking the words, and if you try to read a newspaper story out loud it will not sound right. This is because the English that is written down is not conversational English. Conversational English uses shortened words, and when written down **verbatim** you will find lots of apostrophes.

Look at the two sentences below. The first shows how it would be written, and the second is punctuated the way it might be spoken:

> It would have been a long time until I would have been able to, but do not give up now.

> It would've been a long time 'til I'd 'ave been able to – but don't give up now.

Written English also lacks the intonation of spoken words, and can be easily misinterpreted if punctuation is not used correctly. Written stories often benefit from having an accompanying photograph, which may help in understanding the text. Comics actually use cartoon illustrations to tell the story and use the text to assist in understanding it.

By repeating a sentence and placing the **emphasis** on a different word each time, you can make the sentence have a different meaning. The following sentence is a good example:

What do you want me to do about that?'

Different forms of English are used in media writing, depending on the context. It could be a formal situation, like news reporting, or it could require a technical style – in a training or promotional video, for example. Other styles include the persuasive style of a commercial, or the storytelling style of an audio book, with its use of direct speech.

Different styles for different genres

The style and delivery of the spoken and written word will also change according to the **genre** (type) of product in which it is included. For the audience, this means that the genre should be obvious from the style.

Genre	Styles used
national news	formal Queen's English (also called 'received pronunciation')
documentary	conversational, holding some surprise element
drama	often serious, over-emphasised tension
live broadcast	confident, assertive
advert	persuasive and pleading, authoritative
promotional video	instructional, directing
information video	conversational, informative
popular music programme	in your face, driving
magazine programme	humorous and flippant
consumer programme	warning and advisory tones
quiz show	anecdotal, conversational, argumentative
talk show	flamboyant, show-off
reality show	personal, direct communication
general magazine	conversational, directly addressing audience
specialist magazine	specialist technical language
popular newspaper	short sentences, brash, sensation-seeking
serious newspaper	formal, intelligent complex language
local newspaper	friendly, neighbourly
local radio news item	degree of formality related to station
column	opinionated
review	superior language

Generating ideas for your written material

The brief

There is usually a client or an employer dictating the type and style of written content that has to be generated. The writer seldom gets the chance to write in their own style or on a topic of their choosing, unless they are a creative writer. The **brief**, which will be the result of a **commission** from a **client**, will dictate the **style** and the **medium** (which could be broadcast, corporate or print, whether hard copy or electronic). The **slot** will be defined and the target audience identified in the brief, along with deadlines by which certain writing tasks must be completed. (Your tutor will take the place of the client.)

Brainstorming your ideas

First collect examples from your chosen medium of the type of written material that you are to write – the more, the better. If you are writing as a team, for a big product, you will all need to understand the overall style and know exactly what your part is in the whole. Hold a **brainstorming** session with other members of your class, to think of all the possibilities that you can. Write them down in your own **spidergram**. You should make notes of all decisions and discussions.

Try this ...

With one or two classmates, brainstorm some ideas for a script for radio or television, or for an article in a print publication. Write up your ideas into a draft script or article.

Your research and preparation

Researching the specific written form

The best way to find out about different writing styles is to gather some secondary research data in the form of examples of radio or television scripts, newspaper articles, promotional or training video scripts, newspapers, magazines or website copy. You should collect written material in a portfolio. You will need to identify the differences between texts for your chosen medium. Different styles of writing are also laid out differently on the page.

Look at ...

The CD-Rom contains examples of radio scripts (consumer, discussion, factual, drama) and TV scripts (news, discussion and film review).

Researching the content

You will need some background material on the topic for your text, so some content research is needed next. Before you do this you will need to be sure of exactly what you are being asked to write. Look at Chapter 2, Research for Media Production, to remind yourself about how to gather **secondary** published data, both **qualitative** and **quantitative**. You will need to read the material, validate it, and sort and catalogue the relevant parts. You will then need to write your interpretation of it, in your own words.

Gathering **primary** qualitative and quantitative data will mean talking to people, either in a general conversation, or asking them questions with a questionnaire that you have prepared earlier. You will need to interpret this data and compare the results with your interpretations of secondary data, in order to form your views about what you are going to write.

It is important that what you write can hold the attention of your target audience, and it is useful to test some of your initial attempts on a typical **sample group**. You should do this while you are still writing, to confirm that you are writing in the most appropriate style.

Preparation

Writing cannot be accomplished in a single attempt. When you have researched the ideas, you should set them down in a series of notes, as they form in your mind. Don't spend time trying to get the opening sentences right at the expense of working on the main part of the text. Write down some broad headings for the topic you are writing about, and jump about between headings as the ideas form.

You will need to have a clear idea of the **style** and **treatment** that you should apply to the writing. The **narrative structure** will depend on the media product, but it is worth remembering that all texts have a narrative structure, not just those written as fiction. It is useful to write out an order, an **outline** or **synopsis** of your text, so that you can grasp the overall **structure** before you begin.

Saving drafts

You will make many revisions to your text before it is finalised. These revision stages are called drafts, and four or five drafts are common in professional writing. You should save each draft for your tutor, to show how you have developed the text from initial ideas to final draft. This is easy if you are using a word processing application, as you simply save the original document under one name, and create another document to work with.

Producing your written material

Form

The form that your written material should take will depend upon the product and the medium for which it is being written. The table below shows the types of script layout used for different purposes.

Medium	Type of written material
radio news programme	script
radio documentary	script
radio discussion	scripted intro, close and questions
radio drama	script with directions
TV studio news	single-column script
TV studio makeover	double-column studio script
newspaper feature	article, columnised
newspaper story	report
newspaper 'what's on'	review/preview
web news item	text

Style conventions

The style conventions that you use when writing your material will depend on the medium for which you are writing.

The conventions applied to the way a script is written, to make it appeal to its particular audience, will be seen in the style and complexity of the language used, the use of technical terms and jargon, the tense, the person (first-person or third-person), the voice (active or passive), the degree of familiarity with the audience and the manner of delivery. If the writer takes an authoritative stance it will be different to a conversational style. The content may be presented in a way that leads the audience and suggests an interpretation, or it may present an unbiased account of two sides of an argument and leave the audience to reach its own conclusion.

Layout conventions

The layout conventions that you use when writing your material will, like the style conventions, depend on the medium for which you are writing. The layout conventions used for specific written texts are shown in the table on page 154.

Type of text	Layout conventions
Script (single-column)	Title, running time. Usually 12 or 14 point Arial font, double-spaced. Paragraphs don't go over page. Content of next page prompted at the bottom of the previous page. If news – one story only per page.
Script (double-column)	Page divided into two distinct columns with camera and technical directions on the left, using specific points to identify shot changes. Dialogue on the right, usually 12 or 14 point Arial font, double-spaced. Paragraphs don't go over page. Content of next page prompted at bottom of previous page.
Bullet point script	Pre-scripted programme opening, introduction and menu. Key points listed as bullet points. Questions with anticipated content of answers. Possible extended questions and expected answers. Pre-scripted summing-up and closing statements.
Radio and TV insert cue sheets	In cue (up to six words). Out cue (up to six words). Running time of insert clip, written as 00:00 (minutes:seconds).
Music in scripts	Music has its own notation for start point, end point and running time.
Continuity-link scripts	Written verbatim, usually 12 or 14 point Arial font, double-spaced. Running time written as 00:00 (minutes:seconds).
Newspaper copy	Typed 12 or 14 point Arial font, double-spaced. Editing conventions handwritten or overtyped.
Print article	Headline in bold text. Body text in columns, font dependent on audience, mixed case, single-spaced. Images cropped to style of publication. Paper dependent on product.

Accuracy

The text that you are writing should be spelt correctly and punctuated accurately, and it should use grammatical structures appropriate for its audience. All word processing applications have spelling and grammar checkers built in, but their value is limited. There is no substitute for reading over what you have written very carefully, and using a dictionary to check any word you are not sure about.

Look at ...

The CD-Rom contains sample scripts from radio news programmes, documentaries and discussion programmes, TV studio programmes, magazines, newspaper articles and web pages. For each one, make notes about the layout and conventions they use.

Summary

In this chapter you have covered what you need to know to achieve the three of the four Learning Outcomes relating to Unit 11 of your course. You should now:

- know about different types of writing produced in the media industry
- be able to generate ideas for written material
- be able to produce written material.

When you have finished your writing you will need to review it to achieve the final Learning Outcome. To find out how to do this, turn to Chapter 19, Reviewing Your Work.

17 Photography Techniques

Introducing photography techniques

There are many applications of photography in the photo-imaging sector of the media industry. The sector includes photojournalism, where pictures are used to tell or support a story in a newspaper or magazine. There is a large market for fashion photography, and photography also plays a large part in advertising. There are other areas of photography that might not immediately seem to be part of the media industries – a local wedding photographer, for example, or a medical photographer working in a hospital.

This chapter allows you to learn about traditional film-based photography as well as digital image making.

Photographic equipment and materials

You will use a wide range of equipment in photographic work. This includes:

- cameras: either digital or film-based.
- tripods: used to hold the camera steady.
- artificial lighting: either on a camera flashgun or floor-standing floodlights. You can also diffuse the light using filters or gels.

If you are using a film-based camera, you will need to process your film, using:

- tanks and spools: the film is wound round the spool (in total darkness) and then placed in a lightproof tank.
- measuring cylinder: used to measure out exactly the right amount of chemicals needed to process your film.
- thermometer: you need to process your film using chemicals at the correct temperature.

When you have processed your film you will need to make positive images on photographic paper. You will use:

- enlarger: to project the negative image from your film. It also allows you to produce larger or smaller images.
- frames: the devices that hold your printing paper flat and mask off any unwanted areas of the image.
- contact printer: allows you to place the film in contact with the photographic paper, producing an exact replica of the film images on the paper in a positive format. A contact print is often used by a professional photographer to make decisions about which negatives to print.
- dishes: light-sensitive photographic paper is placed in a dish of developing chemicals to produce a positive print.
- tongs: used to manipulate the printing paper in the dish, to avoid having to touch the developer or other chemicals with your hands.

Traditional photographic materials

Film stock

Film is made for different purposes and comes in a variety of sizes and types:

- 35 mm
- 6 cm x 6 cm
- 5 inches x 4 inches
- 10 inches x 8 inches.

- black and white
- colour print
- colour transparency

In general you will be working with 35 mm film. This film fits most current cameras and accounts for 90% of the film-processing market.

Printing paper

Printing paper comes in a variety of sizes: A4, 10 inches x 8 inches and 6 inches x 4 inches.

Photographers usually buy larger size paper and cut it to the size they want to use. Printing paper is sensitive to daylight and can only be used under 'safe lights'. This is a light that will not 'fog' or ruin the paper before you have an opportunity to use it to make your photograph.

Chemicals

The chemicals you will need for processing your film and printing paper are:

- developer: turns the latent, undeveloped, image on the film or paper into a visible negative or positive image.
- stop bath: stops the action of the developer and stops the image from over-developing.
- fixer: ensures that any unwanted material left on the film or paper is neutralised and fixes the image permanently.

Mounting and finishing

Your finished photographs can be mounted on to board or cardboard. They can be glued in place or you could use a mounting spray that fixes the photograph in place. You may decide to put your photograph in a frame with a bevelled piece of mounting card.

Try this ...

Produce a photogram. This is an image that does not require a camera and is made in a darkroom. Working under safe light conditions, place a piece of photographic paper under the enlarger. Place some everyday objects on the paper, e.g. a key, a pen, etc. and then expose the paper by turning on the enlarger. Use photographic chemicals to develop the image on the paper. You will be amazed at the results!

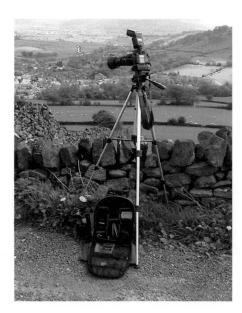

Digital equipment

Digital cameras

The latest technology in photography is digital technology. This involves the use of image capture sensors that replace the film used in traditional photography. These sensors capture the image seen through the camera lens and save it as a digital file. On most digital cameras you can immediately see what image you have captured, on a small screen on the camera. You can choose to keep this file or discard it, or try to capture the image again.

Digital cameras have very much the same functions as a film camera. However, the digital camera has sensors that determine how clear the final image will be. The more 'pixels' the camera can capture, the clearer the final image will be. Cameras today can range from 1 million pixels to 10 million pixels.

Computers

In digital technology a computer transfers the information from the camera to the software from which the final image will be printed. This transfer might be achieved by using a memory stick, flash card or USB cable, which allow the computer to take the information from the camera. Software applications can then be used to manipulate the image and turn the digital information into a finished print.

Scanners

A scanner can be used to convert a traditional print or other flat artwork into a digital image. The scanner records all the information on the material and converts it into a digital format. This is then transferred to a computer for the image to be manipulated and printed.

Printers

A printer turns the digital information into a printable form using inkjet or laser technology. The printer receives the information from the computer and converts this into patterns of dark and light images with colours and shades that match the original image captured by the camera.

Digital materials and software

Memory cards

A digital camera may have a built-in memory store but generally this is quite small. This means that it can only store a small number of high-quality images. Many cameras have a removable storage device such as a memory card, memory stick or flash card. These enable the camera to store lots of information that can then be removed from the camera so that a new card can be put in to capture more information.

These memory cards can be inserted into card readers on a computer and the information transferred on to the hard drive. The cards can then be reformatted after the information has been transferred and used again.

Image-manipulation software

There are many image-manipulation software packages on the market. Generally, they all perform the same functions – changing the file size, altering the contrast or colours of the original image, and cropping (removing) some of the image.

Printing paper

In order to produce your finished digital photograph you will need to use printing paper that is suitable for your printer and appropriate for each image. The paper can be:

- matt or glossy
- lightweight or heavyweight
- textured or smooth finished.

Generating ideas for your photographic images

You will need to consider what you would like to use as a subject for your photographic work. This could be:

- portraits: images of people taken in a studio or on locations.
- creative: images that make people think and challenge the way they view your work.
- documentary: photographs that record an event or place
- press: photographs that you might see in your local newspaper – a local flower show, for instance, or someone receiving an award
- advertising: e.g. a pack shot (used to sell food or packages) or images for a poster or billboard
- fashion: studio or catwalk-based photography.

Try this ...

Take a series of six different images on a digital camera, based around one theme, e.g. portraits or flowers. Download the images on to your computer and then use different manipulation techniques on each image. Try stretching the image, changing the colours, etc. Keep these images as a guide for yourself when you produce more manipulated digital images.

Try this ...

Find at least six examples of photographs from a range of newspapers, magazines and catalogues. Cut them out and make a poster display. Under each photograph, write where you found the photograph, what it portrays and what you think about it.

Here is a mind map for a professional photography idea to advertise Cornish Blue pottery:

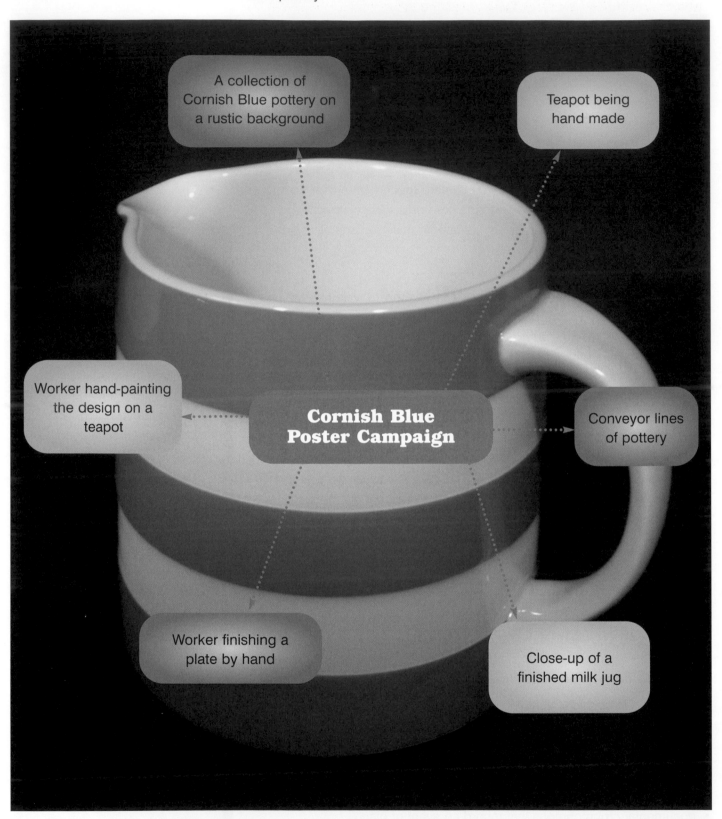

A collection of Cornish Blue pottery on a rustic background

Teapot being hand made

Worker hand-painting the design on a teapot

Cornish Blue Poster Campaign

Conveyor lines of pottery

Worker finishing a plate by hand

Close-up of a finished milk jug

Try this ...

Do a mind-mapping exercise: write the style of photography you would like to try in the middle, and then put ideas into boxes around the central idea. Start to eliminate ideas that cost too much to undertake, where resources are not available or where you do not have sufficient time to complete the work.

The photographers made a visit to the factory and made notes about what they saw. They then took these notes and thought about the way in which they could transfer these into images. They slowly went though each idea on the mind map and dismissed each one until they came to the best idea.

The photographers took a small digital camera with them on the visit to the factory. They used this to record images they saw and this helped them later to choose their idea. The images they captured were produced as rough images without any manipulation, almost as a traditional contact print would have been produced to make decisions about which negatives to print larger.

Influences

It is often claimed that there are no new ideas – simply recycled ideas. This can be true of photography, because photographers are often influenced by what they have seen produced by other photographers.

In 1855 Roger Fenton arrived in Balaklava (Ukraine) to record the Crimean War. He recorded the aftermath of the famous 'Charge of the Light Brigade'. It is said that this was the first attempt to record the horrors of war. His work created a genre that was to stimulate many photographers to follow in his footsteps.

Many great photographers have been influenced by the work of others. Don McCullum is a photographer who has taken many images about war. In some ways they are no different from the work of Roger Fenton, except that they use modern techniques to produce the photograph.

One of the great documentary photographers of our time is Henri Cartier-Bresson, who coined the phrase 'the decisive moment' – the moment in time when all the elements in an image come together to make a photograph. One website describes him as 'The Daddy – a genius. Cartier-Bresson is to photography and photojournalism what Mozart is to music. His lighting, composition and timing are the benchmark'. Many photographers have used the techniques developed by Cartier-Bresson to produce truly memorable photographs.

Try this ...

Find a range of photographic images from across the last century. What do you notice about the style of the photographs, the content of the photographs and the image quality?

Try this ...

Find examples of Henri Cartier-Bresson photographs. What do you think about these images? Do they capture a moment in time?

Planning

In order to create photographic images you need to plan carefully. It is not sufficient to simply take out a camera and hope to find some interesting images. You should:

- make sure that any equipment you need is booked
- book a studio space (if required)
- ensure that any materials you require are available
- check that any models you need are available
- check that you have permission to use a location (you must check that you have a valid permit to take photographs – in some locations you need a licence, e.g. the Royal Parks in London)
- undertake a risk-assessment exercise.

Choosing your film and camera settings

You will need to consider what type of film you will be using to take your photographs. Film is made to ISO or ASA ratings, and these provide a variety of film types to use under different conditions. Low ISO/ASA rating films can be used in bright lighting conditions and give excellent clear results. Higher ISO/ASA ratings can be used in poorer lighting conditions and these tend to give a slightly less clear image. Film can also be rated as suitable for daylight shooting or for tungsten lighting in a studio or room setting. If you shoot on the wrong type of film you will have a **colour cast** on all your photographs. Check carefully that you have the correct film for the job.

You should experiment with loading and unloading a film before taking your photographs. Some cameras have an automatic system for loading the film and some are manual. Some cameras will automatically rewind your film when it reaches the end and some require you to rewind manually. If you get this wrong – and open the camera to remove the film before it has been rewound into the lightproof film case – your film will be ruined.

You must also experiment with the controls on your camera. Some cameras are automatic and you simply point and shoot. With these, you can just concentrate on getting the image right in the viewfinder. Other cameras are manual, and you will need to set the:

- aperture: the control that increases and decreases the size of the hole in the lens that lets in light. The aperture is indicated by an 'f' figure – for example, f22 or f2. The larger the number, the smaller the aperture. The larger the aperture the less depth of field you will achieve.
- depth of field: the measurement of how much is in focus in front of and beyond the image that you are focusing on. If you want the image to stand out from the foreground or background you would use a shallow depth of field (f2). If you want all the foreground and background to be in focus you would use a greater depth of field (f22).
- shutter speed: the time that the shutter is open and letting in light. If you want to capture movement, you would use a fast shutter speed, e.g. a 250th of a second. If you wanted to create movement with blur, you would use a slower shutter speed, e.g. a 30th of a second.

The images below demonstrate depth of field and shutter speed.

Shallow depth of field

Greater depth of field

In this photograph, the shutter has been left open for a long time.

In this example, the movement has been captured with a short shutter speed.

Try this ...

Use a camera to produce ten shots that demonstrate your understanding of aperture, depth of field and shutter speed. Print these photographs and annotate them with the details of how you took each one.

Try this ...

Think of an idea for a photographic exhibition. This could be a set of photographs of your school or college building, the local park or portraits of your friends. Plan how you will take the photographs, what resources you will need and book the equipment. Produce your photographs in the best way you can and mount them on to a display board. Invite people to look at your photographs and ask them for their comments on your work.

In order to achieve the correct exposure you will need to balance the shutter speed and aperture. This can be achieved by using an onboard exposure meter, which will adjust the shutter speed according to the aperture you want to use, and vice versa.

Manipulating your digital images

As you will have seen earlier in this chapter, a digital camera captures images in a file format. Once you have transferred the file to a computer you can:

- manipulate the colour, size and contrast of the image in the file
- add special effects
- output the file to other applications, e.g. a website
- print the file as a traditional photograph on paper, using a printer.

Presenting your final prints

Once you have printed your photographs, from traditional film or digital media, you can exhibit them. To do this you can:

- trim the photographs to the correct size
- glue them on to card or frame them
- present them in a folder or hang them on a wall for people to view.

You should ask people for their views on your photographic work.

Summary

In this chapter you have covered what you need to know to achieve three of the four Learning Outcomes relating to Unit 9 of your course. You should now:

- understand photography techniques, equipment and materials
- be able to generate ideas for photographic images
- be able to create photographic images

When you have finished your photography you will need to review it to achieve the final Learning Outcome. To find out how to do this, turn to Chapter 19, Reviewing Your Work.

18 Animation Techniques

What is animation?

You may have seen examples of animation like *Shrek* or *Toy Story*, but did you know that, as long ago as the Stone Age, artists were trying to depict movement in their cave drawings? Animation, as we know it, began in the 1890s with the first experiments in animating images on film. One of the earliest animated films was *Steamboat Willie*, featuring Mickey Mouse. This was the first sound cartoon to attract widespread attention. Today animation is all around you – in feature films, music videos and computer games.

In this chapter you will be studying historical and contemporary animation, and techniques such as stop-frame animation, claymation and digital animation. You will also look at computer-aided and computer-generated animation techniques.

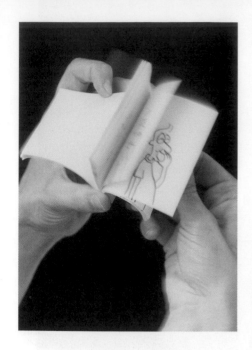

Animation technology

The technology of animation has changed dramatically from the early days of the zoetrope. The zoetrope was a mechanical device that had many still images fastened around the inner rim of a drum. The images were arranged in order, showing the slightly different stages of a simple movement. The drum had slits in the sides and, as the drum revolved, the viewer looked through the slits to see the sequence of images opposite. This quick succession of slightly changing images gave the impression of movement. The zoetrope was a forerunner of the film projector, which used the same technique to produce the illusion of movement.

Today, full-length animated feature films can be seen in cinemas, live-action films can include animated sections, and computer users can view animation sequences online. In fact, anyone with a computer and the appropriate software can use their skills to produce their own short animated sequence.

Animation can be recorded in a number of different ways, the most common being the recording of one **frame** (picture) at a time, using a camera. The camera is attached to a tripod, and the model or drawing is positioned in front of it and photographed once. This makes one frame. The model or drawing is then moved or changed slightly before another photograph is taken. The number of frames gradually builds up, until a completed sequence has been recorded. It is a long process, however, because each second of film needs 25 frames.

Video cameras attached to computers can also be used to record animation directly on to the hard disc. There are various software programs which allow the camera to capture one frame at a time and store them digitally, ready for playback.

Try this ...

Make a flick book animation. Take several pieces of stiff paper or thin card and draw your animation in the corner of each page. Do not try to be too ambitious with your drawing – a simple stick person will be sufficient to demonstrate the technique.

Animation techniques

A good way to understand how animation works is to put together a flick book. A flick book has a series of images drawn on the corners of its pages which are viewed by quickly flicking through the pages. The images you draw will be sequentially different. If you were drawing a stick person, for example, you could show their arms moving up and down. Each page would have the arms in a slightly different position, and when the images were viewed at speed it would look like the arms were moving. This is the basis of animation – still images moving at speed to produce the illusion of movement.

Have you ever considered how a film is made? This is a series of still images that are projected at speed to give the impression of movement. (In a conventional film, of course, the images are photographs of people actually moving, rather than models or drawings.)

Today, there is growing use of computer technology to produce animation. The TV show *Futurama* uses computer animation, whereas *The Simpsons* (an older show) is produced using **cell animation**. Each scene of *The Simpsons* is drawn by a team of animators. One will draw the characters, one will draw the backgrounds, and another will blend the two elements together.

You could produce an animated sequence using a software application such as Flash. This system uses the same principle of frames displayed at speed, but in this case they are files that are run at speed. The software allows you to make changes to each frame, save them as files and then run the sequence on your computer display.

Historical and contemporary practices in animation

To understand the historical and contemporary practices in animation we will look at three case studies of animators: Lotte Reiniger, Bob Godfrey and Aardman.

Lotte Reiniger

The German animator Lotte Reiniger was born in 1899, and her involvement with animation began in 1919. From her very first film, she devoted her life to making silhouette films based on fables and fairytales. She was already an accomplished creator of cut-out silhouette pictures and used this talent at acting school to impress her hero, the actor Paul Wegener. Reiniger produced the captions for Wegener's 1918 film *The Pied Piper of Hamelin*. In 1919, Wegener introduced her to a group who were setting up an experimental animation studio. These included Carl Koch, her future husband and working partner, and the animator Bertold Bartosch, for whom she became an assistant. In 1923, Reiniger worked closely with Bartosch and the director Walter Ruttmann on *The Adventures of Prince Achmed*, the first European animated feature film. The 90-minute film was an adaptation of the *Thousand and One Nights* stories from Arabia and was made entirely with back-lit paper cut-outs, arranged in different layers to provide a three-dimensional look. Ruttmann created the backgrounds and Reiniger cut out the silhouette figures. She was immensely skilled at this – holding her scissors in her right hand, she moved the paper so that she always cut in the right direction. Some of her articulated figures consisted of up to 50 pieces held together with thin wire.

Try this ...

Think about the images you used for your flick book. Can you put these images into a software application such as Flash? Try to produce a short sequence using software to produce an animated sequence. Store this animation in an appropriate file.

Try this ...

Use a search engine to look for an interview that the *Guardian* newspaper did with Bob Godfrey. Have a look at the interview to find out more about him and his animated films.

Bob Godfrey

Bob Godfrey's work reflects his humorous approach to life. You might know his name from the television series *Roobarb* and *Henry's Cat*. He was born in 1922 and started work in animation as a background painter. In 1954, shortly before the start of commercial television in Britain, he co-founded Biographic Films. The company made many television commercials, with Godfrey himself appearing in commercials for a brand of beer. In 1965 he formed his own company. His children's television series *Roobarb*, made in the 1970s, features his own style of continuously moving outlines for the characters. He produced this by drawing in felt-tip pen on paper and changing the shape of the outline in every frame. He called this technique 'boiling'. Stan Hayward, Godfrey's long-time collaborator, wrote the 1980s series *Henry's Cat*.

Aardman

Aardman is a company founded in Bristol in 1972 by two young animator friends, Peter Lord and David Sproxton. The company was named after a character in one of their early films made for BBC Television. They specialised in model animation, using Plasticine – a technique perfected by the American animator Will Vinton, who coined the term 'claymation'. Aardman established its reputation with a children's television character, Morph, so-called because of his ability to change shape. Morph first appeared in 1976 with Tony Hart in the BBC programme *Take Hart*. The character proved so popular that Aardman made a series, *The Amazing Adventures of Morph*, in 1980.

Meanwhile, Lord and Sproxton were developing a novel approach to animation, aimed at an older audience. In their series of *Animated Conversations* (BBC, 1978) and *Conversation Pieces* (Channel 4, 1982) they developed their technique of using real-life conversations, recorded documentary-style, as the basis for character animation. This technique was taken a step further by Nick Park, who joined Aardman in 1985, in his Oscar-winning *Creature Comforts* (1989) where real-life interviews were 'spoken' by zoo animals.

With his Wallace and Gromit films, Park rapidly became the star animator of the studio. Aardman has also nurtured the talents of other animators like Steve Box, whose *Stage Fright* (1997) won a BAFTA Award, Richard Goleszowski, responsible for *Rex the Runt* (1998 and 2001) and *Creature Comforts* (1995–2003), and Darren Walsh with his Angry Kid (2000–2003).

Try this ...

Make a list of animations from the early days of animation up to modern examples. Name the animation, who made it and the style of animation used.

Developing your idea for an animated sequence

Which technique will you use?

Before you choose an idea for your animation project you should think about which animation technique you want to use. A technique may suit certain projects more than others. An animation for young children about toys that 'come alive' might be better using claymation techniques (see page 168). A cartoon-style animation could be done using cell animation, where each shot of the animation is drawn on cells (clear transparencies) and then filmed though a light box. These shots are then joined together to make the animation. An example of this is *The Simpsons*.

An animation that uses your skills in other media or art and design work could use stop-frame animation. This technique uses the process of filming an activity or event over a length of time. A shot is taken at regular intervals and produces an animation effect when run together. This technique has been used in the introduction to music videos, for example, where you see the stage being built in just a few seconds – but it really took six hours.

Animation	Technique used	Comments
Chicken Run	Claymation	The chicken figures and the humans appeared to be alive. Their movements were ealistic and I forgot that this was an animated film.

Try this ...

Find examples of as many contemporary animations as you can. Using a form like the one started here, identify the animation technique and add your comments on how effective it is.

What narrative will you use?

As in any film or video project, there will be a narrative (story) for your animation. How the narrative moves on is an integral part of an animation project. *Chicken Run*, for example, has a narrative about a group of battery chickens wishing for a better life outside their run. The narrative involves a stranger coming to their aid and the film has a happy ending.

169.

You will need to produce a narrative for your animation project. It could be a simple story of two people meeting and then leaving, or a complex narrative about a day in the life of a teenager. There are various types of narrative, for example:

- a children's bedtime story
- a love story
- a horror story
- animated images of a band.

When you plan your animation project you will have to consider the audience. Some narratives will be suitable for young children and some will be more suitable for adults. You will also have to consider the style of your animation project – comedy, fantasy, straight, satirical, etc.

Deciding on your characterisation

In order to give life to your animation project you should consider the way in which you want your characters to work. Do you want them to be human or non-human? Do you want them to be realistic human forms or animals? Do you want them to be fantasy figures?

It is important to make a decision about the characterisation of your animation at an early stage in development. You may want the characters to have a particular way of talking and to behave in a particular way. If so, you will need to ensure that this is carried through the whole animation project. There is nothing more disturbing for a viewer than a character that changes in the middle of an animation.

Producing your animated sequence

Pre-production

This is an important stage in the production. You must plan your animation project carefully, thinking about:

- script: the narrative storyline of your animation.
- sketches: ideas that you have for characters and scenes for your animation. You could make sketches that experiment with characters and scenery. These could then be used to develop your final ideas.
- models: you could experiment with models for characters or the sets you want to build. These models could be used to estimate the size of characters in relation to their sets.

- storyboards: thumbnails of the scenes in your animation. Each frame of the animation could be drawn out to give you (or your client) an idea of what the finished animation might look like.
- music: identify the music you might want to use during the animation or over the titles and credits. You could use your storyboard to try and imagine how the animation will look whilst listening to the music.
- sound effects: gather sound effects you want to use in your animation. If you cannot find ready-made ones you could try to record them yourself.

It is important to produce clear plans for the production of your product. You must ensure that any resources and equipment you will need are available. You could use a form like the one below to identify which resources you will need and where they are located.

Try this ...

Identify the resources and equipment you will need for your animated project. Make a list of them, stating whether they are available in your school or college. Find out how you can book or reserve these resources for your project.

Resource/equipment	Available?	If yes, where they can be found? If no, where can they be bought?
Sound effects CD	Yes	Drama Department
Plasticine for models	Yes	Art Department

Production

When you produce your animation you will have to consider how you will record your material. Will you be using a still camera to take individual frames to be animated in the post-production stage? Will you be using a video camera that requires software to allow it to record frames to a hard drive? Will you be using a MiniDisc to record your sound effects?

You will need to practise using this equipment if you are going to produce a good animation sequence. When you record your animation sequence you will need to consider:

- viewpoint: Will it be shot from a high or low viewpoint? Will it be shot as a whole room or concentrating on one character?
- perspective: looking at eye level and using a reference point – from the viewer's point of view, for example, or from the point of view of one of the characters.
- key frames: this is like storyboarding – the key frames are the major points of action in a sequence, so that it moves from 'point A' to 'point B' to 'point C'.

Try this ...

Think about the animation technique you would like to use. Which one do you think you could use to produce your chosen animation sequence? Produce a short animated sequence using appropriate animation techniques and technology.

171.

Post-production

You must edit your animation material, joining all the shots together and doing some fine tuning to make a piece of animation that flows. Editing involves:

- cuts: straight joins between shots.
- transitions: joins that fade in and out, fade up and down from black, or mix together.
- timing: getting the shots in the right order and moving between shots to produce a realistic story.

You may want to bring in special effects at the post-production stage. This might be reality footage that mixes with your animation. Imagine a scene where two toys have come to life and are looking out of a window at fireworks lighting up the sky. You could add footage of a real firework display to your animation sequence.

You can add music, sound effects and narration at the post-production stage. If your animated characters have voices you will need to synchronise their movements to the voices you have recorded. Often, in the animation industry, the characters' voices are recorded after the visuals have been produced. The animators use a simple guide track of what the characters say to produce the images and then once the animations have been drawn and edited together, the voice artists produce the voice characterisations by watching the characters on screen and recording the words 'in sync'.

Throughout the whole process, remember to keep careful notes on all your planning and production work. This will help you to review your animation work.

Try this ...

Take your animated material and edit it together to make a finished animation piece. What do you need to add to the visuals – music, sound effects or a character's voice? Use the post-production process to remove any visual material you do not need – the start and finish of frames, for example, or clapperboards and mistakes.

Summary

In this chapter you have covered what you need to know to achieve three of the four Learning Outcomes relating to Unit 10 of your course. You should now:

- understand historical and contemporary animation technology, techniques and practice
- be able to develop an idea for an animated sequence
- be able to produce an animated sequence.

When you have finished your animated sequence you will need to review it to achieve the final Learning Outcome. To find out how to do this, turn to Chapter 19, Reviewing Your Work.

Reviewing Your Work

On BTEC First Certificate and First Diploma courses you have the opportunity to become involved with making media artefacts, and following professional production processes in order to do so. It is also possible to make a product that is fit for purpose but does not follow the recognised professional processes and procedures. The problem with this approach is that you may not always get the artefact right every time and for a professional media person this is too hit and miss. You must be able to follow the same procedures and get the same end product right every time you do it. It follows, then, that the way you do something is as important as the product you make.

That is why you will find a Learning Outcome 'Review your own work' in the production units where you have to produce: video, audio, print, advertising, interactive media, photography, animation, writing, web authoring, factual media and digital graphics products. You will also find the same Learning Outcome in production units 13 and 17, covered in the section on the Production Process.

19 Reviewing Your Work

Reviewing your own production work

If you are considering a National Diploma, Higher National Diploma or going to university after this course, you will be expected to analyse and think critically about the world around you and the work that you produce.

This chapter is about looking at your own work in the same objective way that you look at the work of others – when asked to give an opinion on a media product, a production process or an information source. The only way to know that you have done work of a high enough standard is to be realistic about what others – particularly your tutor – may feel about what you have produced, and how it compares with professionally produced artefacts and practices.

To be able to review your own work you need to understand which aspects of it to examine, what to comment on and how to give an **objective** opinion rather than a **subjective** one. An objective opinion is one that compares the work in question with a particular standard of work, whereas a subjective opinion is an individual's own view.

A piece of classical music on a CD is being performed professionally, to a standard expected by its typical target audience. If you don't like the music you might say it's not good. In fact it is good – it's simply that you don't personally like it. This is a subjective opinion. If, however, you recognise the skill and technique required to play such music and state that it is professionally played – even though you don't like it – this would be an objective opinion.

A piece of music of a type that you like, being played by a new, inexperienced band who make mistakes, in a hall with poor acoustics and equipment, might be poorly played. You may, however, state that you like the performance. This would be a subjective opinion. If you said that, although you like the type of music, the way they performed it was unprofessional, you would be giving an objective view.

There are three areas of your work that you will need to review objectively:

- The finished product, and whether it is fit for purpose.
- The production process involved in making the product.
- The sources of information used for the product content.

Reviewing your finished product

To review your finished product you will have to compare it with your original proposal. This contained your first intentions and was the basis on which you were given approval to make the product. You should be answering the question, 'Is this what I intended to make?'

The proposal will have listed a number of criteria that should have been met. Have you met them? Answer the following questions about your product:

- Target audience: does it target the identified audience?
- Content: does it contain the information that was intended?
- Style: is the style appropriate for the audience?
- Format: does the format work for the audience and content?
- Technical quality: is it technically well produced?
- Creative or aesthetic quality: is it attractive to the audience?

You need to answer each of the bullet points as objectively as you can, giving reasons supported by reference to the work of other professionally produced products. You need to ignore your personal likes and dislikes, and think only about the intended audience of the product.

Reviewing the production process

Remember that the production process is time-based. Answer the following questions, thinking about your own media product:

- Which part or parts of the process were you involved in?
- How well did you fulfil the roles you had?
- Check your **production diary** to see how closely you followed the **planning documentation**. In most cases the two won't match, but this doesn't matter as long as you are close, or can explain why there is a large difference.
- Did you do what you planned to do? In the case of working for a real client, did you meet their expectations?
- Did you meet the requirements of the target audience?

Look back at Chapter 4, The Production Process if you need a reminder of the production process.

175.

When explaining significant differences between your original intention and the actual product, it is worth remembering that most things can be planned for. 'Forgetting' to do something is a reason, but not a good reason for straying off-track. Admitting that you didn't do what you should have done is better than saying it was out of your control. It is important to recognise whether you managed your time efficiently, because bad **time management** is often the reason for things going wrong.

Your contribution to the team, whether it is creative or technical, is also important. Think about these questions:

- How productive was your individual contribution to the team effort?
- Did each member of the team do what they should have done?
- Did every member of the team fulfil their role?
- Did you make the team aware of anything you couldn't do?
- Did you use your time well?
- Did you participate actively in production meetings?
- Did you keep a detailed, accurate production log?
- Did you make correct production decisions?
- Did you listen to advice and guidance?
- Did you produce your product on budget and to schedule?

Reviewing sources of information

In this part of the review process you should examine your research skills. Ask yourself how well you completed your research, and answer the following questions:

- Were your sources of information reliable, valid and current?
- Did you keep accurate records of your research?

Summary

In this chapter you have covered everything you need to know to achieve the Learning Outcome 'Reviewing your own work', which is present in most production units. You should now:

- know about reviewing the finished product, the production process and your sources of information.

Glossary

ABC: Audit Bureau of Circulations, organisation that publishes circulation figures for newspapers

Acquisition: getting or gathering what is needed

ADC: Analogue to Digital Converter, an electronic circuit that changes analogue signals into digital signals

Agency: company that provides a specialist service for other companies

AI: Artificial Intelligence, the science of making computers do things that normally require human intelligence

Ambience: atmosphere, surroundings

Ambient background: background sounds

Amplify: make an electronic signal bigger and louder

Analogue: method of recording sound and images using varying electrical signals to represent the sound or image

Analysing: finding out what the information you have really means

Anchor: key presenter on a radio or TV programme who holds the programme together

Annual salary: total income earned in a year from an employer

Artefacts: things that have been made – programmes, newspapers, etc.

ASA: Advertising Standards Association, the regulatory body for all advertising

As-live: in radio or television, recording under the same conditions as if the programme was being broadcast live

Assets: in computers, the elements that go together to make a game – sprites, backgrounds, etc.

Audience: people who will consume a media product

Audit: a systematic assessment of something, e.g. the resources needed for a production, to get a clear and complete picture

Banner ad: strip advertisement found on websites and in print products

BARB: Broadcasters' Audience Research Board, the body that collects information on television viewing habits in the UK

Bibliography: detailed list of sources of information

Billing: charging a customer for broadcasting a radio commercial

Body language: non-verbal communication that reveals your feelings

Body type: type used for the main text in print, as opposed to the headings, etc.

Brainstorming: quickly generating as many ideas as possible, without thinking each one through in detail

Breakfast show: in radio, music sequence format broadcast every morning

Brief: client's outline description of the media product they want a production company to produce

Budget: breakdown of all expected costs of a planned project

BWAV: Broadcast WAV, type of broadcast-quality, uncompressed audio file format that the BBC has chosen as its standard for radio programmes

Cell animation: an animation technique where each frame is drawn on a clear plastic cell, which can be changed in small steps for subsequent frames

Chair: person who controls and guides the contributors in a discussion

Character map/web: in computer games, a visual plan indicating a character's interaction with other characters

Clearances: authorisations to use other people's copyright material in your product

Client: the person the product is being made for

Closed question: question where the answer is chosen from a given list

Code of practice: a set of rules which people in a particular profession are expected to work by

Collate: combine and put into some sort of order

Colour cast: the effect produced when the wrong type of film is used, e.g. using daylight film in artificial light results in images with a yellow cast

Commissioner: the person the product is being made for

Commission: authorisation to make a product for a client

Composition: the way in which the content (of a film or TV image) is arranged

Compressed: made smaller – so that e.g. an audio signal occupies less space on a CD

Conjecture: a personal opinion or guess

Construction: the way in which elements are put together to form a product

Consumer: member of an audience or person who buys media products

Content: the material that a media product contains

Content acquisition: gathering content for a media product

Context-sensitive: in computer games, relevant to the situation – to what the player is doing

Contingency: something unwanted that might happen, and needs to be planned for, e.g. bad weather

Contributor: someone who provides content for a media product, e.g. an interviewee

Conventions: established practices, often so familiar that they appear natural, e.g. newsreader facing to camera

Copy: the text produced for print products

Copyright: the system by which you legally own what you create

CPU: Central Processing Unit, the main information processor in a computer

Cue sheet: in radio production, a list of start words and end words to the items in a programme

Current: belonging to the present time (especially if likely to change later)

Current affairs: events happening now, of political and social interest

Curriculum Vitae: brief written account of a person's education, experience and skills

Cut-scenes: in computer games, scenes that the programme might show to illustrate a point

DAC: Digital to Analogue Converter, electronic circuit that changes digital signals into analogue signals

Data: information that has been gathered for analysis

Decoding: understanding or interpreting the meaning of a message

Defamatory: describes statements that are likely to damage the reputation of someone, can be oral or written statements

Defamation: saying or writing something false about someone

Digital: method of recording sound and images using electrical pulses to represent the sound or image

Digital Betacam: a professional digital video format used to broadcast television programmes

Direct addressee: mode of address where the producer communicates directly with the audience, by asking their opinion, vote for a contestant, etc. Documentary: a programme that tells a factual story without dramatising or changing the facts in any way

Draft script: an early version of a script that will be changed to a final script as the production process moves on

Dramatised: describing factual material presented in the style of a drama or film to make it more interesting

DTP: desktop publishing, making printed publications using a personal computer and printer

Dubbing: adding a new soundtrack, e.g. a voice-over or music, to existing footage

Editing: arranging the parts of a media product so that it is right for the audience

Editorial: in newspapers, short article on a topical issue, which represents that paper's view

Elements: parts of a product that together make up the whole product, e.g. scenes in a radio or television programme

Embellishments: additional material that is added to expand the original item

Empathiser: mode of address that puts the viewer, reader or listener 'in the shoes' of the main character

Emphasis: the focus on a particular point

End user: person who uses (consumes) the product in question

end user device: the hardware used to view electronic files or programs e.g. computer, mobile, television

Engine: in computing, the core software that controls and drives a product, e.g. a video game

Ethical: correct, fair and decent

Evidence: the material gathered and submitted for an assignment

Executable file: in computing, a file that is interpreted by the computer as a program, often used to download a program to a to a computer

Expletives: swear words

Expression: way in which you speak, stand or look

Feasibility: whether a proposed project can actually be carried out

Feature: in radio, a free-standing programme item based on fact, which may be dramatised

Fine edit: the last stage of editing a programme

Font: typeface or style of text used in a print product

Footage log: in film, a list of scenes that have been shot, including the timecode, description and suitability

Formal qualifications: BTECs, GCSEs, A levels, degrees, etc. awarded by recognised bodies

Format: way in which something is arranged; particular method of storing data

Format radio: style of radio playing the same type of music (perhaps just 40 tracks) throughout the day

Frame: in film, a single picture (out of thousands) representing 1/25th of a second.

Genre: type, style or category of media product

Health and safety: legislation to protect workers in their workplace

Hoardings: large flat boards displaying advertisements in public places

Horizontal integration: the merging of two or more similar companies

Horror: a media genre based on fear and shock

Icon: an object or symbol that has a universal meaning beyond its original use

Iconography: the way in which visual images and symbols represent a wider universal meaning, beyond their original concept

Idents: visual and musical items designed to 'identify' the presenter, programme, channel or station for an audience

Immersive: in computing, generating such a realistic image that the viewer/player becomes totally involved

Incidental music: in film, television and radio, music that is playing during the action but not part of it

Inclusive addressee: mode of address where the producer uses unconventional approaches to emphasise that their media product is artificial or unreal

Independent: in television and radio, companies that make their money on the open market rather than from licence fees or government grants

Industry standard: at a level appropriate for the professionals in that business

Information trail: sources searched when gathering information

Initiation stage: first part of the production process in which the idea for a media product is formed

Intelligent speech radio: radio that is speech-based, with little or no music

Jingle: in radio, short musical item used to link items within a programme

JPEG: Joint Photographic Experts Group, a form of compression used for images

Landscape: the format for horizontal images – those that are wider than they are high

Language register: the quality and level of language used, varying according to the purpose and standing of the speaker

Layout: in print production, the way that the text, pictures, etc. are arranged on the page

Legal restrictions: conditions that apply, enforceable by law

Legislation: laws and regulations

Linear time-based: running in sequence as time passes

Linguistic codes: language and words used to identify and communicate in a particular way

Listen Again: facility on websites of many radio stations that lets you listen to previously broadcast programmes

Location recce: (reconnaissance) first visit to check that a location is appropriate

Log: write down details of what happens during an event or project

Logistics: organisation and coordination of a complex operation, involving people, equipment, etc.

Lossless: form of audio (or video) compression that keeps all of the original signal when reversed

Lossy: form of audio (or video) compression that loses some of the original signal when reversed

Media codes: descriptions of the techniques used in a media product to communicate its meaning

Media conventions: established ways of doing things in particular media products

Media products: radio and TV programmes, films, newspapers, magazines, periodicals, websites, interactive CD-Roms and computer games

Medium: the format used to present a product to an audience e.g. radio, print

Message: main point or theme that a producer wants to put across

Middleware: a class of computer software produced by developers to provide basic systems which can then be used and developed by other companies

Mise-en-scène: arrangement of set, props and performers in a scene

Misquote: to state or write something that gives the wrong idea of what a person said

Mock-up: a model of a product

Mode of address: way a producer communicates with the audience, varying according to the producer's purpose

Mood board: visual representations, used to show how a product will look

Multinational: a big corporation, owning companies in more than one country

Music bed: in radio, instrumental music used as a background to speech

Music sequence: in radio, a music-based programme, usually 3 to 4 hours long, presented by a DJ

Narrative: story

Narrative structure: way in which a story unfolds

National press: the main newspapers, which are distributed all over the country

Navigation chart: plan or schematic diagram of a website or CD-Rom

Negotiating: trying to reach an agreement

News bulletin: broadcast summary of news stories, delivered formally without comment or opinion

News magazine: in radio, a programme made up of news items connected by a common theme, e.g. local items

Objective: an evaluation that is not influenced by personal feelings or opinions but is purely based on fact

Observation: watching what happens at an event or during an experiment

OCR: optical character recognition, a computer program that produces a digital file by scanning printed text

Open questions: questions where the answers are not limited by set options

Outline: a brief description of the main points

Ownership: when a company or person owns another company

Page-assembly: in print, adding text, graphics and photo-images to a page layout on a computer

Page layout: a draft of a page from a newspaper, magazine, etc. showing the basic design – margins, text size, images, etc.

Parameter: boundary or limitation

Paste-up: prototype of a print product, using real content, to give an idea of what it will look like

Permissions: documents authorising a producer to use someone else's property or material, e.g. equipment, talent, locations, images etc.

Personnel: the people involved in a project or organisation

Photo-image manipulation: changing an electronic photograph or image

Pitch: present ideas for a media product

Plagiarism: using someone else's words or ideas and taking the credit for them

Planning documentation: drawings, lists, budgets, schedules, permissions, releases and clearances required to make a media product

Point of use: place where a product is used by the consumer

Portfolio: collection of documents, images, etc. created by someone to display their skills, especially to a potential employer

Portrait: the format for vertical images – those that are higher than they are wide

Pre-production: first part of the production stage, involving the creative tasks needed before content acquisition can begin, e.g. writing scripts, producing shot lists, etc.

Pre-rendered: in computing, images that are produced using software and then played back like a short film, e.g. as an introduction to a game

Presenter: person or voice that introduces and holds together a programme

Primary codes: basic codes of a specific medium, e.g. writing, pictures, sounds

Primary research: gathering information first-hand, e.g. by questioning experts or conducting surveys

Production diary: day-by-day (or even hour-by-hour) account of a specific production process

Production process: the method of creating a product

Production schedule: the planned timeline for the production process, showing when each step will take place

Professional development: the experience and skills gained during relevant employment

Professional standards: level of quality produced by professionals

Program: software application that computers use to carry out a specific function

Proofread: read a finished print product to check for mistakes

Proposal: brief description of a planned product or project put forward for consideration by a client

Ofcom: Office of Communications, regulatory body for independent radio and television

Qualitative data: descriptive information that has been found by research, e.g. notes on why someone likes a particular magazine

Quantitative data: numerical information that has been found by research, e.g. the number of people who buy a particular magazine

Questionnaire: set of questions that a researcher gives out to people, asking about their behaviour and opinions

RAJAR: Radio Audience Joint Research Limited, the body that gathers information on radio programme listening

RAM: (random access memory) part of a computer that rules how much processing can be done at once

Raster files: files made up of grids of pixels, which are particularly suitable for photo-realistic images

Readme file: in computing, an introductory file that gives information about a program, including how to install it

Real time: the actual time during which a programme is broadcast

Record level display: scale showing audio signal levels, used for monitoring during the recording process

Recruitment agencies: companies that specialise in finding people to do particular jobs

Regulatory body: official organisation that oversees the standards of a specific industry sector

Relevant: appropriate to or directly connected with the issue being discussed

Reliable: good quality, able to be trusted

Renders: in computer games, illustrations that demonstrate the idea of a proposed character or object, useful when trying to sell an idea for a game

Research: gather and analyse data from a number of different sources

Research methods: ways of doing specific types of research

Running order: in radio and television, order in which items in a programme are broadcast

Rush: unedited video footage that will be edited to make the final product

Sample group: a small set of a large number of people (e.g. a whole audience) that is used to represent all the people in the audience

Schedule: the planned timeline for a job or project, showing when each step will take place

Schematic: for websites, a diagram that represents the various pages, showing the links that make the navigation work

Sci-fi: (science fiction) a media genre based on an imagined future

Secondary research: gathering information from previously published sources

Selection: deciding which elements to use, e.g. which scenes in a film

Self-presentation: the way in which someone puts themselves across to others

Shooting script: a comprehensive script, including camera positions and angles, stage directions and lighting directions

Show-reel: a set of film or video clips created by someone to display their skills, especially to a potential employer

Sign-off: the way an item or whole programme is ended, e.g. 'That's all from me. Goodbye'

Slot: a programme's scheduled date and time for broadcasting

Source: the original place that re-used material is taken from

Speech package: in radio, a brief speech item pre-produced to be included in a specific programme

Spidergram: (spider diagram) diagrammatic way of organising a 'web' of ideas on paper, similar to a mind map

Sting: in radio, a musical phrase that ends a commercial

Storyboard: a sequence of drawings, often with directions and dialogue, used to demonstrate how the product will look

Strategy: plan of action, the way in which a complex task is going to be completed

Structure: the way a media product is arranged

Style: the distinctive way that a product is made, e.g. formal, funny, serious

Subjective: describing an evaluation that is influenced by personal feelings and opinions

Sweeper: in radio, short sound effect that changes tone

SWOT analysis: a way of considering something's strengths, weaknesses, opportunities and threats

Symbols: images (characters, letters, numbers) with a specific meaning

Synopsis: a brief summary

Tag line: in an advertisement, the part of the dialogue that provides the main detail of the product or service

Technique: a way of carrying out a task, especially a creative task

Thumbnail: small visual representation of a proposed product, to show how it will look

Time management: way of organising time when completing a task

Trade publications: newspapers and magazines produced for people in a particular trade or industry

Trade unions: organised associations of workers in one or more professions, formed to represent those workers' interests

Transferable skills: skills that can be reused in another sector, e.g. the skill of writing, perhaps developed in radio, can be used in television

Transition: in video, the visible change from one scene to another, e.g. slow fade, fade to black, etc.

Treatment: a document, developed from a proposal, that provides evidence of the director's intentions, costs, timescales and people that may be used in a production

Typeface: style of lettering

Upload: send or copy files from one place to another, e.g. from a recorder or camera to a workstation

USP: (unique selling proposition or point) the feature of a product that makes it special

Validate: check to make sure something is correct, true and accurate

Vector files: files using geometric principles to join points together, which are ideal for simple drawings that do not require photo-realism

Verbatim: in the exact, original words

Vertical integration: the merging of companies that are linked along the production–distribution chain

VFD: (Verified Free Distribution) the part of ABC (Audit Bureau of Circulations) that publishes the circulation figures for free newspapers

Viability: the ability of a product to be successful, especially financially

Visual codes: descriptions of the rules for using visual images

Voice-piece: in radio, pre-recorded dialogue insert for a programme

Voluntary: without payment, e.g. doing a job just to gain work experience

Voyeur: (also called 'observer') most common mode of address, where the producer expects the audience to watch, listen to, or read what is happening

Walkthrough: in computer games, a testing process, normally done on paper, allowing the designer to try out the elements they want to use

Watershed: before 9 pm, when programmes unsuitable for younger viewers cannot be shown on television

Waveform: diagrammatic representation of a sound or sounds in an audio file

Westerns: a media genre, based on cowboys in western North America

Working title: the name given to a project until a final name is fixed

Word processing: writing using a computer

Work patterns: ways of working in different companies

Zip file: a popular data-compression and archival format, useful when you have lots of separate files to send by email

Appendix

Media bodies and organisations

Media professional bodies fall into four categories: regulatory, data gathering, trade unions and trade bodies.

Regulatory bodies

ASA, Advertising Standards Association: the regulatory body for all advertising in the UK. It guards against false claims being made about products and services provided. See www.asa.org.uk for more information.

BBFC, British Board of Film Censors: regulates the amount of violence, gratuitous sex, nudity and bad language used in films and permits them only where appropriate using the film classification system of numbers and letters. See www.bbfc.co.uk for more information.

CISAS, Communication and Internet Services Adjudication Scheme: regulates the Internet in the UK. It is difficult area to police the Internet across the world because the laws of each country are different. Negotiations are in progress to try to impose some degree of regulation but it is not easy to get every country in the world to agree. See www.cisas.org.uk for more information.

PPC, Press Complaints Commission: regulates the British press. They issue the code of practice for journalists and deal with any complaints against the press. See www.ppc.org.uk for more information.

Ofcom: the regulatory body for independent radio and television. It also issues broadcasting licences to all independent radio and television companies throughout the UK. Ofcom replaced the former ITC (Independent Television Commission), RA (Radio Authority) and BSC (Broadcasting Standards Commission) in 2003. See www.ofcom.org.uk for more information.

Ofcom does not regulate the BBC, which has its own regulation service called the Programme Complaints Unit.

Data research bodies

ABC, Audit Bureau of Circulation: gathers circulation data for distribution of newspapers in UK. See www.abc.org.uk for more information.

BARB, Broadcasters' Audience Research Board: gathers audience data for all television channels in UK. See www.barb.co.uk for more information.

NRS, National Readership Survey: gathers audience data for all newspapers and consumer magazines in the UK. See www.nrs.co.uk for more information.

RAJAR, Radio Audience Joint Research Limited: gathers audience data for all radio stations in UK. See www.rajar.co.uk for more information.

Trade unions

BECTU, Broadcasting Entertainment Cinematograph and Theatre Union: represents television and film workers. See www.bectu.org.uk for more information.

MU, Musicians Union: represents musicians. See www.musiciansunion.org.uk for more information.

NUJ, National Union of Journalists: represents journalists. See www.nuj.org.uk for more information.

Trade bodies

Tiga: represents the business and commercial interests of computer games developers. See www.tiga.org for more information.

ELSPA, Entertainment & Leisure Software Publishers Association: represents the video games industry in UK. See www.elspa.com for more information.

CRCA, Commercial Radio Companies Association: represents commercial radio in the UK. See www.crca.co.uk for more information.

Legal and ethical issues in the media

Defamation is saying or writing something about someone that isn't true. The person must still be alive for a statement to be defamatory. Celebrities often suffer defamation and some have been successful in suing for damages when this has happened.

Libel is the crime of writing or recording something false about someone (a form of defamation).

Slander is the crime of saying something false about someone (a form of defamation).

Equality laws prevent anyone from taking advantage of or discriminating against someone on grounds of their race, sexual orientation, gender or age. These include the **Race Discrimination Act** and the **Age Discrimination Act**.

Privacy laws prevent journalists from publicising private facts about individuals, unless it can be proved that knowing the fact is in the public interest.

The **Data Protection Act** prevents any confidential information or data held on electronic computer files being distributed without the permission of the person concerned.

The **Freedom of Information Act** allows an individual or a body to request access to information that is held on computer files by a professional organisation or government body.

You can find information about the Acts mentioned above at www.direct.gov.uk.

The **Copyright Act** and associated laws are very important to media producers. Copyright is held for most assets that are used as part of a media product, including music, words, recordings, archive footage, photographs or newsreel clips. A producer using such material to make a media product must seek permission from the copyright owner and pay them royalties. The main organisations that deal with copyright in music are the **MCPS-PRS Alliance** (an alliance between **PRS**, **Performing Rights Society** and **MCPS, Mechanical Copyright Protection Society**) and **PPL**, **Phonographic Performances Limited**. See www.mcps-prs-alliance.co.uk and www.ppluk.com for more information.

The **BBC Producer Guidelines** are a comprehensive set of regulations that apply to any media product produced by the BBC for radio, television, merchandise or their website. They cover everything from programme content to the way in which the titles and credits are written, from programme running times to the technical quality of the media product. They are very complex and occupy hundreds of pages. See http://www.bbc.co.uk/guidelines for more information.

Further study

The **BTEC First Certificate and Diploma (Level 2)** are your first steps into the world of the media industries. During your course you will look at the media industry, and how and why media products are produced, and you will learn to make your own media products.

The next step in your education could be a move up to a **BTEC National Award National Certificate** or **National Diploma in Media Production (Level 3)**. These qualifications are similar to the BTEC Firsts, as the units are structured in a similar way and so are the assessment opportunities. There are also specialist pathways in television and film, radio, print production, sound production, interactive media and computer games.

You may consider progressing to a vocational GCE (A Level) such as **GCE Media: Communication and Production (Level 3)**. This provides an opportunity to take an AS or full A Level qualification. This would help you to further develop your understanding of the media industry as well as to make your own media products.

In all these qualifications you will be able to use and further develop the skills you are learning in your **BTEC First Certificate or Diploma**.

Once you have your Level 3 qualification, there are many universities that offer degree programmes in media production, e.g. the University of Sunderland. They have courses in television production, radio production and new media. Why not have look at some university websites to see what they offer?

An alternative to a degree is the **Higher National Diploma in Media**, a qualification that is recognised throughout the world. It provides a vocational approach to media production (just like your BTEC First qualification), together with some academic studies. The HND provides a good platform from which to find employment in the media industry. In fact, some employers allow their staff to attend HND and other Level 4 qualifications as part of their staff training programmes.

You may, of course, want to work in the media industry right away. You will find that with a Level 2 qualification like yours, you will only be able to work in junior positions in the industry. Many employers want their staff to have higher level qualifications. Why not start by working in a voluntary capacity for a local media company? The experience you will get – and the contacts you make – will be invaluable.

Whatever route you choose, you should remember that media professionals can work long and unsociable hours, spend long periods away from home and work very hard. Working in the media industry, however, is one of the best jobs in the world!

Index